THE COST OF THE VOTE

THE COST OF THE VOTE

George Elmore and the Battle for the Ballot

CAROLYN CLICK

THE UNIVERSITY OF
SOUTH CAROLINA PRESS

© 2025 University of South Carolina

Published by the University of South Carolina Press
Columbia, South Carolina 29208

uscpress.com

Printed in the United States of America

Library of Congress Cataloging-in-Publication Data
can be found at http://catalog.loc.gov/.

ISBN: 978-1-64336-512-1 (hardcover)
ISBN: 978-1-64336-513-8 (ebook)

To the children of George Elmore,
who carried the memory
of their father's boldness and
their mother's sacrifice

And for
Jay, Catherine Ann, and Henry

CONTENTS

LIST OF ILLUSTRATIONS

Introduction

If any testimonials were to be given and any purses
distributed, surely George Elmore deserved to be on
the receiving end. He has suffered many indignities
and his family has had to undergo many hardships
because of his willingness [to] prosecute for the
freedom of his race.

—C. Arthur Pompey to South Carolina NAACP
President James Myles Hinton, August 16, 1948

George Elmore was an optimist by nature, not someone to dwell on the
daily humiliations of segregated life in South Carolina's capital city. But
he was also impatient. And he was offended that he could not cast a ballot in the state's Democratic Party primary, the only election that had
mattered since the turn of the century.[1] This was a white man's country, a revolving cast of boldly brazen politicians had emphasized year
after year since the end of the Civil War and federal Reconstruction.
But Elmore and others sensed change in the air, in this, the year of
our Lord, 1946. The United States had defeated Nazism and fascism in
the greatest military conflict of the century. Elmore's people, who had
labored under seventy years of second-class citizenship and endured
prejudices so pervasive they had become routine, had fought honorably. They were now at a crossroads with their white countrymen.

"This War is crucial for the future of the Negro, and the Negro problem is crucial in the War," the Swedish social scientist Gunnar Myrdal
wrote in a sweeping study on race published in 1944. "There is bound
to be a redefinition of the Negro's status in America as a result of this
War."[2] The use of the word "Negro" to describe people of color seems
now quaint and pejorative in the modern age, a way to separate people
and render judgment at the same time. But for much of the twentieth
century, at least into the late 1960s, Black Americans were commonly

1

referred to as "Negro" or "colored." In headlines, Black-owned and white-owned newspapers noted the advancements made by "Negro Americans," not Black Americans or African Americans as the race would become known in the advancing civil rights movement of the 1960s and beyond.

George Elmore, a man of limited education but dogged aspirations, may not have considered himself or his neighbors part of the "Negro problem" that Myrdal and dozens of other distinguished scholars examined in *An American Dilemma: The Negro Problem and Modern Democracy.* He was simply trying to earn a decent living and improve his family's life. But Elmore grasped what Myrdal and his formidable team of researchers had revealed: that the ideals of the "American Creed" rested uneasily alongside segregation, assaults, lynchings, and the absolute dominance of white supremacy, particularly in the South. Elmore had only to read the newspapers and look around his own Columbia, South Carolina, neighborhood to see glaring inequities in employment, in housing, in schooling, in policing, in recreation, in the utter futility of regular city trash collection. Parents had to beg for school crossing guards at busy intersections.[3] ("White children will be guided across the street by officers, while Negro children will be told to '*come on*,'" one activist noted.) Their children could not play in white-only parks filled with modern jungle gyms and equipment. Those who represented him in Congress and on city council did not care about the Negro because the Negro could not vote. A legal challenge to the doctrine of white supremacy enshrined in law and custom since 1895 was perilous. But Elmore, fortified by conviction, a measure of boldness, and the backing of the National Association for the Advancement of Colored People (NAACP), registered, went to the polls—where he was turned away in August 1946—and then to federal court. In the case that became *Elmore v. Rice,* he demanded entry for himself "and others similarly situated," into the primary conducted by and for white Democrats, the election that mattered in the one-party South. Amazingly, just over a month after his June 1947 trial, a federal judge sided with this man of modest means who sold penny candy and dispensed dry goods in the shadow of the state capitol. Negroes were voting in the primaries of Texas, Georgia, and Louisiana, US District Judge J. Waties Waring wrote. "I cannot see where the skies will fall if South Carolina is put in the same class with these and other states."[4]

Why did Elmore take the risk? Perhaps he was moved by the stirrings in post–World War II America. Returning soldiers, white and Black, had seen the world and were not about to return to the old ways of doing things. Migration and mechanization had begun to alter the landscape of South Carolina. The Great Depression, so devastating to South Carolina's rural families, white and Black, was in the rearview mirror and there was money to be made. George Elmore had seen that as he juggled work as operator of a five-and-dime store and two liquor establishments. He also moonlighted as a taxi driver and a photographer. His immersion into politics and his association with leaders of the South Carolina Conference of Branches of the NAACP, as well as an upstart group of Black activists who had formed a new party called the Progressive Democrats, certainly swayed him. Perhaps he was moved to act because he had high hopes for his young children and wanted to ensure better prospects for succeeding Elmore generations.

For all his optimism, Elmore had not reckoned with the fury of white political leaders for the simple act of going to the polls that hot August day in 1946. In their world, the skies *were* falling, and the "southern way of life" was in jeopardy. They believed that the customs of the South were acceptable to both races and that disruption of the old ways was the work of outsiders stirring dissent. In subsequent legal appeals, white Democrats argued that the primary was a private club whose members could erect "keep out" signs to Negroes, Republicans, Communists and others who might be masquerading as true Democrats.[5] They devised an oath that required Democrats—including the newly enfranchised Black Democrats—to swear allegiance to segregation and opposition to federal fair employment laws.[6] The rise of the States Rights Democratic Party, or "Dixiecrat" movement, and the quixotic presidential campaign of US Senator Strom Thurmond hardened the segregationist stance.[7]

Still, there was that glorious moment in August 1948 as Elmore stood in the midst of Columbia's Ward 9 and watched as hundreds of his Black neighbors voted for the first time. Thirty thousand Black South Carolinians cast ballots on that historic day. It would be the high point of his personal legal fight and came in the same month that more than six thousand States Righters gathered in Oklahoma to endorse a platform that called for "segregation of the races and the racial integrity of each race." Feted at a NAACP dinner in Georgetown, South Carolina, George

Black voters in front of the Sunshine Laundry and Cleaners wait to cast ballots for the first time in a statewide Democratic primary, Aug. 10, 1948. From the John Henry McCray Papers. Courtesy of South Caroliniana Library, University of South Carolina.

Elmore quoted the famous heavyweight boxer Joe Louis, known as the "Brown Bomber,": "I'm glad I win."[8]

To paint a picture of the times in which George Elmore lived and labored is akin to walking through a misty fog. The outlines of his life are there in newspaper accounts, a few letters, and hazy recollections. Understanding Elmore's inner world, his motivation and drive, and his hopes and fears is only an educated conjecture. But we know in detail what he was up against. He was born into a state that for centuries had treated its Black inhabitants as lucrative chattel, illiterate tillers, troublesome afflictions, quarrelsome millstones, and uppity invaders. "Violence, terror, and intimidation have been, and still are, effectively used to disenfranchise Negroes in the South," Myrdal wrote in *An American Dilemma*. "Physical coercion is not so often practiced against the Negro, but the mere fact that it can be used with impunity and that it is devastating in its consequences creates a psychic coercion that exists nearly everywhere in the South."[9]

George Elmore chose to drop a pebble into the turbulent river of twentieth century America despite the "psychic coercion" that defined life for the nation's nearly thirteen million Black inhabitants. His public action effectively destroyed his private life and altered the lives of his children and grandchildren. Evidently that was a price he was willing to pay. He saw himself as fully American and deserving of more than second-class citizenship.

The writer Zora Neale Hurston wrote, "There is no agony like bearing an untold story inside you." The children of George Elmore—Essie Naomi Elmore Green, Cresswell Delaney Elmore, Vernadine Veranus Elmore Quan-Soon, and Yolande Anita Elmore Cole—carried their father's untold story. They were children of South Carolina but had to leave to flourish in other places. When they left South Carolina, they carried little with them except for the remembrance of a distinct, perhaps prophetic, boldness about their father that defied the times in which they lived. They, like their parents, endured much in the cause of democracy and justice.

CHAPTER 1

The House on Tree Street

That was all the medicine that I needed.
—George Elmore to the *Lighthouse and Informer*, April 25, 1948

The April morning dawned with a chill in the air that soon gave way to balmy temperatures rising into the 70s. Monday, April 19, 1948, was the kind of promising South Carolina spring day that might have lured neighbors on Columbia's Tree Street outdoors to sit on porches or exchange a pleasant word across clotheslines. Most weekdays if you had inquired at 907 Tree Street, George Elmore would have been at work, juggling his labors as a shopkeeper, photographer, and taxi driver. His wife or young children might have pointed you around the corner and up the street to the Waverly Five-and-10-Cents store Elmore operated on Gervais Street, a bustling thoroughfare that bisected the neighborhoods fanning out from the state capitol building. On this April day Elmore was home, inside his one-story white frame home, recuperating from a cold. He was reclining in his easy chair when he heard the news from Washington that would reverberate from his modest dwelling in Columbia's segregated lower Waverly neighborhood, down Gervais Street to the majestic capitol building, and across the South.

Newspaper and wire service reporters raced to file the story out of the US Supreme Court that would dominate the next day's headlines: the high court had buried the "white primary," the electoral process that had stitched white supremacy into the fabric of southern life.[1] The decision in *Elmore v. Rice* was revolutionary because the primary election, held months before the November general election, was the only election that counted in a South controlled by white Democrats since Reconstruction. For years those same white Democrats had crafted a system that eliminated Republican-leaning citizens, illiterate white

7

people, and almost all Black people. No more could a Black person be turned away from the polls because of the color of his skin. Black women and men, long denied the vote through decades of legal subterfuge and legislative sleights of hand, were no longer to be spectators to democracy. It was Elmore, a gregarious, self-made man with his hand in a half dozen ventures from the dime store to a photography business, who had hammered the last nail in the coffin. What that held for the future of South Carolina was anybody's guess.

Who informed Elmore of the decision by the nation's high court is long forgotten. Perhaps it was his Columbia attorney, Harold R. Boulware, who a year earlier had represented Elmore "and others similarly situated" in a federal district courtroom where it was standing room only, three-fourths of the room made up of Black spectators. Perhaps, although unlikely given his intense work and travel schedule, it was the peripatetic NAACP attorney Thurgood Marshall who had traveled the South stamping out white primaries through dogged persistence and a string of federal lawsuits. Marshall had pressed South Carolina civil rights leaders to find someone willing—and, to be honest, brave enough—to bring down the curtain on the last Southern Democratic Party primary restricted to white voters. Elmore had stepped forward and was now stepping into history.

Since the 1920s, the NAACP had embarked on a decades-long legal struggle to open the white primaries that reigned from Texas to Virginia. The nation's high courts had played what one historian aptly described as a "game of constitutional tag"[2] with the states of the old Confederacy to excise labyrinthine provisions aimed at excluding eligible Black men and women from participating in the primary elections. The NAACP had finally managed to derail the white primary in Texas with the landmark decision in *Smith v. Allwright*[3] that now threatened to undermine the power of the white South. South Carolina's white leaders had become so alarmed over the outcome of the Texas white primary case that they had hustled to the capital city in April 1944 at the behest of the governor. Over a period of six days, lawmakers wiped out any reference to primaries in state statutes, believing their actions might pacify the nation's high court and allow the Democratic Party to keep its primary white.[4]

Elmore, a genial man with an almost indefatigable optimism and energy, was among several Columbians who had considered placing their names on the federal lawsuit that became *Elmore v. Rice*. Elmore understood the effort would carry some personal cost, although he might not have reckoned with the deepening travails that would follow. He endured a three-day trial in the US District Court in Columbia in June 1947. A month later, Judge Waring sided with him, stunning South Carolina party leaders with the ferocity of his legal ruling and his disdain for their "private club" shenanigans. Appeals followed, first to the US Court of Appeals for the Fourth Circuit in Baltimore and then to the US Supreme Court. Through it all, Elmore had dispensed dry goods and candy at the brick-front dime store and waited patiently. Now, on this April day, less than a year after his trial, the nation's highest court had spoken: the Supreme Court stood by the decision of Judge Waring and refused to review the case further.

As wire services dispatched the news across the South, there was unrestrained jubilation in the living room of 907 Tree Street. The forty-three-year-old Elmore leaped up from his easy chair and let out a whoop of joy. His son, Cresswell, then a boy of nine, remembers the joyous scene as his father celebrated and wept over the triumph.

"That was all the medicine that I needed," Elmore declared to John H. McCray, founder and editor of the *Lighthouse and Informer*, one of the city's two Black-owned newspapers. The news roared through the Black community like a rocket. "Telegrams, phone calls, local and long distance, buzzed all over the city," McCray reported in the April 25, 1948, edition. "Attorney Boulware's office had received 106 calls by noon. They didn't count them at the *Lighthouse and Informer*, but the phone rang and rang and rang. The same was true of other places."[5] The *Pittsburgh Courier* and the *Afro-American* in Baltimore dispatched reporters to cover the explosive news.

The following day, the headline in the capital's newspaper, *The State*, declared the verdict in unequivocal terms: "Highest Court Says Negroes May Vote in Primaries." The Associated Press dispatch from Washington began: "The supreme court today cut the last ground from under Southern Democratic groups which had sought to bar Negroes from their primaries by operating as private clubs outside the legally established election machinery."[6] Across town in the office of the *Lighthouse and Informer*, editor McCray was gleeful. He had founded the *Charleston Lighthouse* in 1939, and in 1941 merged it with the *People's Informer*, a Sumter newspaper founded by the Reverend E.A. Parker.

McCray had moved the newspaper to the capital city that same year and quickly established himself as a fierce advocate for the vote, unafraid to challenge the white political system in biting reports and editorials.

He had publicly railed against South Carolina's election system and the white political establishment which had aimed, since the turn of the century, to exclude Black citizens from voting through a toxic mix of intimidation and artifice. McCray, Elmore, South Carolina NAACP President James M. Hinton, and NAACP Secretary Modjeska Monteith Simkins were among those who had decided to fight the charade on a number of fronts. They formed their own political party in 1944, the Progressive Democratic Party (PDP), which white newspapers characterized with pointed parentheses as the Progressive (Negro) Democratic Party. With the high court's decision on Elmore, there were no more paths to subvert the 1944 *Smith v. Allwright* decision, McCray told his readers. "This time, it (the high court) had before it a device concocted to get around that decision and clothed in holy cloth," he wrote. "It had before it the argument of the 'private club' and the absence of statutes controlling primaries. It had before it the brazen threat of former Gov. Olin Johnston to commit violence if 'white supremacy' was not recognized under 1944 primary repeals of statutes." By upholding the Elmore decision, "on the record and in the law books, the white primary, the white party, are both dead ducks. They have gone. The next step is to make certain that the victory was not half a loaf, an empty one."[7]

The *Afro-American* in Baltimore employed even loftier language in its May 1, 1948, edition, noting that the US Supreme Court, in upholding Judge Waring's decision, had tolled the "death knell" of the white primary.[8] Waring, the seventh-generation Charleston aristocrat who would soon be labeled the "turncoat judge" for his willingness to recognize the constitutional rights of Black South Carolinians, was outraged that Democratic Party leaders would equate membership in the Democratic Party with that of a country club. In his written decision issued on July 12, 1947, Waring found that the "private club" apparatus Democrats had installed in 1944 still accomplished the purpose of electing public officials. Sloughing off the official skin of the Democratic Party did not obscure the fact that qualified Black voters, because they could not gain admittance to the white voting clubs, were being denied the right to vote in the only election that really mattered in South Carolina. "Racial distinctions cannot exist in the machinery that selects the officers and lawmakers of the United States; and all citizens of this State and Country are entitled to cast a free and untrammeled ballot in our elections," Waring wrote, "and if the only material and realistic elections are clothed with the named 'primary,' they are equally entitled to vote there." He had a final word for the political establishment so keen on keeping South Carolina's elections in the hands of white people. "It is time for South Carolina to rejoin the Union. It is time to fall in step with the other states and to adopt the American way of conducting elections."[9]

In the twenty-first century, the concept of a political primary that operated as an exclusive "whites only" club seems anathema to the American democratic spirit. But Elmore and his contemporaries were all too familiar with the ways of white South Carolinians. The political establishment had, since the turn of the century, defined how Black South Carolinians would live, work, and play. Tree Street, like nearby Pine and Oak Streets, was a "colored" street, its dirt road dividing two rows of modest, mostly white-framed shotgun dwellings, some still employing outhouses in the back for bathroom facilities. A few streets over, white families dwelled in two-story houses, although in post–World War II white and Black South Carolinians shared equally in the dust that rolled up from unpaved roads.

Elmore's two oldest children, Naomi and Cresswell, walked to segregated Waverly School while white children attended their own grammar schools. The children went to Union Baptist Church every Sunday, their mother, Laura Delaney Elmore, hauling the children in the family's 1938 black Pontiac to the segregated sanctuary on the corner of Blossom and Assembly Streets. George Elmore preferred to stay home, telling his son that he disliked that some of the men in the congregation bought whiskey on credit from his liquor store to slyly sell in the church basement. The Elmore children freely raced and played with the children of other Waverly families—the Artemuses, Fitzgeralds, Holleys—amid a robust and aspiring Black community that served as a reassuring cocoon for working and raising families. But the boundaries of their exuberant play were well established. They did not venture to play at nearby Valley Park, skirting the green lawns and playground of the city park reserved for white people. (Even as teenagers they would

Two boys watch a Little League baseball game from a perimeter wall at Valley Park on June 16, 1955. The city parks were segregated for decades, and Black children were not allowed into the park to play or participate in sports. Tom Nebbia, photographer. The State Newspaper Photograph Archive. Courtesy of Richland Library.

take care to walk around the park on their way to Booker T. Washington High School.)[10]

Perhaps most galling of all, Black voters who had tasted the fruits of the ballot box after the Civil War were totally shut out of elections after the ratification of the 1895 South Carolina Constitution, which stripped Black South Carolinians of the few gains they had made since the war's end. A few obtained election certificates to vote in South Carolina's general election, but the real electoral drama took place months before in the primary. As Waring noted in his opinion, 290,223 votes were cast for governor in the August 1946 Democrat primary that Elmore was barred from. In the general election later in November, less than one-tenth of that ballot number—26,326 votes—were cast for the same offices.[11]

Elmore was born into a state led by avowed racists such as Benjamin Ryan "Pitchfork Ben" Tillman, the architect of the 1895 constitutional convention that disenfranchised Black voters; Ellison D. "Cotton Ed" Smith, a longtime US senator; and Coleman "Coley" Livingston Blease, a bombastic, often vulgar, two-term governor. They made no bones about where they stood on the color line. Smith, who was born in 1864 during the Civil War and went on to serve six terms in the US Senate, was said to have two goals: keeping Negroes down and the price of cotton up. Smith had walked out of the 1936 Democratic National Convention because a Black minister delivered an invocation at an afternoon session.[12] Smith left for good the next day after learning that Congress's only Black member, Illinois Representative Arthur W. Mitchell, was set to speak. When Smith lost his seat in 1944 after a bruising battle in the South Carolina Democratic primary, *Time* magazine described him as "a conscientious objector to the 20th century." He was a man, the weekly news magazine noted, who delivered "oratorial omelets" full of "southern corn, overblown poetical allusions, rough waggery, and incoherent rambling" and never overcame his horror of a Black man voting.[13] Blease, born in 1868, served in the state legislature before his election to governor in 1910 and 1912, promoting white supremacy and lynching with a fervor that reached fever pitch in his appeals to white mill workers. He also served in the US Senate, scandalizing his colleagues in 1929 by reading a poem called "Niggers in the White House" after First Lady Lou Hoover entertained Jesse DePriest, the wife of the lone Black congressman, Oscar Stanton DePriest, at a White House tea. The vulgar doggerel was later expunged from the Congressional Record because of its offensiveness.[14] But the event generated national headlines and spawned hundreds of letters to the White House complaining that the Hoovers were attempting to impose social equality between the races.

Elmore's white contemporaries—those who were born, as he was, at the turn of the century—were as insistent on maintaining white power as those born in the shadow of the Civil War. Olin D. Johnston, a two-term governor, beat the aging Smith in the 1944 Democratic primary, mainly by touting his part in preserving white supremacy at the 1944 special legislative session. (A decade earlier, when Smith departed the 1936 Democratic National Convention in a huff, the more vigorous Johnston had lamented the theatrics, telling a reporter, "You can tell the senator that we will never be bothered with Negro equality in South

Carolina.").[15] In his speech to the 1944 special session, Johnston had declared: "History has taught us that we must keep our white Democratic primaries pure and unadulterated so that we might protect the welfare and homes of all the people of our State."[16] Strom Thurmond, elected governor in 1946, was deeply alarmed by President Harry Truman's decision to desegregate the military and Truman's advocacy of a civil rights plank in the Democratic Party platform. That summer of 1948 Thurmond would become the presidential standard bearer for the newly formed "Dixiecrats" and thunder against the ongoing assaults on the "southern way of life." These were men with deep roots in the past, keepers of a glorious, mythical narrative of prosperity, war, and redemption concentrated in an antebellum nineteenth century vision of South Carolina. The legacy of the fiery pro-slavery, states' rights politician John C. Calhoun hung heavy over historical remembrance. "I have come to the conclusion that our generation got very little real history taught us," James A. Hoyt Jr., a longtime South Carolina newspaperman working in Washington as the auditor and reporter for the United States Court of Claims, wrote to his friend Fitz Hugh McMaster in December 17, 1938. In an exchange of letters debating the greatness of South Carolina leaders, Hoyt lamented, "It was all colored with Calhoun and with secession, and the other side did not get a show."[17] A few days later, McMaster wrote to his friend, newspaper editor William Watts Ball: "I think Ben Tillman did more to suppress talent in South Carolina and elevate mediocrity than any other man who ever lived in the state."[18]

Elmore, born in 1905, entered a society where white and Black people operated in two strictly separate societies, attending separate schools and separate churches. Most South Carolinians labored on farms and most Black laborers were tenant farmers or sharecroppers, working on shares and beholden to white owners in a system of peonage not far removed from enslavement. In the state's few urban centers such as Columbia and Charleston, Black men were subservient to white bosses in factories and mills. Black women served as domestics and nursemaids to white households. Black household income was a fraction of that of white households, with white non-farm common laborers earning 29 cents an hour and black non-farm workers earning about 23 cents per hour.[19]

The return of Black and white World War II veterans, many impatient for change, and the growing industrial and financial power of the United States signaled opportunities, even for South Carolina, so rooted in its agrarian ways. Elmore had already succeeded at exploiting the booming war economy, ferrying Fort Jackson soldiers to and from their destinations in his taxi and trading ration coupons when he could. He was a fixture in the Black business community that anchored Gervais Street and Millwood Avenue, his Waverly Street Five-and-10-Cents store a place to obtain everything from ice-cold Coca-Cola to canned goods and sewing notions. He operated a liquor store and a photography business, setting up a back room of 907 Tree Street for his darkroom. He was a fourth degree Mason and regularly attended lodge meetings. He could afford Buster Brown shoes for his growing family and keep his wife, Laura, supplied with the almond Hershey chocolate bars she loved. On this joyous April day, when moviegoers at the downtown Carolina Theatre were laughing at the comedic antics of William Powell in *"The Senator Was Indiscreet,"* about a bumbling, crooked southern politician,[20] Elmore could be forgiven for believing that the future was spreading out generously for his family and for other Black South Carolinians.

The 1947 trial and subsequent appeals had not been easy, although Elmore seemed to have the same personal fortitude that other men of his era possessed. America had defeated Nazi Germany, and change was in the air as returning military veterans were poised to shape postwar America. Black soldiers had helped secure the victory, and those coming back to South Carolina were determined to change the entrenched segregation that defined an agrarian economy where plodding mules still outnumbered tractors in the fields. Elmore had come to the capital city sometime in the 1920s from his home in Holly Hill, leaving the rural farm life behind. In Columbia, he met Laura Delaney, the young woman he would court and marry. Early in their marriage, they had rented small unpainted wooden houses on Read and Lyon streets. But by 1943, with two children in tow, Elmore had purchased the Tree Street home, although the city directory reference misspelled "Tree" as "Free" Street.[21]

Elmore had discussed with NAACP leaders the risks of placing his name on a lawsuit, which would be viewed as a a high-profile legal assault against the white political establishment. At that time lynching was still a horrible consequence of stepping outside of the rigid system. Hinton, the NAACP state president, was routinely the target of threats, as was editor McCray. Before the decade was out, Hinton would be kidnapped and beaten by members of the Ku Klux Klan (KKK), released only because the kidnappers had heard that police were searching for them. A returning World War II veteran, Isaac Woodard, had been beaten and blinded by police in Batesburg, South Carolina, in February 1946, hours after being honorably discharged from military service in Georgia. McCray was among the first news-papermen to tell the story, reporting that Woodard was pulled off the bus for having the temerity to ask the Greyhound bus driver to wait as he used a restroom. As Elmore and other Black business and political leaders contemplated the best means of penetrating the political life of their state and discussed who among them would be best situated to take up the challenge, he relied upon his light skin to grant him entrée. "They don't know if I'm white or black," he told NAACP leaders.[22]

George Elmore's arrival to register to vote might have seemed a mat-ter of routine to the Millwood Avenue store clerk, although she likely was frazzled on this day because there had been a concerted effort by Black Columbians across Columbia's wards to register. When that hap-pened, the registration book would be quickly stashed under a counter and declared unavailable. Because he was light skinned, Elmore was welcomed, even though she may have recognized him talking with a group of Black men attempting to register throughout the day. As she had done for countless white citizens, the clerk pulled out a big ledger from behind a counter and assisted Elmore in filling out the proper paperwork for the much-coveted voting certificate. Elmore completed the application, leaving only his address blank. "She told him, 'Why you did everything right except you forgot your address,'" Cresswell Elmore, George Elmore's son, recalled. When his father wrote down his 907 Tree Street address, the demeanor of the registrar changed. "Why you're a nigger!" she exclaimed.[23]

Nevertheless, Elmore was able to obtain the certificate that allowed him to cast a ballot in the general election. (He was appar-ently so persuasive that she allowed the other Black men who had been attempting to register that day inside to complete enrollment.) In a 1962 speech recounting the memories of that day, McCray noted wryly, "Quite often one finds that these Southern whites who declare so firmly that they know Negroes and what Negroes need and want, demonstrate overtly that actually they can't even tell a Negro from a white person."[24] On August 13, 1946—the date of the SC Democratic primary—Elmore presented himself at the polling place, requesting a ballot and permission to vote. He was rebuffed on the grounds that he was not a white Democrat. His action was a key maneuver in the upcoming lawsuit—NAACP lawyers needed someone who had registered successfully and attempted to vote in the primary. In the sworn affidavit he made on that sweltering summer day, the forty-one-year-old Elmore testified that he was directed to John I. Rice, chairman of the Richland County Democratic Executive Committee, who stood at his Ward 9 precinct. The deposition, taken by civil rights attorney Boulware, noted: "John I. Rice stated to him that he could not and would not permit him to vote; that John I. Rice further stated that he (the deponent) was not a member of the Democratic Party and that the said party was for white people only; that he asked the said John I. Rice why he was not permitted to vote and that the said John I. Rice stated to him that no Negroes were permitted to vote in the Democratic Primary."[25]

When the *Elmore v. Rice* case opened in Waring's courtroom June 4, 1947, Elmore seemed a mystery to the lawyers intent on keeping him out of Democratic Party politics. Christie Benet, a South Carolina football standout who had served a brief five-month term in the US Senate following the death of Senator Tillman, was one of a cadre of attorneys representing the Richland County executive committee. He argued that "George Elmore, Columbia Negro five-and-ten cent store operator, did not testify to anything in the case 'and makes no showing of what he is,'" *The State* reported in its June 5, 1947, edition. "Elmore does not show whether he is a Democrat, Republican, Populist, Communist—or what not," Benet was quoted. "Elmore doesn't say he believes in the principles of the Democratic Party. He simply comes before the court and asked that he be infiltrated into the Democratic primary."[26]

Benet's choice of words was no accident. Implying that Elmore could be a Communist or infiltrator was part of the larger narrative that the southern white power structure had utilized throughout the century to keep Black people from exercising the ballot. (In the 1950s and 1960s, it would expand to include the accusation that those demanding change were "outside agitators," even if they were native-born South Carolinians.) Given the opportunity, white politicians emphasized in speeches and campaign harangues that naïve Black citizens, if given full access to the vote, would fall prey to foreign elements. The fear that Black people would somehow join in a powerful bloc to topple those in power

kept uneducated white people in line too, even if they might have bene-
fited from aligning their economic interests with Black people.

Democrats who had smarted from Judge Waring's blistering July
1947 opinion, became more alarmed when the federal appeals court
in December 1947 upheld Judge Waring's decision. The lawyers,
despite the ruling in the Texas white primary case, had held out hope
that the US Supreme Court would come to their rescue in 1948, seeing the Elmore case in isolation. Stunned by the high court's rebuff,
Democratic Party leaders had no immediate comment. But Hinton,
the powerful state president of the South Carolina Conference of the
NAACP and a member of the Progressive Democratic Party, argued it
was time for Black people and white people to come together. "It is the
wish of all Negroes that the South Carolina Democratic party will bow
in obedience to the courts and will as good citizens, good sports . . .
now welcome Negroes into the Democratic primaries," he told the city's
newspapers. "They could do no less and Negroes expect no less."

McCray, who was also chairman of the Progressive Democrats, told
the daily newspapers: "The question of subterfuges and denials based
on class and race is now forever settled as far as voting by classes is
concerned." Any attempt "to void the rights of Negroes . . . will be challenged with the same vigor which characterized the now-ended struggle for the Democratic ballot in South Carolina."[27]

Three days later, Governor Thurmond returned from a trip to Washington where he had lobbied for the deepening of the Beaufort-Port
Royal harbor. He said he was shocked at the high court's refusal to
review the case.

"I predict that Americans everywhere will live to regret the prin-
ciple of law which has been laid down," he said in a statement published in the April 22, 1948, edition of *The State*. "The result is unsound
and un-American, and denies to our people their constitutional right
of peaceful assembly." He went on: "We in South Carolina will be faced
with many serious practical problems in the days ahead. These we will
solve with the coolness and determination of our forefathers."[28]

Shortly after the Supreme Court decision, Elmore finally exercised
his newly won right. State Democratic Party Chairman W. P. Baskin
decided that anyone—Black person or white person—who was in possession of a city registration certificate could properly cast ballots in
the Columbia municipal election set for the following day, April 20.
Elmore, who moonlighted as a photographer, also recorded the historic

The State: South Carolina's Largest Newspaper COLUMBIA, S. C., WEDNESDAY, AUGUST 11, 1948

Negroes Line Up in Ward 9 to Vote in Democratic Primary

Shown above is a portion of the voters casting their ballots in Ward 9, where the greatest proportion of Negro Democratic voters is enrolled, as evidenced by the long line at the right. A portion of the line for white voters may be seen at the left. (Photo by Munn.)

George Elmore (foreground, center of image) watches as hundreds of Black voters turn out to cast ballots on August 10, 1948, the first statewide primary since his successful lawsuit, *Elmore v. Rice*. The State Newspaper Archive. Courtesy of Richland Library.

moment, photographing the first Black voters to cast primary ballots in the city's Ward 9 in at least half a century. Four months later, on August 10, 1948, the opportunity to vote in the statewide Democratic primary drew thousands more Black voters to the polls, although Waring had to weigh in once more on a loyalty oath that Democrats had engineered that would require all voters to affirm the separation of the races. In *Brown v. Baskin*, he imposed a temporary injunction against the oath and threatened South Carolina officials with jail if they attempted to violate the spirit of the Elmore decision. Newspaper photographers captured the faces of patient, expectant voters on that historic day. One photograph in *The State* shows men and women waiting in long lines to cast ballots in Columbia's Ward 9. Elmore was there too, a lone, rotund figure standing under an umbrella and surveying the scene.[29]

Eventually, George Elmore, the man behind the counter of the five-and-dime, the moonlighting photographer and taxi driver, the husband

and father who made a courageous and ultimately life-altering calculation, became lost to history. The flesh-and-blood activist who rose up from his easy chair to hear the news that the "white primary" was no more, simply became a name on a crucial legal case. The lives he and his family, his neighbors on Tree Street, and his contemporaries in the NAACP and Progressive Democratic Party lived became part of a gauzy, irretrievable past. The trials that were to come were chalked up to "the times" and his challenge to segregation one among hundreds in those years before the full national flowering of the civil rights movement. Elmore's participation in the dismantling of rigid segregation shaped his life and, likely, his death. His story is both a South Carolina story and an American story.

CHAPTER 2

Amid a Rural Landscape, Spasms of Violence

After this nothing was known of the affair until a
volley of perhaps 500 shots rang out just west of
the town of Badham, and when the correspondent
arrived at the scene the lynching party had all
departed. . . .

—*The State*, August 24, 1906

George Augustus Elmore was born on a late winter day in March 1905,
his mother, Sadie, likely attended by a midwife in a one-room cabin
in rural South Carolina.[1] Sadie Johnson was nineteen or twenty years
old at the time of his birth and unmarried. Family lore suggested that
the baby's father was a Jewish man, although that was never substanti-
ated, and the father and son never crossed paths in their lifetimes. A
few years later Sadie wed George W. Elmore, a man more than twice
her age. By the 1910 census, when little George was five years old, the
household included the elder George Elmore, 51, Sadie, 25, and children, Ben, 12, George, 5, Willie, 1, and an infant daughter, Ines. It is not
clear from census records whether Ben Elmore was George's or Sadie's
son from a previous relationship. The elder George Elmore, a farmer,
was listed as a Black man; the race of Sadie and the children was listed
as mulatto, a common term of the times for someone of mixed race.
George, sometimes identified as George Johnson or Johnston in census records, would take his stepfather's name. But stories swirled in
later years about the paternity of the five-year-old, whose skin color
was a few shades lighter than that of his brothers and sisters. George
Elmore always rooted his family in Holly Hill, in Orangeburg County,
on the border of Orangeburg and Dorchester Counties. The family
likely moved in his early years; he attended school in Harleyville in
Dorchester County. The Elmores were always listed in the Dorchester
County census.[2]

The pastoral Lowcountry world that young George was born into was one of seemingly endless fields of cotton and corn, swamplands, hot humid summers, and a pattern of life that had long revolved around the seasons and agricultural production. His maternal ancestors had been freed from enslavement four decades earlier, but most of the Black families who remained in the region still worked the land as farmers and field hands. Many could not read or write. As the nineteenth century ended, Black residents of Dorchester County outnumbered white residents, a reminder of the thousands of enslaved men, women, and children who had toiled on the sprawling rice and cotton plantations of earlier times. Those plantations, with lyrical names of Middleton Place, Newington, Tipseeboo, and Clear Springs, were long gone after dominating the bustling agricultural economy of the Lowcountry before the war. But the land, now divided into smaller agricultural ventures, was still being farmed. By 1900, 42 percent of Black farmers in Dorchester County operated farms as owners or tenants, and George Elmore, listed as a farmer and employer in the 1910 census, was likely one of them. But while the census designation of farm owner created an illusion of limited but growing prosperity, the title was obscured by the harsh reality of farm life. Census enumerators were instructed to report as a "farm" any tract of three or more acres, as well as any tract under three acres that produced at least $250 worth of farm products in 1909. Census writers in 1910 noted that the number of farms grew exponentially between 1850 and 1910, mainly because of the breakup of the old plantation system. "In the case of many plantations, although most of the land is now worked by tenants, each of whom is reported as a farmer and the land operated by him as a farm, yet there is supervision by the owner, so that, in a sense, the entire plantation may be said to constitute a single farm."[3]

The 1910 census reported 176,434 farms across South Carolina, the majority, 111,221, listed as tenant farms. There were 64,350 classified as owner farms and 863 as farms operated by managers. The tenant structure included "share" tenants, those who paid a certain share of the products they raised in exchange for rent of the land; share-cash tenants, who paid a share of crops as well as cash for rent of the land; and cash tenants, who paid "a cash rental or stated amount of labor or products such as $7, 10 bushels of wheat, or 100 pounds of seed cotton per acre," according to the census report. Across South Carolina, as farm operators increased from 93,864 in 1880 to 176,434 in 1910, the number of tenants expanded from 47,219 to 111,221. In the 1910 census, "colored" farmers owned just 21 percent of farms while tenants "of color" operated 78.8 percent of the farmland.[4]

Dorchester County, where federal census workers recorded the Elmore family, was officially created by an act of the state legislature in 1897, originally part of the vast tract of Lowcountry lands that included Colleton and Berkeley counties. But settlers had lived along the Ashley River since 1676 when Congregationalists from Massachusetts first settled there and created the village of Dorchester. The 1897 act also divided the county into townships instead of parishes, which had been the tradition in the past centuries. The new townships included Burns, Dorchester, Carns, George, Givhans, Koger, and part of Collins. The Elmores resided in Givhans township in the 1910 census.

As it had been for decades before and after the Civil War, life for the Elmores was dictated by the seasons and the crops that were the lifeblood of the region. Elmore's stepfather, born about 1856, had been witness to the brief spurt of progress for Black people during the Reconstruction period. He left no account of his memories of enslavement, the Civil War, or the postwar period, but to be a youngster at this juncture in history must have been illuminating.

In 1865, South Carolina and other rebel states came under federal control, although that may have been too mystifying for a nine-year-old to grasp. But he would have been witness to the confusion and celebration of freedom that the end of the war brought as well as the upheaval to the old plantation way of life that was played out in the Lowcountry and beyond.

Union surgeon Henry Orlando Marcy, who served with the 35th Colored Troops, recorded some of the confusion and mayhem in his diary as federal troops under Union General William Sherman methodically worked to confiscate and destroy Lowcountry plantations. In January 1865, federal troops burned the Beaufort County District Courthouse, prompting Marcy to write: "I trust this blasted (blasted is crossed out in the text) state has hung its last slave under its code of black laws—and the blackened ruins of court house and all would seem to appear a fit monument of their injustice, and pound out the vengeance of heaven visited upon their legal crimes." A few days later on February 12, 1865, he set fire to the jail at one of the plantations belonging to Charles

Heyward. While Marcy lamented the destruction of the grand river homes, "this I did with pleasure. Some of their means of punishment are worthy of the old Inquisition."[5]

Marcy arrived at Middleton Place, the palatial Dorchester County home and gardens of Williams Middleton along the Ashley River, on February 23, 1865. "All here was confusion," he wrote. Middleton had already taken his family and abandoned the plantation when the 56th New York Regiment of Volunteers arrived and informed the enslaved that they were now free. Marcy observed the house both before and after its burning and lamented the loss of its library, containing more than eight-thousand volumes, as well as the state of the house with its goods and furnishings strewn about the ground. But he spent time explaining some options to those newly emancipated who wanted to leave Middleton: "My first object was to get the people together and advise them what to do—find there is a schooner and several flats here and as they are all determined to leave I advise them to load the boats and proceed to the city."[6]

White southerners looked on in horror at the swath of devastation wrought by the Union army, a destruction that would turn Sherman's name into a bitter gall for generations. They wrung their hands and lamented the future of a state where those who had labored for free were now abandoning their toil in fields and grand houses to seek shelter and guidance from the Union soldiers. One Union soldier, surveying the chaotic scenes as Sherman's army marched from Georgia through the Carolinas, saw the Union troops as "God's instruments of justice." Brevet Major General George Ward Nichols, an aide-de-camp to Sherman, scorned the evils of the plantation system and the haughty southern aristocrats who had degraded Black people beyond his comprehension. While house servants showed some education, Nichols wrote in his diary, "the plantation negroes are the most ignorant and debased of any I have ever seen. As nearly as I can ascertain, it has been the effort of the South Carolina master to degrade his slaves as low in the scale of human nature, and as near the mules and oxen which he owns in common with them, as possible." He added: "It makes one's blood boil to see the evidences of the heartlessness and cruelty of these white men."[7]

Nichols was equally appalled at the appearance and living conditions of white factory women at the Saluda Factory as they passed through that town on the way to Columbia. "In the old times it was a favorite argument of the slaveholders that their 'peculiar institution' was a blessing to the negroes, and it was their habit to make comparisons between the condition of their slaves and that of our well-bred, intelligent factory operatives, asserting that the slaves were the higher and happier class of the two," he wrote. "We have seen what the slaves are; but here is a shocking exhibition of the disgrace and degradation which is visited upon white labor in the South."[8]

As the soldiers made their way to Columbia, amassing a growing herd of livestock, more and more formerly enslaved people joined them despite efforts by their former enslavers to hide them and the horses from the Union advance. "The latter, however, when they could do so, have hidden in the swamps, coming out to join us as we passed along," he wrote. "As usual, they are our best friends, giving invaluable information of the roads and the movements of the enemy. They are always our safest guides, and their fidelity is never questioned."[9]

But the "best friends" of the invading Yankees were soon pawns in a post-Civil War reorganization of society marked by a devastating and concentrated rollback of gains in voting and education as well as ongoing violent physical attacks by the Ku Klux Klan. This process at times took the form of physical violence, while at other times the mechanisms were legislative and judicial. The goals were the same: to deny the humanity, or at very least the citizenship, of Black people. While the wartime Emancipation Proclamation and the Thirteenth Amendment had officially ended enslavement, the status of newly freed people remained uncertain. Would they be recognized as full citizens by the federal and state governments? And how would white southerners react to the new realities? In South Carolina, as in other southern states, initial answers came in the form of the Black Codes, a series of laws meant to define the place of Black people within a post-enslavement society.

South Carolina passed its version of the Black Codes in December 1865, the same month the Thirteenth Amendment to the US Constitution, which abolished slavery, was ratified. It had been just eight months since the laying down of arms at Appomattox on April 9, 1865. President Abraham Lincoln was assassinated shortly after on April 14, 1865, roiling the country into further upheaval and plunging the country into national mourning. Lincoln was succeeded by Vice President Andrew Johnson, also a target of the assassins who harbored sympathies for

the defeated white plantation owners. The legislature's act, "to establish and regulate the Domestic Relations of Persons of Colour, and to
amend the law in relation to Paupers and Vagrancy,"[10] outlined the
realities of a world for the more than four hundred thousand newly
freed people in South Carolina. The Black Codes delineated certain limited civil rights to the newly emancipated, while ensuring they would
remain as farm laborers to white bosses. Black workers, called "servants" under the law, were required to enter into labor contracts with
white employers. The contracts ensured that the workers remained on
the employer's farm and work sunup to sunset except on Sundays. No
one wanted to be picked up as a vagrant because sheriffs could then
"hire out" the imprisoned to work off their punishment.

While the newly free were now servants, not slaves, the legislation
made it clear that the people for whom they would be toiling would
be known by that familiar, fear-inducing title of master. The hours of
labor remained as during slavery. If the servant and master disagreed
over the work or pay or misconduct, a district judge or magistrate could
mediate the dispute. But the laws were written with the old plantation
order in mind:

> For any acts or things herein declared to be causes for the dis-
> charge of a servant, or for any breach of contract or duty by him,
> instead of discharging the servant, the master may complain
> to the District Judge or one of the Magistrates, who shall have
> power, on being satisfied of the misconduct complained of, to
> inflict, or cause to be inflicted, on the servant, suitable corporal
> punishment, or impose upon him such pecuniary fine as may be
> though fit, and immediately to remand him to his work; which
> fine shall be deducted from his wages, if not otherwise paid.[11]

The intent was to keep Black workers subservient to white "mas-
ters" and without redress in the courts. Opportunities for meager economic advancement were slim to none and secret organizations were
now afield terrorizing Black citizens. The Thirteenth Amendment was
meant to lay to rest the centuries-old claim that one race could enslave
another, but it also included a crucial phrase that would come to haunt
the newly freed for the next 150 years. Slavery or involuntary servitude
could no longer be practiced in the United States "*except as a punishment for crime whereof the party shall have been duly convicted.*" And so

petty crimes, from stealing a pig to vagrancy, became grounds for what modern historians consider a second slavery, setting the stage for mass incarceration of minorities in the twentieth century.

Northern outcry mobilized efforts in the Black community, and the response of South Carolina's military district governor, General Daniel Sickles, led to the abolition of most of the formal Black Codes in the fall of 1866, less than a year after the measure's passage. Earlier that spring, in April 1866, Congress passed the Civil Rights Act over the objections of President Johnson, who shared the attitude of most white South Carolinians that the lives of freedmen should be tightly regulated. Two months later Congress passed the Fourteenth Amendment and required that legislatures of the southern states ratify the amendment before the state's congressional representatives could be seated. Passage of the Fourteenth Amendment was aimed at ending such feudal discrimination. Section 1 of the Fourteenth Amendment stated: *All persons born or naturalized in the United States, and subject to the jurisdiction thereof, are citizens of the United States and of the State wherein they reside. No State shall make or enforce any law which shall abridge the privileges or immunities of citizens of the United States; nor shall any State deprive any person of life, liberty, or property, without due process of law; nor deny to any person within its jurisdiction the equal protection of the laws.*

Again President Johnson objected, saying it was unfair to the former Confederate states. The South Carolina Legislature, which wanted to maintain some dominance over the freedmen but pacify the federal government, repealed sections of the Black Codes in the fall of 1866 at the behest of Governor James Orr. The new legislation removed the racial taint and made equal for Black and white people the right to own land, make contracts, and inherit. Laws concerning vagrancy remained on the books, however, as did the prohibition on intermarriage between the races. Two-and-a-half years after the passage and repeal of the Black Codes, the South Carolina General Assembly ratified the Fourteenth Amendment on July 18, 1868.[12]

Promises made to the newly emancipated—of land ownership and perhaps a surplus army mule to till the fields—were also abandoned before the first anniversary of the end of the war. Union General William Sherman, after meeting with formerly enslaved people in Savannah, had issued his famous Field Order No. 15 in January 1865, which transferred land ownership of thousands of acres of rich and idle land along the coast of Georgia and South Carolina. The field order read:

> The islands from Charleston south, the abandoned rice fields along the rivers for thirty miles back from the sea, and the country bordering the St. John's River, Florida, are reserved and set apart for the settlement of the negroes now made free by the acts of war and the [Emancipation] proclamation of the President of the United States.
>
> Whenever three respectable negroes, heads of families, shall desire to settle on land, and shall have selected for that purpose an island or a locality clearly defined, within the limits above designated, the Inspector of Settlements and Plantations will himself, or by such subordinate officer as he may appoint, give them a license to settle such island or district and afford them such assistance as he can to enable them to establish a peaceable agricultural settlement, the field order noted.[13]

But even as the freedmen planted fields that spring and watched their crops mature in summer, southerners were in Washington seeking the ear of the president. Months later President Johnson reversed Sherman's field order and required that some forty thousand Black freedmen return the lands to the original plantation owners.

For Elmore's Black ancestors, enslaved on Lowcountry farms, federal Reconstruction offered the great hope that they would take their places as full American citizens. The passage of the 1868 state constitution, a document which offered real, tangible democracy to newly freed enslaved people, was revolutionary, including elegiac language in Section 1 that echoed the Declaration of Independence: "All men are born free and equal—endowed by their Creator with certain inalienable rights, among which are the rights of enjoying and—defending their lives and liberties, of acquiring, possessing and protecting property, and of seeking and obtaining their safety and happiness."[14] The new South Carolina state constitution, adopted in March 1868 by a majority of Black voters, breathed hope in the hearts of the newly freed men and women. They were now allowed to vote and to be educated. Women had the right to retain property and to be divorced. But many white South Carolinians, ruined by war and undone by the toppling of the social and economic order, would not accept the changes that came with federal Reconstruction of the South. They could not fathom that

Black South Carolinians were now leaders of the constitutional convention that opened in Charleston on January 14, 1868. Albert G. Mackey, a white Republican, was elected president of the convention, and the proceedings suggest the gravity and earnestness possessed by the delegates. The *Charleston Mercury* ridiculed the gathering as the "Great Ringed-Streaked and Striped Convention" composed of men who were only elected because white voters could not, or would not, exercise their vote because of federal Reconstruction. The newspaper offered up sketches that aimed to poke fun at and diminish the work of the delegates.[15] The "piebald Convention, so far as heard from, will consist of two-thirds negroes and one-third whites," The *Charleston Daily Courier* wrote in its November 25, 1867, edition. "To call this a Convention of the people of South Carolina is a farce that deceives no one."[16] Of the one hundred twenty-four delegates gathered, seventy-six were Black and more than half of them had been enslaved. Forty-eight white delegates were present.

In a 2003 interview, James L. Underwood, the late distinguished professor emeritus of constitutional law at the University of South Carolina (USC) and an expert on the state constitution, said the document had "a lot of earmarks of our national constitution. It had a better delineation of separation of powers." The document eliminated most barriers to voting. There were no mandatory poll taxes or literacy tests, devices that would be employed liberally in coming decades. There was even a call for female suffrage, although that was turned aside.[17]

The delegates to the 1868 constitutional convention engaged in eloquent debate over the merits of establishing literacy requirements in the new constitution, namely whether to require voters who came of age by 1875 to be able to read and write—and the fairness of imposing such restrictions on a race that had been denied education for so long. "I think it would come with bad grace from any individual in this state, who has helped to deprive men for two centuries, of the means of education, to demand that in seven years all unable to read should not be allowed to vote," Delegate Francis L. Cardozo argued in urging defeat of the literacy requirement.[18]

His fellow Charlestonian, Delegate Richard H. Cain, agreed saying:

> A man may not be able to educate himself. The circumstances
> of his childhood may possibly have prevented the acquisition of
> knowledge, but for all that he is a man, the noblest work of God;

and I would not deprive any being, rich or poor, of the enjoyment of that franchise, by which alone he can protect himself as a citizen.

Too long, he said, tyrants had ruled over men. "I believe, we have entered upon a new era, and obliterated those peculiar distinctions which made the ruling class the tyrants of those held in subjection."[19] The poll tax, seen by some as a means of financing education for newly franchised Black and poor white people, also came under intense scrutiny. It remained in the document as a means of supporting public schools, but nonpayment could not be used as an excuse to deprive a man of his vote. Because the constitution was crafted by a majority Black delegation—the Radical Republicans having made sure those who had participated in the Civil War were ineligible to vote—it was doomed to destruction. "The most lasting legacy was the beginning of the educational system. That part of it survived," Underwood, the USC professor, said in the 2003 interview. Voter registration books from the period speak eloquently of the pent-up fervor of the hopes of Black people. In Beaufort, where thousands of formerly enslaved people sought refuge with the Union Army during the war, the ledger lists hundreds of names with those identified as "colored" far outnumbering those identified as white.

Passage of the 1868 constitution was a watershed event in the state's history, allowing the entrance of Black men into government positions hardly dreamed of a decade earlier. By 1870, twelve of the thirty-two members of the South Carolina Senate were Black men; seventy-five of 124 house members were Black men. But festering resentments toward Reconstruction, growing Black political influence and claims of State House corruption erupted throughout the late 1860s and 1870s, resulting in Ku Klux Klan raids on voting places and other acts of horrific violence. Among those killed was R. B. Randolph, a Black lawmaker slain while campaigning at Hodges Station in Abbeville County on October 16, 1868. His final resting place would be in the capital of Columbia, where he was reburied in a cemetery that now bears his name. This epitaph was carved into his tombstone: "Killed by assassins." Randolph Cemetery, lodged between an old city cemetery that had become a "potter's field" and the more prosperous white Elmwood Cemetery, would be a final resting place for at least nine Reconstruction-era lawmakers and many ordinary Black South Carolinians. Eventually it would be the place where George Elmore would be buried nine decades later.

In the fall of 1871, six years after the end of the Civil War and thirty-four years before George Elmore's birth, the Convention of the Colored People of the Southern States met in Columbia. The delegates, led by Robert B. Elliott, a South Carolina lawmaker newly elected to Congress, called on the United States to live up to its constitution for people of all races. It was time, delegates said, to grant full citizenship to the country's four million Black citizens, most of them newly freed from enslavement. Elliott, who had helped draft the 1868 state constitution, prepared the final address to the public.

The rights that would place the newly emancipated "on a common footing with all other citizens of the nation" have been withheld because of "the prejudices and passions left in the hearts of a portion of our fellow-citizens," the convention explained in the public statement circulated after the convention.

> Since the close of the war a settled policy has controlled the public and private action of the great body of the white people of the South towards us. They have sought to hold us in a condition of modified servitude, so that we should not be able to compete with the industry of the country.

Even more alarming was this report to the convention:

> We have been hunted like beasts by armed and disguised bands. Many, both men and women, have been killed; vast numbers have received severe corporal punishment; and many more found shelter in the swamps, by day and by night, from this storm of human hatred.[20]

Northern sympathy for the plight of former enslaved Black southerners gradually diminished under the enormous financial burden of transforming these individuals into citizens, especially as lurid and exaggerated stories of life in the South migrated north. James S. Pike, an antislavery journalist for the *New-York Tribune*, traveled to South Carolina in 1873 and reported to his northern readers that the state was under siege by "the most ignorant democracy that mankind ever saw."[21] His book, *The Prostrate State*, did much to fuel northern antagonism toward the administration of President Ulysses S. Grant and the southern Reconstruction governments.

"The overshadowing mass of black barbarism at the South hangs like a portentous cloud upon the horizon," he wrote. No one longs for the return of slavery, not even in South Carolina, he argued, because now the southerner realized that Black people had been the cause of the region's downfall. Pike continued:

> It is the Negro who has been the innocent cause of their despolia-
> tion. . . . It is the man from Africa who today bestrides them like
> a colossus. He came in helpless, he has risen in strength. He was
> the servant of South Carolina; he has become her master."[22]

Any stirrings of Black political ascendency would not last long. White South Carolinians relentlessly chipped away at the Black citizenship that Cardozo, Cain, Elliott, and others so eloquently desired. Southern planters gained reentry into the union and reclaimed lands that would now be plowed by laborers paid the cheapest daily rate possible. The white men who vowed to "redeem" the state from federal Reconstruction promoted and enlivened claims of government corruption against the Republicans, particularly Black officeholders such as Cardozo, the elected state treasurer who endured a show trial aimed at ridding the capitol of Black Republican politicians. Cardozo, who was born to a free Black woman and a Jewish father, had been educated in Scotland and Great Britain. He had served honorably as a member of the 1868 South Carolina Constitutional Convention and was elected secretary of state in 1868 and state treasurer in 1872 on the Republican ticket. But he and others could not withstand the onslaught of charges leveled at Republicans over their handling of government.

To oust the Republicans from power and return South Carolina to home rule, former Confederate General Wade Hampton III, a wartime hero who had grown wealthy on the hard labor of thousands of enslaved people on his cotton plantations in South Carolina and Mississippi, was persuaded to run for governor in 1876. As the bewhiskered war veteran traveled around the state, he was cheered by hundreds of men on horseback, who aligned themselves in rifle clubs and called themselves "Red Shirts" in defiance of those whom they believed to be destroying the white supremacy they had enjoyed. The Red Shirts stuffed ballot boxes and intimidated voters as they engaged in likely the most brazen election fraud in the state's history. They surrounded and threatened those who attended Republican meetings, firing pistols in the air. Brawling broke out in Aiken and Barnwell Counties, resulting in the deaths of between twenty-five and one hundred Black people.[23]

Hampton eventually emerged victorious over Republican Daniel Chamberlain after months of dispute, but few would remember the details of the chicanery or the violence. It was the triumph of the white "Redeemers" that would lodge in the collective memories of most white South Carolinians. The Redeemers would become, in legend, the real emancipators of the state because they had reimposed white supremacy and sent federal troops packing. Years would pass, yet successive generations of South Carolinians would tell stories of ancestors who rode with Hampton as if the action was part of some mystic search for a holy grail. Third District Congressman William Jennings Bryan Dorn was one of them, recalling how he was raised on stories of his grandfathers, who "rode like the wind" to vote eight and nine times on that eventful day in 1876.[24] Some Black voters were persuaded, through intimidation or self-preservation, that casting a ballot for Hampton was the best means of avoiding run-ins with armed Democrats. Eventually those Black Hampton voters would be the only ones with a clear path to the ballot box in the twentieth century.

Frank Adamson, a formerly enslaved man living in Winnsboro, South Carolina, told an interviewer with the Federal Writers' Project in 1937 that he stayed clear of Black Republicans during those times. In dialect interpreted by a white interviewer, Adamson said: "Didn't ketch me foolin' 'round wid niggers in radical times. I's as close to white folks then as peas in a pod. Wore de red shirt and drunk a heap of brandy in Columbia, dat time us went down to General Hampton into power." He went on: "I 'clare I hollered so loud goin' 'long in de procession, dat a nice white lady run out one of de houses down dere in Columbia, give me two biscuits and a drum stick of chicken, patted me on da shoulder, and say: 'Thank God for all de big black men dat can holler for Governor Hampton as loud as dis one does." In a touch of irony, the eighty-two-year-old Adamson told the researcher: "I'll be rockin' 'long balance of dese days a hollerin' for Mr. Roosevelt, just as loud as I holler then for Hampton."[25]

Viewed by some white South Carolinians as a racial moderate who had pledged his help to the state's fledgling Black citizens, Hampton publicly decried efforts to rig the ballot box and renege on the Democratic promise to expand Black suffrage, even as he allowed those efforts to flourish. Campaigning for reelection in 1878, he reiterated his beliefs in a Fourth of July speech in Blackville, chiding those who were attempting to prevent potential Black voters from joining Democratic clubs:

If you are to go back upon all pledges that I have made to the people—if you are to say that the colored men that have sustained us are no longer to be citizens of South Carolina—if you require me to go up and give my allegiance to a platform of that sort, then, my friends, much as I would do for you and for South Carolina, earnestly as I would desire to spend or be spent in her service, willing I am to give even my life for my State, I shall have to decline. I would give my life for South Carolina, but I cannot sacrifice my honor, not even for her.[26]

Hampton reminded the extremists in his party that the Black man had helped secure the redemption of the state from Republicans: "And now would you turn your backs on them, and after trying for ten years to convince the colored man that his true interests lay with the Democratic party, would you say, 'Now we have no use for you. You shall not vote even at the primary election?'"[27]

But in the years following his election, Hampton could not—or would not—control the extreme elements of his party, who were bent on excising Black South Carolinians from the political process and promoting the idea of Black inferiority. Soon after the 1878 election, when Hampton secured a second two-year term, he agreed to go to Washington to take the place of US Senator John Patterson, ceding the power he had accumulated as a Bourbon Democrat to Tillman and the Edgefield cabal. Historian George Tindall argued that Hampton's removal to the nation's capital, away from the day-to-day political infighting of Columbia and its environs, diluted his moral influence just as "he was within reach of his objective of establishing interracial good will on such a permanent basis that it would become the standing policy of the state."[28]

With Hampton's departure, chaos reigned when it came to race relations. More restrictions were placed upon voting, including adoption of the Two Box Law and then, in 1882, the Eight Box Law crafted by the conservative Edward McCrady, a Charleston lawyer and war veteran who believed that participation of poor white and Black citizens in elections should be limited. The Eight Box Law required voters to cast ballots separately for each office and ensure their ballots were placed in the correct box, which meant the voters also had to know how to read. Gerrymandering was used to limit Black voter influence in congressional elections. Registration was complex. While the law allowed illiterate voters to ask for help in reading the box labels, poll managers could opt to mislead Black voters and assist white voters. While these laws were "colorblind" on their face and did not outrightly violate the Fifteenth Amendment, they did not operate that way fairly in practice and were meant to strengthen white supremacy.

Hampton's reputation was altered because of those chaotic decades. He was "canonized in the white folklore not as a man of generous sentiments and great moral courage so much as the leader of a violent campaign to remove the Negro from the government of the state," according to Tindall.[29] Years later, modern historians would also portray him as an enthusiastic enslaver and a learned-at-the-knee son of a wealthy father who had put down a rebellion by those enslaved and expanded the family's South Carolina plantations into Mississippi lands to take advantage of the exploding antebellum cotton economy.[30] A monument to Hampton III's exploits remains as the centerpiece on South Carolina's State House grounds. Immortalized in bronze and sitting astride a horse, the bewhiskered Hampton is attired in his Confederate uniform, the cavalry battles he fought for the Confederacy etched in bronze along the granite pedestal. The fifteen-foot statue was first placed across the street on the grounds of Trinity Episcopal Cathedral in 1906, during what has come to be known as the era of the Lost Cause. The old antebellum South and the Confederacy were romanticized and enlarged during this period following the war and into the early years of the twentieth century, and Confederate heroes such as Hampton were venerated. The statue was moved to its current location, south of the capitol building, in 1969 and remains there today, even as Confederate statues in other states have been removed in modern times.

The apparent paternalism Hampton and his lieutenants held toward Black people would soon give way to the virulent strain of racism practiced by men such as Martin Witherspoon Gary and Ben Tillman, both from Edgefield, who held a fanatical view of white supremacy and the absolute necessity of intimidating Black individuals. Tillman advocated lynching as a means of keeping the Black population subservient and, with his rise to power in the 1880s, virtually ensured the end of the progress Black people had made since the Civil War. Elected governor in 1890 by a combination of agrarian interests and anti-Black people sentiments, he set the stage for the elimination of Black individuals from public life. In his second term, Tillman, who would earn the nick-name "Pitchfork Ben" for his threat to stick the farm implement into President Grover Cleveland, secured legislative authority for a constitutional convention in 1895, which was specifically aimed at eradicating the suffrage rights so eloquently embraced at the 1868 convention.

The methodology for disenfranchising the Black population made up a good portion of the debate, with solutions running the gamut from outright fraud to what George Tillman, a former congressman and brother to Ben Tillman, described as "honest" means of diluting the Black vote and securing a white majority. Those devices included literacy tests administered by white officials, lengthy residency requirements, and property qualifications—all ostensibly aimed at elevating the electorate without raising the alarm of the federal government. "Why do they say that the negro must be disfranchised?" Delegate Thomas E. Miller of Beaufort asked in an eloquent rebuke to the convention. "Is it because he is lawless? No! Is it because he is riotous in the discharge of the right of suffrage? No! They answer, 'Because his skin is black he should not vote. Because his skin is black he is inferior. Because he did not fight for the ballot he should not have it. Because we are a conquered people and were conquered by the National Government, in the name of the negro, he shall not vote.'"[31]

James Wigg, one of six Black delegates to the convention, exposed the machinations of the delegates for what they were as he offered his own suffrage plan. (Interestingly, his proposal still included a demonstration of literacy or property holding and no barrier to female suffrage.)

"White supremacy, you say, must be secured, by honest means if you can, by dishonest means if you must. To this, I believe every white delegate here stands pledged." Wigg acknowledged that his hope lay with the grand language of the US Constitution and the Fourteenth and Fifteenth Amendments, which

> stand like the two angels at the gates of Paradise with flaming swords, barring the way. They warn you in tones of thunder that you must make no change in the suffrage which will discriminate either directly or indirectly against any citizen on account of color or previous condition of servitude.[32]

Nevertheless the majority of the delegates at this defining moment in South Carolina history agreed to shutter the most precious of American rights to its Black citizens. A year later in 1896, the white primary was written into law. In Washington, Tillman, now a United States senator, brazenly described the view of his fellow white South Carolinians:

> We of the South have never recognized the right of the Negro to govern the white men, and we never will. We have never believed him to be equal to the white man, and we will not submit to his gratifying lust on our wives and daughters without lynching him.[33]

In Dorchester County, as in counties and cities across South Carolina, elections came and went as regularly as the seasons of planting and harvesting, with the majority Black residents of the county having little influence in the elections that would shape their lives and those of their children.

Tucked away on a rural farm setting, the Elmore family likely knew the danger of stepping out from under segregation's rigid code. Baby George's birth in 1905 was bracketed by two lynchings in Dorchester County, the January 13, 1904, killing of thirty-year-old General Lee and the slaying of Willie Spain on August 23, 1906. Both men had been arrested for the alleged crime of illegally attempting to enter residences, one the home of a Reevesville widow with small children and the other a Badham lumber owner. Both men were taken from sheriff's custody by armed men and lynched before any serious police investigation could unfold.

According to a January 16, 1904, newspaper account in *The State*, Lee, described as a "negro of bad reputation," was apprehended because his foot matched that of a track left at the home of Mrs. A. P. Wimberly on Tuesday evening, January 12, 1904. She had been startled by loud knocking at her door and saw a man fleeing her yard. Although news accounts suggest she was familiar with Lee, Wimberly never identified Lee as the culprit and never suggested it was Lee who was running from her yard.

A day after the incident, a delegation from Reevesville went to the magistrate to swear out a warrant for Lee's arrest. Soon after, the magistrate's constable, St. George's Chief of Police R. E. Mims, drove to Reevesville in a buggy and arrested Lee at 6 PM. According to the Columbia newspaper's account, the pair left in the buggy at midnight and, after going about a mile, was surrounded by a mob of fifty men who overpowered Mims and took the prisoner. "The last he saw of the mob it had left the road and was making for some woods nearby," according to the news account.

The following day, a Thursday, a delegation searched for Lee but to no avail. But on Friday, January 15, 1904, Lee's body was found lashed to a tree about a hundred yards from where he was taken. A newspaper account relayed events as follows:

> It was reported to the correspondent that the condition of the body indicated that the mob, after tying the victim, retreated some distance before firing, thus sprinkling the body with small shot; the mob, it appears, then advanced to a few feet and discharged their shotguns into the dying man's face and body.

The reporter conveyed a weary resignation and, perhaps, cynicism, concluding: "The usual inquest was held last night. And the usual verdict rendered—that General Lee came to his death from gunshot wounds rendered by unknown persons."[34]

A year after George Elmore's birth, just as he was beginning to toddle about in the hot August summer of 1906, a Dorchester County mob engineered an even more daring and horrific capture of Willie Spain. Spain was a young Black man accused of trying to break into the home of S. L. Conner, the manager of Dorchester Lumber, near the town of Badham. The quadruple decker headline in the August 24, 1906, edition of Columbia's *The State* was alarming in its chronological detail: "Negro Boy Murdered by Dorchester Mob." Then this: "Taken From Jail Soon After Being Arrested by Sheriff," "Had Attempted to Enter Residence at Badham," "Willie Spain Shot to Pieces After Identification By Frightened Little Girl—the Sheriff Tells the Governor."

Conner had been alerted to the attempted break-in and wrestled with the culprit in a sugar cane field near the home where his eleven-year-old daughter had witnessed the home invasion. As he fought with the alleged burglar, ragged clothing fell from the assailant's body, prompting some to think he was looking for food. A posse rounded up Spain and turned him over to Dorchester County Sheriff R. M. Limehouse.

According to the newspaper:

The prisoner had not been in jail more than 30 minutes when, without warning, a lever car on the Southern railway, which runs within 150 feet of the county jail, was stopped, and a crowd of determined men went into the jail and took the prisoner out, placed him upon the hand car and sped away.

The mob took Spain to the Conner's home where he was brought before the little girl. She identified Spain as the culprit.

After this nothing was known of the affair until a volley of per-haps 500 shots rang out just west of the town of Badham and when the correspondent arrived at the scene the lynching party had all departed and there remained nothing to tell the tale but the life-less body of Willie Spain, hanging on the limb of a small oak tree, shot beyond recognition in the face.[35]

Spain's lynching was the third lynching in South Carolina in a span of two weeks during the summer of 1906.[36] It was a grisly phenomenon that could not be stymied even by appeals from South Carolina Governor Duncan C. Heyward. In each case the governor sent pleading messages to members of the lynch mobs to avoid violence and allow the courts to determine guilt. According to a newspaper account in the *Times and Democrat*, a teenage boy from Saluda County, identified in newspaper accounts as Robert or Dan Etheredge, was taken off a train and lynched in Batesburg on August 20, 1906, for an alleged attack on a six-year-old girl. The boy's demise merited only a small mention under a separate, and much more lurid, account of the capture and lynching of Bob Davis in Greenwood County, on August 16, 1906, about 150 miles northwest of Dorchester County. The Etheredge lynching did get front page coverage in *The State* on August 21, 1906, a day after the lynching. "Etheredge was a mite of a Negro, about 15 years old, according to his father's statement, although the boy claimed to be only 12 years old," the newspaper reported. "He was thoroughly cowed when caught and his long stay in the swamps and woods had exhausted him so that he was unable to longer resist the temptation to give himself up and have it all over with," *The State* reported. The newspaper reported an intrigu-ing fact, noting that Etheredge was captured by H. G. Wright, the newspaper's correspondent for that community, although presumably journalistic ethics precluded him from writing the dispatch. The mob of about 150 men built a fire to provide light and shot Etheredge about

9 PM. "There was not a suggestion made that the Negro be burned," the newspaper reported. "There was no indiscriminate firing of pistols or guns. The crowd was grimly determined to have the life of the negro, but they made it as painless as possible."[37]

The *Gaffney Ledger* provided more details of the Etheredge and Davis lynchings, noting that the grisly details of the mob slaying of the teenager resembled the circumstances of the Davis lynching a week earlier. Both Etheredge and Davis were suspended by ropes into a tree and fired upon indiscriminately. Davis, branded a "fiend" in newspaper accounts, was accused of a brutal knife assault on a young white woman, Miss Jeanne Brooks, and of a sexual assault on an unidentified "colored girl" who lived nearby. Miss Brooks was minding a country store run by her parents when Davis entered seeking some bacon and other goods. According to the newspaper accounts, he lunged at her and attempted to assault the woman as they tussled with a knife. She was seriously wounded, and the assailant fled when a passerby approached and heard the attack. As word of the alleged assault spread, a mob gathered. As the mob swelled, the governor was kept apprised of the worsening situation. He contemplated calling out the National Guard. Instead, he raced to the scene, taking the 4 PM train to Ninety Six and arriving on the same day that Davis was captured. The mob laid boards across a fence to make a platform for Governor Heyward to stand upon and address the crowd. They listened to him courteously, according to news accounts, as he argued eloquently for the courts, not vigilantes, to ascertain Davis's guilt or innocence.

"In God's name," he implored, "do not put another stain on the name of your State. I beg you, I implore you, I plead with you, let this man have a legal trial. The case can be tried in two weeks' time, and your own jurors will try him and no one will interfere with the verdict of your jury."

Finally, according to an August 22, 1906, account in the *Manning Times,*

> Governor Heyward asked the crowd to reason together as Carolinians and see the wrong that was about to be done by lynching Davis. He told them how he was circumstanced, and how he had always felt that there was something higher and nobler than vengeance on a brute of a negro devil and that was the vindication of the law. He went on: "Gentlemen, after you have killed this poor

negro, as you may do, you will not enjoy it. Let there be a legal trial and you will all feel better."[38]

The crowd, including women in the house attending to the wounded Miss Brooks, was unmoved.

According to the *Manning Times* report, repeated a day later in the August 23, 1906, edition of the Orangeburg *Times and Democrat*, the mother or aunt of the Black victim had asked to fire the first shot at Davis. Her nerve failed, but it did not matter. At the signal, one thousand bullets were fired into Davis after his body was hoisted into a tree. An August 21 news report in the *Gaffney Ledger* lamented the actions of the mob, noting that they brought disgrace upon themselves and the state. The report noted:

> A humane man pulled the negro's hat over his face and stepped to one side and waived [sic] his hand. A perfect sheet of flame lightened the deepening twilight and a roar dulled the air, and the miserable, brutish life of Bob Davis, rapist and would-be murderer was hurled into the great unknown.[39]

Days later, the *Ledger* editorialized against what it described as lynching "mania." The newspaper noted, "When a negro commits a crime, mobs form, assume the role of judge, jury, executioner, and to sate their abnormal desire for human blood they are not content to merely murder their helpless victim, but that murder must be done in fiendish and brutal manner." But the Cherokee County newspaper also printed a response from the "Colored Citizens of Greenwood County," which endorsed, in a backhanded and contorted fashion, the mob killing as a means of preserving the lives of "respectable negroes." "We can't afford, as a race, to uphold anything that tends to lower our Christian or moral standing, and the quicker we show that we are ready to help trace the rascal to his den, the quicker will we have the sympathy of the white man when we are intruded upon."[40] We do not know what conversations took place in the modest Elmore house at the turn of the century about this arc of violence and the continued diminishment of the social and political lives of Black folks. It remains unknown whether George Elmore's mother or stepfather ever voted, although both could read and write. It may have been unfathomable to them, as they raised up their household of children, that in another fifty years their son would step up to challenge segregation and injustice.

CHAPTER 3

Hard Work, Racial Uplift, and Card Parties

> With two exceptions there had been no visible
> check placed on the advancement of negroes in
> business and other vocations. The two blots on
> Columbia's record are the denial to the negro of the
> plumber's license and of the privilege of voting in
> the democratic primary.
>
> —C. A. Johnson, Supervising Principal of
> Colored Schools, *Columbia: Capital City of
> South Carolina, 1786–1936* (1936)

George Elmore's adult life in Columbia, with its commerce, social life, and promise of a better life even for those living in the shadow of segregation, was far removed from the rural South Carolina landscape in which he had grown up. George Elmore never explained to his children why he had left his rural farm life near Holly Hill in South Carolina's Lowcountry, but he seemed to grasp that as a young Black man he stood to prosper more in an urban setting.[1] His mother and stepfather remained in the country but there were frequent visits. George Elmore's son, Cresswell, recalled as a young boy taking long Sunday drives on meandering roads to visit his maternal grandmother. (Cresswell's paternal step-grandfather, George Elmore, had died in 1938.) Grandmother Sadie, George Elmore's mother, prepared meals for the family inside a one-room cabin—"almost a shanty," he said—with a small vestibule, where they would gather to talk.

The image of his grandmother carrying a tray ladened with food was indelibly etched in Cresswell's mind because of a small birthmark on his left thigh— a mark that appeared to resemble his hunched over grandmother.[2] Sadie may have shared that home with others—the 1940 census placed her in the home of Lucius and Sally James along with her daughter Esther and granddaughter Sadie (Esther's daughter).[3]

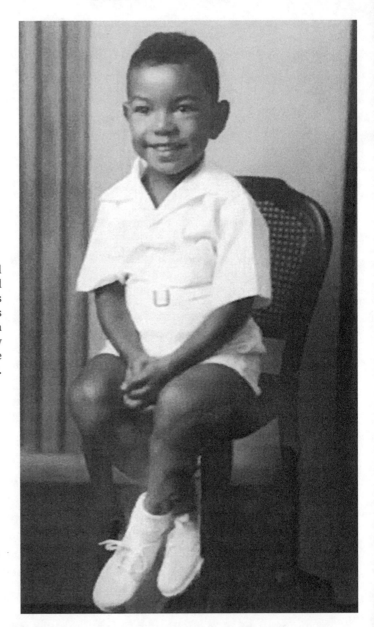

A young Cresswell
Elmore recalled
positive memories
of his early years
growing up in
Columbia. Courtesy
of the Elmore
Family.

Others of George Elmore's generation were heading north for jobs in
urban cities, seeing little future in the subsistence farming and segregated daily life of the South. But Elmore chose to remain in South Carolina and headed to its capital city. The cotton economy had collapsed
after World War I, triggered by declining prices and the arrival in

1921 of the boll weevil, a beetle that feasted on the leaves of the cotton plant and devastated farm owners. Tenants and sharecroppers, already strapped for cash, fared even worse. Those that could accumulate enough money for a train ticket north or hitch a ride in a boxcar going in that direction fled. In 1920, the year Elmore turned fifteen years old, the Black population in South Carolina was 864,719, or about 51.4 percent of the total population of 1,683,724. Ten years later, in 1930, the United States Census would report that the Black population had dropped to 793,681, or about 45.6 percent of the state's residents. Those who left knew if they stayed on the land they likely faced a life of bleak subsistence and back-breaking physical labor. In Elmore's young life, mules were still the farmers' main companion in the fields. The 1920 census recorded only 1,213 tractors on the state's 192,693 farms, vastly outnumbered by the 220,164 mules harnessed to wooden plows and guided by farmers' weathered hands.[4]

George Elmore is believed to have arrived in the capital city sometime in the early 1920s, perhaps armed with the notion, shared by many a toiling South Carolina youth, that he wanted to feed his entrepreneurial spirit and escape those unending cotton fields. He is first listed in the 1925 Columbia city directory within the "Colored department" section behind the pages of white residents. According to *Walsh's Columbia City Directory*, he was employed by Chero-Cola Company and lived at 501 Marion Street.[5] With a population of 37,524 in the 1920 census, Columbia was more of a small southern outpost than a bustling capital city. "Columbia is not as pretty as it looks on postals, but there are two nice streets," a young girl had written to a friend back in 1909, when the population had just topped 25,000.[6] But that postcard scene depicting horse and buggies and women crossing Main Street in long Victorian era dresses was now lodged only in memory, having given way to a bustling city with expansive hotels on downtown corners that featured elegant dining, tea rooms, and salons. The Hotel Jefferson, built in 1912 and situated on the corner of Main and Laurel Streets, boasted marble and terra-cotta tile in the ballroom and lobby. To be sure, there was only a hint of the Roaring Twenties captured on film and in books of the times, but streetcars and buses operated downtown and trains from other cities in and outside of the state arrived daily. There were dance halls, lectures, and theater shows to attend. The new Camp Jackson federal military installation was booming. Columbia was no New York or

Paris, and there were even fewer opportunities for Black people as they attempted to take advantage of the South's version of limited prosperity. But there were upward-advancing and well-educated Black families living in the Waverly area around Allen and Benedict College campuses, although the roads in front of their homes were still unpaved. Most Black families clustered inside Columbia's city limits lived in unpainted wooden row houses with dirt front yards and outhouses in the back.

On New Year's Day in 1925, Elmore might have listened to the stirring words of the Reverend E. A. Adams, pastor of Bethel AME Church, who delivered the Emancipation Day address before the Lincoln Memorial Association at Benedict College. Reverend Adams, quoting the historian Carter G. Woodson, told those attending:

> The hope of the blacks lies not in politics from without, but in race uplift from within in the form of social and economic development. Neither Democrats nor Republicans, say we, are interested in the Negro except so far as the race may be used to enable them to get into office.[7]

Adams's full address was published in the January 10, 1925, edition of the *Palmetto Leader*, the newspaper's inaugural issue.

Reverend Adams was giving a nod to the late Booker T. Washington, who had risen during the turn of the century as the premier national voice for improvement of Black people through industrial education and entrepreneurship. Washington was appointed at the age of twenty-five to lead the Tuskegee Normal and Industrial Institute in Alabama, and immediately students there began to build and expand the institute using the industrial and agricultural skills he championed. His speech at the 1895 Cotton States and International Exposition in Atlanta was met with thunderous applause among both Black and white people in the crowd and soon earned him audiences with presidents and prominent American business leaders:

> To those of my race who depend on bettering their condition in a foreign land or who underestimate the importance of cultivating friendly relations with the Southern white man, who is their next-door neighbor, I would say: "Cast down your bucket where you are"—cast it down in making friends in every manly way of the people of all races by whom we are surrounded.[8]

Washington had traveled to South Carolina in March 1907, two years after George Elmore's birth, as part of a southern tour aimed at inspiring Black men and women and reassuring white people. There was a desperate need of inspiration and uplift in the turn-of-the-century South. The most outspoken South Carolina politicians were crassly racist and made crude anti-Black appeals to white voters, particularly poor white mill workers and farmers. The specter of lynchings and beatings was always present for Black men. Two months prior to Washington's visit, on January 15, 1907, Governor Martin F. Ansel had called in his inaugural address for the legislature to impose the death penalty for attempted sexual assault. It was, Ansel said, a matter "I consider of grave importance at this particular time in our history," an attempt to perhaps replace the lynch mob with legal execution and still control the minority population.[9] During his seven-day South Carolina tour, Washington was welcomed by mayors and other dignitaries and addressed hundreds of people, both Black and white, in Rock Hill, Winnsboro, Columbia, Denmark, Orangeburg, Sumter, Florence, Charleston, Anderson, Greenville, and Gaffney, as well as a few smaller stops along the way. His message of industriousness and education and his emphasis on Black and white people getting along with each other while not raising the prospect of equality resonated with white leaders. Washington "wanted to demonstrate that black men were accomplished in various endeavors, had black wives and did not desire white ones," said historian David H. Jackson Jr. "He intended to show too that that educated and successful African Americans had nice homes and churches that were well maintained, and when left unmolested, they could lead productive lives."[10] The speeches were aimed at defanging the dominant harangues of politicians who demonized Black people, reminding white citizens that their Black neighbors were making steady progress.

Washington's visit was sponsored by the South Carolina State Negro Business League and coordinated by the Reverend Richard Carroll, a Baptist minister in Columbia who, like Washington, could reassure white people of a conservative, pragmatic approach to Black progress. White newspapers could rightly report that Washington exhorted Black men and women to regard the white man as a friend and benefactor. But as historian Jackson noted:

> Washington said things for white consumption even when he
> knew they were not true, but he used his words to soften white

hatred and animosity toward local blacks. He had mastered the art of dissemblance and was adept at delivering his messages to mixed southern audiences.[11]

In later years, Washington was viewed as accommodating white supremacists by not decrying the alarming segregation and disenfranchisement of Black people as the nineteenth century ended and the twentieth century began. But his focus on racial uplift also resonated with rising middle-class Black and white people who longed to improve their economic circumstances and educate their children. Washington's friendship with the nation's richest men, including John D. Rockefeller and Andrew Carnegie, led to substantial financial partnerships with Tuskegee and other Black institutions. Perhaps most noteworthy was his connection to Sears & Roebuck president Julius Rosenwald, a philanthropist who endowed the Julius Rosenwald Fund. The fund built more than five thousand schools for Black children between 1917 and 1932. More than five hundred of the two-room white frame Rosenwald schools were built in rural South Carolina alone, replacing some of the weary unpainted shacks that passed for "separate but equal" schoolhouses. Washington's tactics infuriated some of the nation's influential Black leaders such as W. E. B. Du Bois, who insisted that Black people should directly confront the white political structure. But there was some support for Washington's philosophy among South Carolinians who understood that they would have to rely on their own thrift, fortitude, and educational resources to advance. That spirit was reflected in a short blurb in the January 4, 1930, edition of the *Palmetto Leader* about the upcoming dedication of a Rosenwald School in Allendale County. The story, under the headline "The Greatest Event in the History of Allendale County" detailed the program that would be held, including presentations by students and teachers in Allendale and surrounding counties, and speeches by distinguished academics. The story exhorted: "Come, contribute largely to education."[12]

If upon his arrival in the capital city, Elmore had begun to read the *Palmetto Leader*, the city's Black-run newspaper, he would have found within its pages' manifestations of both the Washington philosophy of uplift and Christian duty alongside more full-throated calls for direct legal assaults on discrimination. Each week, correspondents would report on church and school news across the state, highlighting special programs that featured singing, recitations, and sermons. There were details of social occasions to suggest that Black women, like their white counterparts, were aware of the importance of gatherings of refined females to celebrate engagements and weddings. School programs were particularly celebrated, reminding readers that the next generation of Black children was engaged in learning Black history and the tangible accomplishments of Black citizens.

On April 11, 1925, the story that led the newspaper's front page, reported by the NAACP news service, detailed the NAACP's challenge to the all-white primary in Texas.

> An attack in the courts on the Texas "White Primary" law which specifically disbars Negroes from voting in the Democratic primaries, and which will constitute the opening of a general attack upon disenfranchisement of colored people in the South, is announced by the National Association for the Advancement of Colored People.

The case brought by Dr. Lawrence A. Nixon challenged a 1923 Texas act that specifically banned Black people from voting in that state's Democratic primary. James Weldon Johnson, then secretary of the NAACP, was quoted in the article:

> It is clearly evident that decision in this case will profoundly affect the Negro in America. So long as Negroes can be deprived of free access to the ballot because of their color, just so long can their economic, legal, political and other rights be disregarded with impunity.

He went on:

> Since the Democratic Primary constitutes the entire machinery of election to office in most Southern states, this case involves the only effective way of striking a blow for the Negro's right to vote. In undertaking a vigorous prosecution of the case known as *Nixon v. Herndon,* the National Association for the Advancement of Colored People feels it is performing a service not alone to the Negro but to all America; inasmuch as the rotten borough system of the South afflicts the entire nation with shameful isolation of the 13th, 14th and 15th Amendments to the federal Constitution.[13]

Laura Delaney Elmore lived in the 1100 block of Blossom Street with her family in an unpainted shotgun house. The homes were later demolished to make way for development of the University of South Carolina campus. Joseph E. Winter Photograph Collection. Courtesy of South Caroliniana Library, University of South Carolina.

That announcement foreshadowed the long fight that the NAACP would embark upon in South Carolina, the last white primary stronghold, two decades later with Elmore as the lead plaintiff.

But in the 1920s, Elmore was a young man, just establishing himself in the capital city where reminders of the past and the power structure that controlled the present were ubiquitous. He had courted and married Laura Belle Delaney, the teenage daughter of Samuel and Maggie Delaney, who lived in a one-story home at 1110 Blossom Street, a short walk from the state capitol building.

By 1927, the twenty-two-year-old Elmore was working as a taxi driver and living at 1300 Wheat Street, according to the 1927 Columbia city directory printed by The State Company, which also published the daily newspaper.[14] This was the first year the directory was developed and printed under local direction and was endorsed by the city chamber of commerce. Black residents of the city were listed as "colored," in a separate section that listed addresses and professions. Houses of worship were also listed under "white" and "colored." Schools for Black children were noted with an asterisk.

That same year, there were thirty-four restaurants in the city (seven operated by Black cooks), five tea rooms, and six downtown movie theatres, according to the city directory. There were fourteen tailors and five shoeshine parlors. Seven photographers enjoyed business in what was a lively period for family photography. It was at Roberts Studio, operated by the Black photographer Richard Samuel Roberts at 1119 1/2 Washington Street, where the young Elmore had his photograph made, the first-known image of Elmore as a young man.[15]

Roberts, who operated his studio from 1920 until his death in 1936, was adept at utilizing light and shadow and employing unusual backdrops to create an atmosphere and mood in his portraits. Well-dressed women, some sitting alone, some holding babies or surrounded by family members, gaze out of portraits with regal bearing. Couples hold hands lightly; a trio of sisters reveal their serious natures; two young brothers share their sporting interests as they perch on scooters. In the photographs some men and women are attired in elegant suits, suggesting a foothold in the Black middle class. Others are pictured in coveralls and work clothes of daily life. Often, light played around the faces of his subjects, as Roberts employed various settings to capture what he called "a true likeness." In his portrait, Elmore is attired in an ordinary tan-colored wool flannel suit, cotton shirt and bow tie. He gazes into Roberts's camera without backdrop or exaggerated lighting. He is seated, his hands resting lightly on his thighs. There is no hint of swagger or artifice; his face shows a quiet determination. The portrait was likely taken in the mid-to-late 1920s, shortly after his arrival in Columbia, when he was a driver for the Blue Ribbon Taxi Club, the cab company that served the city's Black population.

Roberts's pictures lined mantels and graced the pages of private family scrapbooks in Columbia for years, a testament to the upward progression of Black families in the new century. His work in revealing the lives of Black South Carolinians between the two world wars drew wider examination only in the latter part of the twentieth century, in the 1970s and 1980s. That is when an archivist with the South Caroliniana Library paid a visit to the Roberts family home at 1717 Wayne Street, then owned by Cornelius Roberts, one of the Roberts's children, and his wife, Carrie. Conversations with the family, including all of Roberts's four surviving children, unveiled a rich trove of photographs and remembrances, along with this discovery: the family had stored under the home some three thousand glass plates, a sizeable portion of the negatives R. S. Roberts had made in his lifetime. Eventually the book *A True Likeness: The Black South of Richard Samuel Roberts* was published. It revealed, belatedly, another layer of life in Columbia, a reminder of the upward mobility that Black South Carolinians, including Elmore, sought during the decades of the 1920s and 1930s. The portrait of George Elmore captures a resilience and determination that Jim Crow policies could not completely stamp out, even though at the tail end of 1927, one thousand University of South Carolina students marched in the Red Shirt parade commemorating the fiftieth anniversary of the return of white people to power.[16] The university's *Garnet & Black* yearbook also noted the anniversary of the end of Reconstruction on page 383 of the annual under a photograph of the surviving columns at Millwood, the plantation home of Confederate General Wade Hampton, which was burned by Union troops at the end of the Civil War.

The years of the Great Depression were particularly difficult for Black families who had limited access to education and good jobs. In South Carolina, wages for unskilled workers clocked in at under thirty cents an hour; Black workers made about a nickel less per hour. But there were hopeful signs, according to economists who gathered in Washington in May 1933 under the auspices of the Julius Rosenwald Fund. The economists agreed that Black workers had suffered just as white workers had through the worst of the 1930s, but unemployment was due more to economic factors than racial issues. They noted as much, saying:

> However, the fact that the race is still largely found in two of the great occupational groups which have suffered greatly, agriculture and personal and domestic service, has led to a larger amount of unemployment among the colored than among the whites and has forced them to appear in disproportionate numbers among the seekers of relief.[17]

The Bureau of Labor Statistics charted the wages for picking one hundred pounds of seed cotton in the southern states between 1924 and 1934. In South Carolina, over the ten-year period, the wage plummeted, from ninety-five cents in 1924 to fifty cents in 1934.[18] Average monthly wages for a farmer worker, without board, was about twenty dollars, or about ninety-six cents per day.[19]

In his January 31, 1931, inaugural address, Governor Ibra C. Blackwood detailed the dire state of South Carolina's financial prospects and the particular plight of the state's farmers who were abandoning their lands and heading to urban centers. He said:

> Viewing with alarm the distressing condition of agriculture, as manifested by numerous foreclosures and the exodus of thousands of good, honest people from the farms into centers seeking other vocations, and the poverty and desolation in agricultural life generally, I would recommend that, commensurate with sound business policies generally, the State employ its great powers to the fullest extent to relieve the stricken farmers of their distressful plight.

The lofty words, however, did little to fill empty bellies or prevent the migration of thousands out of the state to northern cities.

By the 1930s, George and Laura Elmore had situated themselves in the segregated Liberty Hill area of Columbia, northeast of the more prosperous Waverly neighborhood. US Census records suggests Elmore's sister Esther was also living at the rented unpainted wooden dwelling at 1212 Lyon Street, the first of several rentals the family occupied. (Esther would return the favor decades later when she took in George Elmore's teenage children following his death.)[20] The first of the family's four children, Essie Naomi, who was called by her middle name, was born at home on March 12, 1932, with the assistance of a midwife. Six years later, Cresswell was born on November 8, 1938, at 1405 Lyon Street. George Elmore held a succession of jobs, according to the Columbia city directories over the course of the 1930s, working as a taxi driver, a Belk department store employee, janitor, and service employee.

As Naomi turned four in 1936, the city of Columbia prepared to celebrate the sesquicentennial of its founding amid the Great Depression. Perhaps looking to shake off the effects of the worldwide economic collapse, the four-day celebration was not only a salute to the past but a paean to the future. Festivities began on March 23, 1936, on the State House grounds with a parade of white beauty queens, a cannon salute, and the launch of a sixty-five-unit parade that measured more than five

George and Laura Elmore with children Naomi and Cresswell display their
Easter baskets at their Lyon Street home. Courtesy of the Elmore Family.

miles in length, the *Columbia Record* reported in its afternoon edition.[21]
Christie Benet, a former US senator who eleven years later would represent South Carolina in the white primary case, was the master of
ceremonies at the opening gala, which also recognized the oldest and
youngest citizens of Columbia.

The elder honor went to ninety-six-year-old Jane Dargan of 1314 Laurel Street. A photo of the smiling nonagenarian graced the front page
of the March 23, 1936, edition of the *Columbia Record* along with a short
description of her life that suggested that echoes of the past still resonated in twentieth century Columbia. The caption noted that Dargan
was born on September 15, 1839, in a home that was burned by Union
General Sherman during his brutal 1865 Carolinas campaign that signaled the end of the Civil War. She had gone to Darlington during the
"Confederate war," the newspaper noted, and suffered the loss of her
husband, Alonzo Dargan, who "was killed in 1864 while fighting for
the Confederacy in Virginia." The chair she resided in was 150 years
old, "having been carried from the burning home by a slave."[22]

The next day, March 24, 1936, *The State* reported that at many as sixty-five thousand people had witnessed the opening festivities. Below a bold headline that read "CAPITAL'S GREATEST CROWD SEES SESQUICEN-TENNIAL," the writer noted: "A parade, the equal of which has not before passed in South Carolina, thrilled countless spectators as it passed in review, depicting the history of yesteryear and the progress of today."

The city of Charleston claimed top honors among the parade's judges for a float that featured Miss Charleston and tableaus of characters from the six wars that Charleston had endured, from the Indian wars to World War I. Second prize went to the Cayce Supply Company "which presented in miniature the old Cayce house, which still stands as a monument to the days when Columbia was but an Indian trading post."

The prize for the most original float went to the S. B. McMaster sporting goods store. In typical language of the time, the paper noted: "It was a faithful reproduction of Southern darkies fishing in marshland. A boat was drawn up to the bank and Maude Smith occasionally yanked a fish out of the water. Sam Smith, also fishing, caught a 'picka-ninny,'" a common term used by white people to describe a Black child. Robert Lee Smith, Leroy Smith, and Roosevelt Fleming Smith also participated in the tableau, according to the description in *The State*'s March 24, 1936, edition.

The Evans Motor Company float followed, featuring "a tableau in which a young woman in a predicament was dialing the familiar Evans Motor Company number." Just before a car carrying Congressman H. P. Fulmer and his wife, men on horseback offered up a vision that may have chilled the hearts of Black parade spectators. The newspaper reported: "Then came the klansmen, the Ku klux klan—clad in trailing white robes they sat, mounted regally upon their unruly steeds."[23] The following day, more than three hundred children, Black and white, marched in a pet parade to mark the city's anniversary, carrying animals that ranged from garden-variety cats and dogs to mice, horses, goats, and even a crow. The number of entries so overwhelmed organizers that they had to call out additional numbers as the entrants marched past the judges. "The pet parade was made to order for lovers of originality and variety," the newspaper wrote. "Much hilarity was provoked by a little Negro boy, who, clad in an army coat and overalls, marched along with a crow perched atop his hat. It was one of the

cleverest entries. Ducks riding in wagons and waddling along beside
their tiny owners were also laugh-provoking."[24]

It was clear that in 1936, the Confederacy still occupied a lively spot
in the historic imagination. A pen-and-ink map featuring the city's
most storied landmarks was among the souvenir keepsakes memorial-
izing the historic celebration. The map featured the State House, Trinity Episcopal Cathedral, the US Post Office, the federal courthouse,
and the South Carolina state hospital. Monuments to the Revolution
and the Civil War were featured prominently on the map, including
the George Washington statue on the State House grounds and the
monument to Civil War General Wade Hampton. The monument to
women of the Confederacy was also featured. There was a drawing of
Old City Hall, "built in radical days, burned 1876," and a drawing of the
First Baptist Church, "where the secession convention of S.C. met and
organized Dec. 17, 1860." The map featured institutions of higher education for white citizens, including the University of South Carolina,
Columbia College, Lutheran Theological Seminary, and the Barham-
ville South Carolina Female Institute, but there was no mention of the
historically Black Allen or Benedict colleges. The only nod to Black
life was a description of the house of Charles Mercer Logan, a low-
slung brick structure located near the southwest corner of Assembly
and Senate Streets, where enslaved people were held prior to being
auctioned. The structure stood on that location until 1951 when it was
disassembled and moved to a private location, according to Historic
Columbia.[25]

A history of Columbia, edited by Helen Kohn Henning for the sesquicentennial, detailed the progress of the capital city in business,
education, government, literature, the arts, and sports. C. A. Johnson, supervising principal of the Black schools, wrote the chapter on
"Negroes." He divided his commentary into two sections: "Negroes of
Columbia before 1865 and during Reconstruction" and "Negroes since
Reconstruction." Johnson noted, without a touch of irony, that between
1786 and 1865, "the greatest contribution to Columbia was a desirable
and a much-needed type of labor." The building of streets and houses,
the planting of trees, all went toward building "the struggling little village at Taylor's Hill near Granby into a city," he said. "All of the money
in South Carolina and all of the planning of the architects could not
make these things possible without the labor which the negro helped

to furnish. This service looms even larger when we consider that this was entirely slave labor."[26]

Johnson also defended the reputation of men and women of his race during Reconstruction, reminding readers of those who led the constitutional convention of 1868 and the work of such men as Professor Richard T. Greener at the University of South Carolina. During Reconstruction, he said, most of Columbia's aldermen were negroes and all but the police chief were also Black men. "As to the dishonesty, most of it is traceable to the work of the carpet-baggers and scalawags," he wrote.[27] During Reconstruction, the formerly enslaved "lost the care of his master" and the protection of federal troops "and had to contend with a hatred and prejudice that would not accept him as a citizen." That animosity had been reduced in Columbia, Johnson said, at this juncture in Columbia's history. He said mutual good will exists between Black and white citizens. "With two exceptions there had been no visible check placed on the advancement of negroes in business and other vocations. The two blots on Columbia's record are the denial to the negro of the plumber's license and of the privilege of voting in the democratic primary."[28]

That same anniversary week, Allen University prepared for the arrival of four thousand Black teachers for the annual conference of the Palmetto State Teachers Association. "Perhaps no body of men or women is engaged in work that calls for greater sacrifices and are confronted with greater discouragement than these teachers," the *Palmetto Leader* wrote in a welcome editorial. "But, be it said to their credit, they go blithely to their task and give the best that is within them."

Governor Johnston traveled across town to the Allen campus to welcome the teachers, pledging to work to eradicate the stubborn illiteracy among South Carolina children. But the governor did not address an issue that had festered in the Black community: the state's refusal to pay Black teachers and principals the same as their white counterparts. In saluting the teacher gathering, the *Palmetto Leader* hinted at yet another battle that was to come in the decade ahead as teacher equalization battles began to be waged in the South. "On the average, paid starvation wages, yet required to measure up to the standards of those who get something like a living wage, they do not shirk," the newspaper noted. "They take pride in the fact that the sacrifices they make contribute to the advancement of their race and the welfare of their state, though illy treated by that same state in the matter of compensation."[29]

As the teachers gathered for workshops and keynote addresses, as city residents saluted its past and looked to the next 150 years, there was in that heady spring week of 1936 some small progress in the relations between the Black and white residents. In a front page notice in the *Palmetto Leader*, Belk, the state's largest department store, announced the creation of rest areas for its Black customers:

> Lounging rooms for colored Folks, on Belk's third floor. We invite the teachers of South Carolina to make themselves comfortable and at home in lounging rooms on our third floor (ask elevator operator for directions) . . . Clean, comfortable bright, rest room and lounge . . . make this your meeting place while in Columbia.[30]

It was a small gesture on the road to a decade of change. Through the years, the Belk department store would become one of the Elmore family's favorite downtown shopping destinations, along with Tapp's department store. It was there that Laura Elmore outfitted her children in well-constructed clothing and Buster Brown shoes. Often, Cresswell said he would walk downtown with his father on shopping excursions. As a small child, Cresswell Elmore did recall coming upon a mystifying scene in Belk: two water fountains, one marked "colored" and one marked "white." He couldn't quite picture what "colored water" looked like, he said. That was one of the few times his father explained the racial dividing line.[31]

It was a rarity for race and segregation to be discussed in the Elmore household. Instead the Elmore patriarch seemed to embrace as many entrepreneurial opportunities as he could and encouraged his children to do the same. George Elmore made it clear he did not want his wife to work as a domestic in other people's homes, so he took on a variety of jobs as the young family's sole provider. Like other South Carolinians surviving the Depression, the Elmores had to make the best of hard times. Shortly after Christmas in 1936, the couple entertained the Radio Literary and Social Club at their Lyon Street home. After a brief meeting, there was an afternoon of card games and a robust meal that included baked turkey and dressing, chicken, steamed rice, creamed potatoes, peas, cocktails, candies, and wine. And, finally, there was that favorite pastime to chase the Depression blues away: dancing.[32]

George Elmore and young son, Cresswell, walk along Columbia's Main Street, ca. 1941. The family routinely shopped at downtown clothing and dry goods stores. Courtesy of the Elmore Family.

CHAPTER 4

"Difficulty with the White People"

Everybody knew Mr. Elmore. He was a friendly guy; everybody liked him except the white power structure.

—Melvin S. Hodges, August 2022

Melvin S. Hodges was in sixth grade at Waverly Grammar School when his teacher, Miss Ida Boyd, introduced a social studies lesson that would have set off alarms among South Carolina's white leaders had they eavesdropped on her lecture.[1] Miss Boyd was the type of teacher whose grasp of teaching and confident demeanor lodged in memory. "I had never encountered anyone so intelligent," Hodges recalled in an interview. On that school day sometime during the 1949–50 academic year, Miss Boyd discussed two federal court cases swirling in South Carolina: the explosive school desegregation case emerging out of rural Clarendon County and the *Elmore v. Rice* decision, which had demolished the last southern "white primary" in 1948 and cleared the way for Black people to vote. Judge Waring of Charleston was a central figure in both cases, she told her class, impatient to end the white supremacy that governed every aspect of daily life in South Carolina. He had already ruled that Black and white schoolteachers must be paid equally. He had urged the NAACP in the school's case to forget enforcing "separate but equal" doctrines and simply aim to destroy segregation. Waring considered segregation "per se inequality," a view that made the Charleston judge a reviled figure among his contemporaries who were intent on preserving white supremacy.

"She would tell us how Judge Waring was having difficulty with the white people in Charleston," Hodges, an attorney who has made his home in Oakland, California for many years, said in a 2022 interview. "We talked about that and of course she talked about the Elmore case. We didn't grasp the totality of the circumstances but those of us who were in tune with things knew something important was going on."

Black teachers photographed outside Waverly School at the end of the academic year, June 1954. Ida Boyd is pictured third row, far left, partially obscured. Midlands Memories Collection. Courtesy of Richland Library.

The Elmore decision resonated particularly with the young Hodges because the plaintiff in that case was the father of one of his best friends, Cresswell Elmore. He and Cresswell had become pals in fifth grade when Hodges was transferred across town to the red-brick grammar school on Oak Street, in the heart of Columbia's Waverly neighborhood. Hodges had attended the small, segregated Milford Grammar School in the little community known to its Black residents as Frogtown, about three miles across town. Frogtown was a tiny neighborhood of Black residents that encompassed two streets, Monroe and Heyward, on the edge of the Columbia city limits. Frogtown was tagged onto the east end of the expansive, leafy Shandon neighborhood, an all-white enclave of early twentieth century homes between Rosewood and Devine Streets.

Although they were placed in different homerooms, "we became buddies immediately," Hodges remembered. Cresswell's father was well known to the Waverly school children, particularly children like Hodges and his siblings who had to walk by the store to catch the public bus. Hodges often stopped in to buy ice cream cones and other treats after school before walking to the corner of Gervais and Harden Streets to catch the first of two city buses home.

"Everybody knew Mr. Elmore," Hodges said. "He was a friendly guy; everybody liked him except the white power structure." To Black children like Hodges, Elmore was a role model, an enterprising man, willing to tackle multiple jobs to earn a living.

"I remember every business that Mr. Elmore started," he said. "The suppliers wouldn't give him goods, there were threats of violence. The stress of the lawsuit and all of the other things that spun off from it took such a toll on his health that he could not work, that he could not be gainfully employed."

Young Melvin was the second oldest of eight children born to Hilliard Hodges Jr. and Aubrey Thompson Hodges. His parents divorced when he was nine, and his father died when he was eleven years old.

His grandmother, Bessie Thompson, had purchased the land near the Shandon neighborhood with his grandfather's "mustering out" money from World War I. His grandmother had told him the land had been a gravel pit for the paving of state Route 48, which wound through Rosewood Drive and Bluff Road. The civil engineer on the roadway had purchased the land and laid out plats for homes that were purchased by Black families. Hodges was born in a one-story wooden house at 3814 Monroe Street and grew up in his grandmother's concrete block house at 3822 Monroe. The neighborhood had dirt streets, no electricity, and no public sewer facilities. Outhouses were behind each residence.

Hodges, born in 1940, recalled that many of the family's neighbors were illiterate, often recruiting him to read the daily newspaper out loud to them as they struggled to understand what was going on in the larger world, particularly as World War II ended. Hodges had learned to read at age four and skipped the third grade because he was ahead of his class. "I remember the *Columbia Record* ran a long series in 1946 that raised the question, is Hitler dead or alive. I would read a portion, and they would say, 'That's not true, is it?'" When his family talked about the racial disparities around them or the changes that were brewing in the post–World War II world, they did it behind closed doors and out of earshot of youngsters, he said. "They talked about it out of your presence. It was a subject that could get you in a lot of trouble because your neighbors could talk to the whites and say that you were a dangerous person, that you were talking about things," Hodges said.

Hodges said he was not afraid of interacting with white people and as a young boy began seeking out work to earn money for his family. He learned at a young age how to navigate segregation's convoluted customs. "I started working for wealthy whites doing their yardwork and in their houses, waxing their floors and serving at parties," he said.

Certain alarming events stayed with Hodges and his young contemporaries. The horrifying case of World War II Army Sergeant Isaac Woodard, who was blinded by a South Carolina law enforcement officer on his way home from service on February 12, 1946, had become international news by the summer of 1946, casting a harsh spotlight on South Carolina and segregation.[2] According to historical accounts, Woodard, honorably discharged from Camp Gordon after serving three years in the Pacific theater and having earned a battle star for bravery, was in uniform on a Greyhound bus out of Augusta, Georgia, heading to his home in Winnsboro, South Carolina. As the bus rumbled north through the dark and made short, periodic stops, Woodard asked the driver if he could use the restroom during a stop. The driver, Alton Blackwell, cursed him and said no. Woodard cursed the driver back, telling him, "Goddamn it, talk to me like I'm talking to you. I'm a man just like you." The driver allowed him to leave the bus to go to the bathroom, and he returned without incident.

But at the next stop, in Batesburg, South Carolina, the driver got off the bus and went looking for police. He found Batesburg police chief Lynwood Shull and an officer, Elliot Long, in a nearby patrol car. According to later court testimony, Blackwell told police he had two disorderly and drunk passengers, one Black and one white. Soldiers of both races were in a celebratory mood as they left Camp Gordon and at least one white passenger had complained about the soldiers' behavior, as some passed liquor back and forth among their seats. At trial, Woodard testified he had not been drinking, which was disputed by the bus driver. Blackwell climbed back on the bus and ordered Woodard off. As Woodard tried to explain his actions to the officers, Shull struck him on the head with his blackjack, a weighted baton, and told him to "shut up," then arrested him. As they walked to the jail, Woodard testified that Shull struck him again when he answered "yes" to Shull's question about his discharge from the armed forces. Shull explained to the soldier he should have said "Yes, sir." On the way to the jail, Shull twisted Woodard's left arm behind him and the two grappled with the blackjack until Long, the second officer, arrived with his gun drawn. According to Woodard, Shull took up the club and began beating him around the head and face until the soldier passed out. When he came to, he struggled to his feet while Shull again gouged at Woodard's eyes with the blackjack. At trial, Shull denied striking Woodard repeatedly, saying he only remembered hitting him at most three times.

The next day Woodard awoke in a jail cell and could not see. His face was covered in dried blood. Nevertheless, he was required to appeared in court. Woodard pleaded guilty to drunk and disorderly conduct before H. E. Quarles, the town judge and Batesburg mayor, who ordered him to pay fifty dollars or serve thirty days on the road gang. Woodard had forty dollars in his wallet and an additional four dollars in his watch pocket as well as a check for $694.73 that was his mustering-out money from the US Army. When he informed the judge that he could not see to sign the check, the judge reduced his fine to the money he had. He remained in jail until the following day, the police chief administering drops to his eyes. After a local physician examined Woodard, Shull drove Woodard to the Veterans Administration hospital in Columbia. Woodard's wife, waiting for him in Winnsboro, and his parents anticipating his arrival in New York, knew nothing of his whereabouts for several weeks.[3]

The subsequent publicity of the attack, the federal trial of Shull for allegedly violating Woodard's civil rights, and the photographs of the blind Woodward were seared into the memories of Black children. Five months after the attack, Woodard's case was taken up by Hollywood producer and radio broadcaster Orson Welles, who read aloud Woodard's affidavit on his American Broadcasting Company radio broadcast "Orson Welles Commentaries" on July 26, 1946. The power of Welles's oratory electrified many Americans who only learned of the horrific beating through his fifteen-minute radio monologue.[4]

In the initial broadcast, Welles misidentified the city where the attack took place as Aiken, South Carolina, just as Isaac Woodard had done in its affidavit. Some white southerners, incensed and embarrassed by the spotlight shown on the segregated South, latched on to this error to suggest Woodard's story didn't add up. The mayor and police of Aiken were so outraged that the city sued Welles and banned his new movie in its theatres. Welles, who could identify Woodard's police assailant only as "Officer X" in the initial broadcast, stepped up his investigation.

In his August 11, 1946, Sunday afternoon radio broadcast, Welles dismissed the city's protests in the wake of the larger issue of Woodard's loss of his eyesight and continuing violence and lynching in the South:

> The soldier says he was blinded and the mayor and the chief of police in the place where the soldier says it happened are most indignant with me for repeating what he said and swore to. The *Times* the other day was full of their official protest, sent under seal all the way up to New York City from within the inviolable borders of Aiken County in South Carolina.
>
> If the soldier was wrong about the place, I'm going to do something about it, but he isn't wrong about his eyes. He lost them, and I'm going to do something about that. All the affidavits from all the policemen in the world won't protest his eyes back in his head. Somebody, somebody who called himself an officer of the law, beat that boy with a stick until he lost his sight. Now that somebody is nobody. He's vanished. He's never been heard of. He hasn't any name. Well, he's going to be heard of. The blind soldier has my promise of that. That somebody is going to be named.

Welles summoned outrage that would help spark a slow and hesitant national reckoning on race in postwar America. He reminded white Americans of their complicity if they continued to turn their backs on southern atrocities.

> Editorials in lots of newspapers and lots of people are writing me to demand to know what business it is of mine. God judge me if it isn't the most pressing business I have. The blind soldier fought for me in this war. The least I can do now is to fight for him. I have eyes; he hasn't. I have a voice on the radio; he hasn't. I was born a white man and until a colored man is a full citizen like me, I haven't the leisure to enjoy the freedom that colored man risked his life to maintain for me. I don't own what I have until he owns an equal share of it. Until somebody beats me and blinds me, I am in his debt.[5]

Woodard had gotten the place of his beating and blinding wrong. Welles's investigators, joined by the NAACP, began traveling up and down the bus route from Augusta to Columbia and determined it was the tiny community of Batesburg, about twenty-five miles northeast of Aiken, where Woodard had met the brutal end of a policeman's baton. Reporters discovered it was police chief Lynwood Shull who had beaten the soldier. Many white South Carolinians took Shull's word that Woodard was unruly and obstreperous, another Black man who needed to be subdued. Hodges was just six years old when he learned about the attack on Isaac Woodard, overhearing adults discussing the case behind closed doors. He saw the photograph of the blind soldier, his eyes forever shut, an image seared into his memory. The brutal story haunted him for years. A decade later Hodges matriculated at Morehouse College. He often took the Greyhound bus from Columbia to Atlanta on Sunday evenings after a weekend visiting his family and girlfriend. He rode the same stretch of dark two-lane highway heading south that Woodard had traveled in 1946 going north.

"I would get a feeling of abject fear, a sense of foreboding," Hodges recounted. "I would feel that abject fear thinking about Sergeant Woodard. It was always a real gut-wrenching experience to ride through Batesburg and I always hoped the bus would not stop."

Woodard's blinding was among hundreds of horrific incidents against returning Black veterans that dominated headlines in the year after the Allied victory over Nazi Germany and Japan. National NAACP leaders had hoped the war would galvanize Americans to end segregation. In 1944, the NAACP's Walter White endorsed the "Double V" campaign publicized by the *Pittsburgh Courier*, which expanded the national "V for Victory" campaign that was aimed at enlisting all Americans in the fight to defeat the Axis powers. The "Double V" called for victory over fascist enemies abroad and victory over Jim Crow policies that hampered the lives of Black Americans at home.[6] Just a year after the war's end, that victory was tainted by outrageous attacks on Black soldiers who had returned to the South unwilling to continue as second-class citizens.

As the Woodard saga played out over five weeks on the "Orson Welles Commentaries," Welles reminded his listeners that the attack was one in a long list of atrocities that vigilante mobs were still carrying out across the South. In his August 11 broadcast, Welles linked the racist rhetoric of Georgia Governor Eugene Talmadge to the July 12, 1946 lynching of two Black married farm couples in Monroe, Georgia, in Walton County. The attack came to be known as the Moore's Ford lynchings. The four young farm workers were Roger Malcom, recently arrested for the stabbing of a white man; his common-law wife, Dorothy, who was seven months pregnant; George W. Dorsey, Dorothy's brother; and his wife, Mae Murray Dorsey. George Dorsey had returned nine months earlier from World War II service as a decorated veteran.

Talmadge, already a thrice-elected governor, was locked in a bitter gubernatorial primary battle that year for a fourth term in the first Georgia primary that was open to Black voters. The Georgia state Supreme Court had ruled in *King v. Chapman* that primaries were part of the electoral process in 1945, notching another southern victory for Thurgood Marshall's NAACP legal team. White Georgia Democrats for the first time could not bar minorities from casting ballots. Talmadge, well known as a white supremacist and race-baiter, crowed that he was the only candidate who favored a return to the Georgia white primary. He hoped white Georgia farmers and returning white veterans would put him over the top. In a radio address during the campaign, Talmadge offered up this pledge:

> What do I say? I say it's the law this year, and some of the Nigras will vote, the fewer the better, but I add to it this: If I'm your governor, they won't vote in our white primary the next four years . . . Let's get the great majority, and then come on to the convention in Macon. And there won't be anybody in that convention but white women and white men if I am your governor.[7]

According to written accounts, Talmadge had earlier campaigned at a barbecue in Walton County, Georgia, appealing to about six hundred white farmers against his chief opponent, the moderate James V. Carmichael. Among those in the crowd were Barnette Hester and J. Loy Harrison, a wealthy cotton farmer who employed Malcom and Dorsey. On July 11, Hester was stabbed in an argument with Malcom, who believed his wife was having an affair with Hester. A day after the stabbing and five days before the July 17 Democratic primary, Talmadge returned to Walton County. A witness told FBI investigators that Talmadge allegedly offered immunity to anyone who "took care" of

Malcom, who remained in jail as a suspect in the alleged stabbing. The FBI investigator discounted the FBI tip as "unbelievable" but, nonetheless, circulated a memo about the allegation. Although Talmadge's opponent Carmichael won the popular vote July 17, Talmadge won the primary because of the county unit system, which favored rural counties over urban ones. Talmadge easily won in Walton County. He went on to win the general election but died before assuming office.[8]

On July 26, 1946, Harrison, the white farmer, paid the six-hundred-dollar bail to release Malcom from jail and then drove the two couples toward his farm. They were met by a mob on the Moore's Ford Bridge. The two Black men were taken out of the car and tied to trees. When one of the women screamed out the name of a man in the mob, the women were also tied to trees and shot repeatedly by the mob. According to published accounts in newspapers, Harrison said he had no advance knowledge of the planned attack and did not know the lynch mob would be waiting on the bridge. He told authorities he could not identify any of the men who participated.

The lynching of the four Georgia farm workers stirred President Truman to order a federal investigation and offer a $12,500 reward for information leading to the killers. The lynchings remain unsolved, and no one was ever tried.[9] But the growing violence, including the slaying of another Georgia man, Maceo Snipes, for casting his ballot in the July 17 Democratic Party primary, horrified national civil rights leaders, who believed more was needed from the Truman administration. NAACP leaders illuminated the dire situation in a meeting in September 1946 with Truman. During that meeting, NAACP director Walter White also recounted what had happened to Woodard, a moment that seemed to be a turning point for Truman. Historians suggest the events of 1946 and 1947 represented a change in Truman's thinking about race, which had been rooted in Confederate gallantry and the mythology of the Lost Cause.[10]

In the Woodward case, the Justice Department filed suit against the Batesburg police chief for violating the civil rights of Isaac Woodard. But a lackluster performance by government attorneys in presenting the case against Shull resulted in an expected acquittal and cheers from the southern spectators in the federal courtroom in Columbia on the evening of November 6, 1946. The jury had deliberated for just twenty-five minutes, although Judge Waring had declared he would take a walk around the courthouse so the jury could not immediately vote and report its verdict. The judge was horrified at the federal government's handling of the case, including its failure to effectively counter the defense's argument that Woodard was disruptive, drunk, and unruly on the bus. The federal government had found witnesses who reported that Woodard did not cause any trouble on the bus, but their testimony was lost in light of the police chief's insistence that he had delivered just one blow to Woodard's head in self-defense.[11]

On the stand, the police chief said he was sorry that Woodard had lost his sight. But the brutal police attack on Woodard was overshadowed by what many white South Carolinians saw as simply another example of the federal government's interference in the affairs of states and localities. "Such intercession on the part of the central government in the affairs of the state can lead only to a renewal of argument over states' rights," *The State*'s editorial writers opined a day after the verdict. "It is therefore an unwholesome influence against unity in the Union, and something to be studiously avoided whenever possible."[12]

The *Columbia Record* also weighed in on Saturday, November 9, several days after the verdict. The violation of civil rights that the Justice Department alleged

> seems to involve a sort of racial discrimination. If a white officer in South Carolina or Georgia uses too much force in subduing a white man it is of no concern to the federal government. If a Negro officer uses too much force in subduing a Negro prisoner it probably also would not concern the federal government. But if a white officer uses too much force to subdue a Negro prisoner it becomes a violation of federal law, punishable by the federal courts.[13]

Events later that year would justify the fears of white leaders that the federal government was no longer taking a hands-off approach to the South's persistent racial problems. In late 1946, Truman, reeling from the Republican takeover of both the House and Senate, nevertheless established "The President's Committee on Civil Rights." Months later, in 1947, the committee released its report, "To Secure These Rights," which illuminated racial discrimination in housing, voting, public accommodations and other areas of American life.[14] In

June 1947, Truman became the first president to address the national NAACP, traveling to the Lincoln Memorial to address the thirty-eighth annual convention. "I should like to talk to you briefly about civil rights and human freedom," he told the thousands of delegates who gathered outdoors.

It is my deep conviction that we have reached a turning point in the long history of our country's efforts to guarantee freedom and equality to all our citizens. Recent events in the United States and abroad have made us realize that it is more important today than ever before to insure that all Americans enjoy these rights.[15]

On July 26, 1948, President Harry Truman signed Executive Order 9981, creating the President's Committee on Equality of Treatment and Opportunity in the Armed Services. The order mandated the desegregation of the US military:

It is hereby declared to be the policy of the President that there shall be equality of treatment and opportunity for all persons in the armed services without regard to race, color, religion, or national origin. This policy shall be put into effect as rapidly as possible, having due regard to the time required to effectuate any necessary changes without impairing efficiency or morale.[16]

Black soldiers, including Woodard, Snipes, Dorsey, and innumerable unnamed others, had offered up their lives—or in Woodard's case, his eyes—twice for the United States.

In school, Hodges studied the changes that were taking place in American life, and listened closely to Miss Boyd at Waverly Grammar School and, later, to his teachers at the segregated Booker T. Washington High School on Columbia's Marion and Blossom Streets. But Hodges and his fellow students didn't see much change in their everyday world, even after the May 1954 Supreme Court decision that outlawed segregation in public schools. The *Briggs v. Elliott* case that Miss Boyd had enumerated in Hodges's sixth-grade class was among five cases consolidated into the historic *Brown v. Board of Education of Topeka, Kansas*. The students at Booker T. Washington could not imagine a day when they would attend school with white students. But Hodges clearly remembers the announcement that went out on his school's public announcement system. As the US Supreme Court decision was announced, he remembers it was accompanied by a rendition of "Dixie."

As a young teen, Hodges remembered working as a server at a party given by one of his white employers. Among the guests was then Governor James Byrnes, a distinguished jurist and confidante of President Roosevelt who had served in Congress, on the US Supreme Court, and as US Secretary of State. After a brilliant career during the crucial war years, Brynes had returned to South Carolina and was elected governor in 1950. Despite his worldly experience and his insistence on the spread of democracy abroad, Brynes believed that segregation should be maintained in the South. Knowing the clock was ticking down on the Supreme Court's decision on integrating public schools, Byrnes had persuaded the state legislature to embark on a multimillion-dollar equalization project to bring Black schools up to white standards and allegedly fulfill the "separate but equal" mandate established in the *Plessy v. Ferguson* decision. It was a massive undertaking but destined to be a stopgap measure on the way to the tortured path to equal schools. "I remember when a group were huddled around him talking in hushed tones, 'What are we going to do, what are we going to do?'" Hodges recalled. "And he assured them that he had a plan." Young Hodges also had a plan, which was to go to college, earn a good living, and leave South Carolina behind.

"I remember at Booker Washington, the teacher asked what we wanted to do, and I said, 'I don't want to be poor all my life,'" he said. "When the Morehouse representative came, he said I was known as the smartest boy in the senior class. I knew that I was different from my classmates because certain things intellectually came to me so easily."

Hodges gained admittance to Morehouse College and left for the renowned Atlanta school in January 1957 even though he couldn't afford the books. To get through the semester, he said he would borrow his classmates' books at the beginning, read and return them, and then tutor his classmates as the year progressed. Back home during the summer of 1957, Hodges listened as Strom Thurmond, the junior senator from South Carolina, filibustered the 1957 Civil Rights Act, insisting that there was no need for the federal government to interfere with elections in South Carolina and other states.

"I am in favor of having every qualified voter enjoy the right of franchise. I want to say that in my State every qualified voter has that privilege. No one—white, colored, or anyone else—is denied the right to vote in South Carolina," Thurmond told California Senator William Knowland, the floor manager for the legislation, during his 24-hour filibuster. "The (state) statute I have read protects people from being coerced and intimidated and threatened in any way. If there is any violation of law now, a person who is discriminated against may go to the Department of Justice, and under the statute I have read a violator of that statute will be either sent to jail or fined or both. What the proposed compromise would do would be to take away that right of trial by jury."

Southern lawmakers such as Thurmond were alarmed that the 1957 civil rights legislation would create a new civil rights division within the Justice Department that would wield ultimate power over the thousands of claims of voting intimidation that were well documented in the southern states. Thurmond also resisted the charge that southern juries would not convict in civil rights cases brought by Black voters. Eventually, the southerners were able to weaken the legislation that finally passed.

In his courtly response, Knowland said he took Thurmond at his word that there were no egregious examples of voting suppression, even though Congress had affidavits from hundreds of voters who claimed otherwise. "I have never taken the position on the floor, or publicly or privately, in which I have made a blanket indictment and stated that southern juries would not convict, because I have the highest respect for the people of the South, for their responsibilities of citizenship, for their loyalty to this country, and for the fact that they have served in uniform side by side with citizens from other sections of the country in fighting off our enemies in the various struggles in which this Nation has been engaged," Knowland said. "Of course, I do not know his State as well as does the Senator from South Carolina, but if he tells me that there are no cases where a person is deprived of his right to vote, where a Negro citizen, if he possesses precisely the same qualifications that would be expected of a white citizen."

Thurmond quickly interjected: "None that I know about . . ."[17]

After two years at Morehouse, Hodges returned to Columbia to help support his family following his grandmother's death. Hodges said he eventually earned enough money to complete his undergraduate education, entering the University of California, Santa Barbara, and putting physical and psychological distance from the South of his youth. He graduated in 1965 and entered law school at the University of California, Berkeley. During his long career, he practiced corporate law, worked in the California attorney general's office, and taught law. He established a private practice in 2002.

Hodges said he never forgot Elmore's sacrifice and the legal case that altered his native state. When he was in law school at Berkeley, he cringed when his law professor glossed over the *Elmore v. Rice* case. He asked his professor if he could elaborate on the Elmore case and its impact on South Carolina and his own life. "I was allowed to talk about the case from a historical and personal perspective," Hodges said. Now, he said, he returns to South Carolina occasionally to attend school reunions and visit relatives. During the coronavirus pandemic, Hodges and his Booker T. Washington High School classmates, including his longtime friend Cresswell Elmore, routinely met via Zoom. "I have to say that considering the agony and all that was heaped upon his family, that he has remained someone who is positive and not bitter. It has not taken over his thinking and made him bitter."

The year Hodges left his native state, South Carolina was just beginning to wrestle with the integration of public schools and the dropping of segregation's barriers. It would be January 1963 before the state's colleges and universities would finally admit Black students. Harvey Gantt would be the first, breaking the color barrier at Clemson University, after a court battle that went to the US Supreme Court. In the fall of 1963, Henrie Monteith Treadwell, Robert Anderson, and James Solomon integrated the University of South Carolina. It would be the end of the 1960s and into the 1970s—after protests, a riot in Lamar, South Carolina, that involved overturning a bus full of Black students, and machinations over "freedom of choice" and school assignments—before South Carolina public schools would finally be integrated. It would take another fifty years for most of those schools to resegregate in the twenty-first century.

Years have passed since Hodges's childhood in Frogtown and his days walking up Gervais Street for an ice cream cone at Elmore's store. Hodges has seen, from a distance, the transformation of South Carolina from an agricultural state to an urban, industrialized region. He has witnessed the election of James E. Clyburn to the US House of Representatives, the first Black lawmaker since Reconstruction.

Unthinkable as it may have been to him in 1940s Columbia, he observed the city in 2010 elect its first Black mayor, Stephen K. "Steve" Benjamin, who went on to serve two more terms. Still, as Hodges recalled memories of his time in South Carolina, he remained skeptical of a racial transformation in his home state.

"It's like you fly into Russia and you get off a plane and talk to two men," he said. "The first man will say 'A lot of things have changed, but not much is different.' The second man will say 'A lot of things are different, but not much has changed.' That is how I describe South Carolina."

CHAPTER 5

Battle Lines at Home and Abroad

I would like to see not only the Negro but the white
man in South Carolina free. There are many white
men in Columbia who hope we can accomplish what
we are fighting for.
—Dr. R. W. Mance Jr., April 22, 1942

In the spring of 1942, as South Carolinians immersed themselves in daily news of the war in Europe and the Pacific, James Hinton sent a letter to New York, addressed to NAACP special counsel Thurgood Marshall.[1] "We can see that our only course of action is to resort to a legal battle, for which we are now ready," Hinton wrote on letterhead of his company, Pilgrim Health and Life Insurance Company. "We need advice, and we trust that you will come to us at your earliest convenience, (at our expense), that we might know the best legal course to pursue." In the typewritten letter dated May 5, 1942, Hinton enclosed a clipping from Columbia's afternoon paper, the *Columbia Record*. The story detailed the refusal of Richland County Democrats to consider opening the party's primaries to qualified Black voters.[2]

Hinton was now the president of the state conference of branches of the NAACP. He was a fearless fireplug of a man credited with reviving the civil rights organization in the state and providing collective backbone to the Black struggle for citizenship. Hinton had initially been reluctant to form the statewide conference, a concept promoted by Levi Byrd, a plumber from Cheraw who led the NAACP chapter in his small community near the border of North Carolina. Byrd would be honored years later as the father of the South Carolina NAACP, sharing with Hinton a passion for ending the avalanche of outrages and indignities heaped daily upon the members of his race. Byrd's letters were unpolished and full of misspellings, but when they were read in the New York office, people there detected something bold and brave about the letter writer that suggested he could be called on to act. Byrd had once been beaten in Cheraw by a group of white men for no reason and he chronicled other such unprovoked attacks in letters to the national NAACP office. Byrd believed that uniting the disparate, and sometimes moribund, NAACP chapters around the state would strengthen the organization's will and clout. Hinton finally agreed, but only if he could assume the presidency of the statewide conference. He became the second statewide president, succeeding the Reverend Alonzo Webster Wright. Hinton would prove to be the man for the times, enlisting a cadre of volunteers in the battle for the ballot.[3]

In 1942, the franchise remained stubbornly elusive for all but a handful of the state's qualified Black voters, who could cast ballots in the general election. At its May 4, 1942, gathering, the Richland County Democratic Convention debated a stunning resolution to alter those decades of disenfranchisement. The resolution, put forth by Columbia physician Heyward Gibbes, attorneys R. Beverley Herbert and D. W. Robinson Jr., and others, urged the state Democratic convention to formally "repeal the rule which prohibits Negroes from participating in the Democratic primaries." By a 4–1 vote, the resolution was rejected. In presenting the minority report, Gibbes "declared that he was convinced that a large element of Negro citizens were qualified in mind and character to take part 'in our kind of government.'" According to a report in the May 5, 1942, edition of *The State,* Gibbes stated that South Carolina had the opportunity "to light a spark and find worldwide good in it." Supporters reminded the group that the Axis powers, particularly Nazi Germany, were using the second-class status of American minorities to diminish the Allied cause. But those opposed to opening the primaries recounted a familiar fear: namely, that the Democratic vote had already been "taken over" by Black voters in the North and would likely upend white supremacy in the South. The news of the convention's denial stirred Hinton to write his letter to the NAACP.[4]

It also prompted letters to Herbert, a prominent white lawyer who had served two terms in the South Carolina House and made a run for governor in 1930. "Let me commend you as highly as I know how for the splendid stand you took on Monday regarding giving Negroes the vote in the South Carolina Democratic Primary," Louise Bailey wrote in a May 6, 1942, letter. "Persons who have bothered to examine the record know that the Negro has not assumed, and cannot assume, his rightful place in our society until those who wrong him can be held account-able at the ballot box." Bailey, secretary in charge of the University of South Carolina's short and special extension courses, wrote her letter on university letterhead, a bold move that suggested there were some university employees who had given some serious thought to the glar-ing inequities around them. "Economically, educationally, in fact, in every area of our social order, the Negro is handicapped and cannot speak for himself and few of us will speak for him." She predicted Her-bert's leadership "gives many who have been thinking in the same direc-tion encouragement and makes others who have not been thinking at all heretofore think."[5]

However Columbia businessman E. C. Townsend, president of a Columbia real estate and insurance firm, had his own predictions. Townsend expressed surprise at Herbert's "recent attitude toward the colored people voting in our election" and estimated that if Herbert ran on such a platform "you would be defeated 99%." On letterhead of the E. C. Townsend Company, Townsend said, "As long as there is a South the white people will rule the various political states of the solid South, then when this cannot be done, it will be just too bad." Townsend concluded with this: "Such advocacy, publicity that you all are giving this together with Mrs. Roosevelt arm in arm with the negro women will do more to bring about trouble with the races than any-thing that can be done."[6]

Amid wartime upheaval, Herbert and other like-minded white moderates believed that Townsend and others could be brought along to accept change in the South—if change were gradual and overseen by white leaders. But Herbert, like so many of his white contempo-raries, was worried that too much agitation on the part of Black leaders could topple the fragile progress that had been made. In a letter to the Colored Citizens Committee, dated April 23, 1942, Herbert cautioned the newly formed group:

> "I hope the negroes in their effort to get the vote will show the
> same patience and understanding that they have exhibited in the
> last few years and will not become bitter if it is not given to them
> at once." He went on: "Your people must try to see both sides
> of the question. To throw the door open wide and tell all of the
> negroes to come and vote would probably mean that a vast major-
> ity would be mislead [misled] by the first demagogue who came

along and promised them anything, just as far too many white people are mislead [misled] in the way.[7]

Hinton undoubtedly chafed at such blatant paternalism, well-meaning as Herbert thought himself to be. But Hinton and other Black Columbians who served on the interracial committee that Herbert headed likely stuck with the effort to gain some incremental change. At a moment when democracy was challenged worldwide by Nazis and fascists, the interracial group understood that the time had come to rid the Democratic Party of the arcane rules that led to mass purging of Black names from voter rolls. For years many Black citizens threw up their hands at the convoluted machinations of the white elections officials and declined to even try to register. Others, hearing of intimidation and threats leveled at potential Black voters in rural areas, stayed away out of self-preservation.

Two months before Hinton wrote his letter to Marshall, the newspaper reported that the chairman of Columbia's election commission had instructed city enrollment clerks to permit Black voters to register for the two upcoming city primaries. But there was a catch. Chairman W. M. Perry pointed out the qualifications for voting, adopted on January 22, 1942, by the city Democratic executive committee: "Every Negro applying to vote in the city Democratic primary must be known to have voted the Democratic ticket continuously since 1876."[8]

That explanation, effectively limiting Black suffrage to octogenarians who had cast ballots for Confederate General Wade Hampton, drew "a united roar of laughter" from a large delegation of Black citizens who appeared before the city board of elections on April 22, 1942. Even city attorney Paul Cooper seemed chagrined to note that the local board must follow the rules of the party, although he said he was not sure the state party "had the right to make the rule," according to an account reported in *The State* a day later.

Dr. R. W. Mance Jr., a physician and son of a former president of Allen University, the school founded by the African Methodist Episcopal Church in 1870, led the delegation's members. The men had been requested to appear and explain why their names should not be struck from the voting rolls just days before the April 28, 1942, city primary. "Our great American government is faced with the gravest emergency in its history, torn between dictatorships abroad, and a lack of unity at home. In times like these, all citizens regardless of color should be

Dr. R. W. Mance Jr., a physician and civil rights activist, pointed out the absurdity of white Democratic Party rules, including one requiring Black voters to have cast ballots continuously for Democrats since 1876. From the John Henry McCray Papers. Courtesy of South Caroliniana Library, University of South Carolina.

drawn into closer relationship for the general good of America," Mance said in his address to the city election commission. He continued,

> Millions of young men, white and black, are preparing now to sacrifice their lives on the battlefields of the world, in order that American Democratic philosophy will embrace all peoples, regardless of race, color or previous servitude. It is our hope that the Democratic Party of South Carolina will meet the challenge of the times, and let the world know that democracy which they preach is an actuality rather than a far-fetched idea.

Casting aside the outright silliness of the "Wade Hampton requirement," Mance told the election commissioners he wanted to "bring this question to the common sense view . . . I would like to see not only the Negro but the white man in South Carolina free. There are many white men in Columbia who hope we can accomplish what we are fighting for." He then added: "If this room were made dark right now you could not tell if a white man or a black man were talking. I reason and talk like a white man." Mance noted that he would soon be off to war in the medical service of the US Army, willing to shed his blood for his country. But he said he could not tolerate returning home "where the white people can shove a grandfather clause in my face. . . ."[9] The city commissioners seemed sympathetic to their request and assured the group that the matter would be taken up at the Democratic state convention in May. But by that time, all understood that the city primaries would have passed.

Was George Elmore in the room? There is no record of his presence, although it is possible he would have been in the crowd that nearly flowed from the county courtroom. A formal petition, signed by the Negro Citizens Committee of South Carolina, was delivered to the State Carolina State Convention of the Democratic Party, which held its one-day meeting on May 20, 1942, at the South Carolina State House. The meeting garnered front-page coverage but it was down page and dwarfed by the news from Europe that dominated the front page of the *Columbia Record*.[10] The headline across eight columns screamed "100,000 NAZI PARACHUTE TROOPS POISED FOR DRIVE ON CAUCASUS." The opening paragraph painted a clear picture of what was at stake: "Russia's armies storming toward the great steel city of Kharkov were reported by London sources to have fought their way 'into the heart of the city's defenses' today, while the Germans were massing 100,000 parachutists for a giant air-borne invasion of the Caucasus." As the monster Russian fifty-two-ton tanks rumbled over fields littered with "many hundreds of German dead," the newspaper reported that Pravda, the Russian news agency, had declared: "The Red Army is breaking the fierce resistance of the Hitlerite beast and pushing them back to the West, liberating Soviet soil step by step."

Meanwhile, Brigadier General James H. "Jimmy" Doolittle was pictured at the White House, where President Roosevelt had presented him with the Congressional Medal of Honor for carrying out the US secret bombing raid over the Japanese islands on April 18, 1942. In the Associated Press dispatch, Doolittle made hay over Japanese assertions that the enemy had shot down nine of the American bombers as the squadron "blasted a 40-mile path of fire and destruction through Japan." Doolittle "hooted" at the Japanese propaganda. "The Japanese do not have one of our planes on display," Doolittle said. "They may have painted up one of their own to look like ours, or they have may gotten an American plane from somewhere else, but not from us." A few Columbians reading the afternoon newspaper may have smiled, remembering that Doolittle and his company of seventy-nine fliers had briefly trained for the secret mission in the capital city. Doolittle remained circumspect about where the mission had launched. The story noted that President Roosevelt had declared tongue-in-cheek that the raid was launched from Shangri-La, the fictional Tibetan city portrayed in the novel *Lost Horizon*. Even better, the story noted, German radio had broadcast the president's mythical location as fact.

Amid that backdrop and with a red-hot debate among delegates on whether liquor should be outlawed yet again, the state's white Democrats decided that now was not the time to consider the explosive suggestion of extending the ballot to qualified Black voters. Voting 40–1, the rules committee postponed all "controversial" matters to the 1944 convention. Manning Mayor John G. Dinkins, elected as temporary chair, summed up the feelings of the group in his extemporaneous remarks as reported in the *Columbia Record* and *The State*: "In this crucial hour, I feel our people are more desperately in need of guns, tanks, shells and food than of Democratic speechmaking. I consider it the duty of all parties to unite with the one motive of winning the war, and to brush aside all controversial issues." The Rules Committee took the action after receiving a resolution from A. B. Langley, a delegate from Richland County, and several petitions from groups including the Negro Citizens Committee of South Carolina.

Langley argued that this moment in history was the exact time to finally grant full citizenship to the state's Black voters. The resolution mirrored the words of the failed Richland County resolution but did not ask for immediate opening of the primaries to white and Black people:

> Whereas, it is to the interest of good government and world Democracy that no one be denied the right to vote in the Democratic Primary on account of race, color or previous condition of servitude, now, therefore, be it resolved, that: The chairman of this convention do name a committee from the convention to study the question of permitting Negroes to vote in the Democratic primaries of this state when they are qualified to do so. And that such committee report its findings to this convention.[11]

The decision of the convention was hardly surprising to the petitioners. But Mance was correct in asserting that some forward-thinking white South Carolinians were now publicly aligned with the suffrage battle. Several days before the convention delegates met, twenty-one white citizens of Columbia, including those who had been rebuffed at the Richland County Democratic Convention, urged the South Carolina Democratic Convention to appoint a committee to study the question of Black voting "and try to arrive at some plan by which qualified Negroes may vote in the Democratic primaries of this state."

"We believe that an understanding and sympathetic approach to this problem by the white people of South Carolina will result in making our Negro citizens friendly and co-operative and that they will join good white people in seeking good government," the petition signed by some of Columbia's most prominent citizens noted. The petition was printed in its entirety in the May 18, 1942, edition of The State.[12]

In addition to Gibbes and Herbert, the group included Fitz Hugh McMaster, a former lawmaker, newspaper editor, and historian who, as a boy, had witnessed the 1876 Red Shirt campaign that returned Wade Hampton and the Redeemers to power. While editor at the Columbia Record in the 1930s, McMaster had instituted a new policy that the word "Negro" would be capitalized in all stories, rendering a courtesy title that was acknowledged in an editorial in the Palmetto Leader.

Also included among the petitioners were newspaper executive Frank Hampton, a great-nephew of Confederate General Wade Hampton, and Columbia city schools superintendent A. C. Flora, among others. Their recommendations were modest. The men understood the obstinate audience to whom they were addressing their concerns, and they had their own deep-seated prejudices about the minority race. According to the petitioners,

> We do not believe that it is either necessary or advisable that the Democratic party be thrown open to Negroes indiscriminately. Nor do we believe that anything but good would come from establishing minor educational and character qualifications for membership of whites in the party. We believe that carefully considered qualification of this kind, applied to whites and blacks, might result in a definite improvement in our political institutions.[13]

The Virginia-born Herbert would soon assume leadership of what became known as the South Carolina Committee of the Commission on Interracial Cooperation. The South Carolina committee was part of the Atlanta-based Commission on Interracial Cooperation, founded in 1919 in the wake of post–World War I racial unrest. It aimed to bring together the South's moderate and progressive thinkers on the issues of social justice, if not social equality. (Eventually, the group would merge with the Southern Regional Council and turn its attention to economic arguments for ending segregation and improving life in the South.) The Atlanta commission was led by Will Alexander, a white Methodist minister, but Black leaders, including Morehouse College president Benjamin Mays, a native of Greenwood County, South Carolina, were quickly recruited to join the effort. In the 1920s and 1930s, white southern leaders believed that a more equitable level of segregation could somehow be achieved if the best minds of both races could fashion a solution.[14] But by the early 1940s, it was clear that Black leaders envisioned an end to segregation as the only means of achieving true equality. That left many of their white counterparts struggling to reconcile their own place in southern society and what that might look like amid the upheaval and change of full integration. Some white leaders discovered they were not as progressive as they had believed in their hearts when it came time to share economic and political power.

In October 1942, fifty Black leaders met in Durham, North Carolina, for the Southern Race Relations Conference and issued a call to demolish segregation and discrimination in law, education, jobs, and health. The "Durham Manifesto," as it would come to be called, took aim at the southern white primary, the poll tax, discrimination in the court system, unequal schools, the absolute dearth of good-paying jobs, poor health facilities, and a host of other ills that limited the progress of Black people.

"The war has sharpened the issue of Negro-white relations in the United States, and particularly in the South. A result has been increased racial tensions, fears, and aggressions, and an opening up of the basic questions of racial segregation and discrimination, Negro minority rights, and democratic freedom, as they apply practically in Negro-white relations in the South," the conference announced in its final report. "These issues are acute and threaten to become even more serious as they increasingly block, through the deeper fears aroused, common sense consideration for even elementary improvements in Negro status, and the welfare of the country as a whole."[15]

Conference members were adamant that the old paternalistic relationships between white and Black people must be a thing of the past. "Instead of letting the demagogues guess what we want, we are proposing to make our wants and aspirations a matter of record, so clear that he who runs may read," the final report stated. "We are hoping in this way to challenge the constructive cooperation of that element of the white South who express themselves as desirous of a New Deal for the Negroes of the South." This proposed new Charter of Race Relations would be "fraternalistic and scientific; for the old charter is not compatible with the manhood and security of the Negro, neither is it compatible with the dignity and self-respect of the South."[16]

Black South Carolinians were prominent among those at the Durham conference who were calling for "common sense considerations" during perilous times. Gordon Blaine Hancock, born in Ninety Six, South Carolina, in 1884 to parents who had been enslaved, gaveled the meeting into session. He was a prominent sociologist and professor at Virginia Union University and had a wider audience as a syndicated columnist for Black newspapers, including the *Lighthouse and Informer* and the *Palmetto Leader*. He was among southern Black leaders who were adamant that segregation must end. Among other South Carolinians in attendance were Reverend H. B. Butler of Hartsville, president of the Baptist State Convention; J. B. Blanton, principal of Voorhees Normal and Industrial School in Denmark; J. A. Bacoats, then vice president (later, president) of Benedict College in Columbia; Dr. and Mrs. J. G. Stuart of Columbia; Dr. and Mrs. D. K. Jenkins of Columbia; K. W. Green, dean of South Carolina State in Orangeburg; A. B. Cooke, business agent for Local No. 815 of the Carpenters Union in Columbia; and Modjeska Monteith Simkins, who was identified in the program in the traditional manner as Mrs. Andrew W. Simpkins (a misspelling of her surname).[17] Simkins was well known in her own right in 1942 as a woman who would brook no nonsense in the quest for equal rights. She, NAACP chief Hinton, and newspaperman McCray would soon put distance between themselves and their well-meaning white counterparts as the NAACP's legal fight to overturn the white primary in Texas and in neighboring Georgia ignited Black leaders in the Palmetto State. In just a few years George Elmore would take his place in that struggle.

The decade of the 1940s upended life in South Carolina, as it did in all of the states. Young men who had never left the borders of their home counties were suddenly thrust into Europe and Asia, fighting in places with strange names and terrain far removed from the Lowcountry marshes, the sandhills, and the Blue Ridge Mountains. At home, people found collective purpose in supporting the war effort and sometimes crossed the color line to do so. Black leaders saw an opportunity for real change, and some moderate white people also saw a momentary opening to throw off a way of life that had become unsustainable.

It is clear that the mythology of the Lost Cause and the absolute belief in white supremacy were still uppermost in the minds of most white South Carolinians, led by outspoken demagogues in Columbia and in Washington. But as war raged, even the most rigid white supremacist saw that the sons of Black South Carolinians were spilling blood alongside the sons of white South Carolinians, albeit in still-segregated military units. The state NAACP found its collective purpose in the 1940s, no longer acquiescing to the sensitivities of their white fellow citizens. Now the demands for equality in teacher pay, in education, in voting, even in public life were insistent. The results in the courtroom were soon to be cause for optimism.

CHAPTER 6

"We'll Fight the Negroes at the Polls"

History has taught us that we must keep our white
Democratic primaries pure and unadulterated so
that we might protect the welfare and homes of all
the people of our State.

—Governor Olin D. Johnston, April 14, 1944

On April 21, 1944, the Charleston novelist Josephine Pinckney wrote to her friend R. Beverley Herbert, lamenting the political drama unfolding in the halls of the South Carolina capitol. "The recent antics of the governor, legislators, senators and W. W. Ball have reduced me to a state bordering on despair," she wrote to Herbert, a Columbia attorney. "Aren't there any people in South Carolina who are decent and intelligent about the negroes? There must be but they are pretty hard to find with the naked eye."[1]

Pinckney was horrified that Governor Olin D. Johnston had called lawmakers to Columbia for one stated purpose: to maintain white supremacy in the Democratic primary. Days earlier, on April 3, the US Supreme Court announced that Texas Democrats must open their all-white primary to Black voters, a decision that roared across the one-party South like a freight train.[2] But the state's white powerbrokers from Washington to Columbia made it clear they were not about to lose control of its machinery, and to hell with the nation's high court. "The white people of the South will not accept these interferences," US Senator Burnet R. Maybank declared to his fellow senators in remarks published in the April 14, 1944, edition of *The State*, the day the special session opened. "We know what is best for the white people and the colored people. We are going to treat the Negro fairly, but in so doing we do not intend for him to take over our election system or attend white schools."[3] As governor, Maybank had fought the Ku Klux Klan and worked to improve schools and economic opportunities for the state's

Black citizens, but extending the franchise was a bridge too far. Pinckney, as a literary observer of her native city and the caste system that defined it, also understood that white Charlestonians and the rest of the South were facing a bewildering racial reckoning. "I feel so strongly that we Southerners have to find some working philosophy ourselves for dealing with the negro or else some unpleasant solution will be forced on us from outside," she wrote Herbert, noting, "I am quite willing to write or say anything that would do any good, but where can we begin?"[4]

If there were other white citizens like Pinckney who were beginning to wrestle with the great moral questions of the day, the state's white political leaders were not listening to them. For his part, Maybank said he had never seen South Carolinians "so much disturbed as they are now" and blamed "agitators" who he believed were taking advantage of a nation at war to promote their ambitions. These people, he said, aimed to "upset our election laws and our custom of segregation, which have proved mutually satisfactory to the vast majorities of both races in South Carolina." His garrulous senate colleague and dean of the US Senate, "Cotton Ed" Smith, was less refined in his comments, pounding his fist as he met with reporters in Washington. It was time "for the people of South Carolina to wake up," he said, and denounce the encroachment of President Roosevelt and the federal government into the business of the states. "I foresaw years ago the dangerous tendency of the New Deal Democratic Party. Tariffs have been raised instead of lowered; States' rights have been usurped. And now, boldly, the supreme court has challenged the right of white supremacy in the political and social arena of my state." He hearkened back to the 1936 National Democratic Convention in Philadelphia where he had walked out rather than bow his head as a Black minister offered a prayer to Almighty God to close one of the sessions. In Smith's South Carolina, God in heaven was as white as the primary. And so Smith reached for another biblical reference as he railed against the high court: "All those who love South Carolina and the white man's rule will rally in this hour of her greatest Gethsemane to save her from a disastrous fate."[5]

Pinckney knew that Herbert had been active in modest interracial efforts in Columbia and had pushed Democratic leaders as early as 1942 to open the white primary to qualified minorities. She understood there were at least a handful of South Carolinians who thought Johnston was headed on a collision course with history. Almost immediately after the Supreme Court decision, Johnston huddled with top leaders of the Democratic Party to figure out a way to legally circumvent the nation's highest court and keep the South Carolina primary private and for white people. At first Johnston professed publicly that he was "not alarmed" by the decision. He issued a statement praising the 1943 General Assembly, which, at his behest, had removed state statutes related to Democratic primaries, except for those affecting election fraud. He said he believed the party could handle the fallout from the case in the May Democratic state convention.[6] But just a week later, on April 12, 1944, Johnston changed his mind. He called an "extraordinary session" that would commence two days later. The state's senators and representatives rushed to Columbia to answer the governor's edict. Shouting to the 170 lawmakers gathered in the House chambers on the evening of April 14, 1944, Johnston evoked the memory of the Redeemers, the men who had restored white rule after the Civil War's tumultuous Reconstruction period. "I regret that this ruling by the United States Supreme Court has forced this issue upon us, but we must meet it like men," the governor declared in the evening address.[7] In just six days, the legislature removed all references to primaries in state statutes.

South Carolina newspapers provided day-by-day coverage, reporting scrutinized and analyzed by the state's newspaper editors, none more intently than William Watts Ball, the editor of Charleston's *News and Courier*. Ball, who had long railed against President Roosevelt and his New Deal policies, was so incensed by the high court's ruling, he took the unusual step of publishing a front-page editorial on April 4, a day after the *Smith v. Allwright* ruling. Pinckney was likely referring to that editorial and subsequent writings in her letter to Herbert. The editorial—"To Save State from a Reconstructed Court"—was chock full of language that echoed the political fights of the Redeemers seventy years earlier. In it, Ball argued that Democrats should abolish the primary system and return to a convention system, where conventions or caucuses could meet "in private houses, in sitting rooms or around supper tables."

"The South Carolina negroes are even now preparing to crash the white primaries, as Hinton, a Columbia negro, announces. There should remain no South Carolina primaries to crash," he wrote. Let the high court "break into the doors of white men's club rooms, lodges, private homes, lest white men and women meet in them and nominate candidates."

The primary system is "decayed," Ball asserted. The corrupt "purchasable and herdible" element in the white population was already a threat to honest government. Then his journalistic kicker: "To retain and admit 300,000 negro men and women to vote in it would make South Carolina uninhabitable by decent white people."[8] With one scathing sentence, Ball dismissed nearly half of the state's population and disabused Black subscribers to his newspaper of any notion of evenhandedness in public and political life.

The governor was as overwrought in person as Ball was in print. Never mind that South Carolinians at that hour were fighting a twentieth-century world war with sophisticated airplanes and state-of-the-art tanks and weaponry. Inside the ornate capital, the past was palpable. In citing the urgency of what lay before the legislature, Johnston returned to a post–Civil War wound that still festered in the minds and hearts of those assembled: the majority-Black Reconstruction-era legislature. "What kind of government did they give South Carolina when they were in power?" Johnston asked. "The records will bear me out that fraud, corruption, immorality, and graft existed during that regime that has never been paralleled in the history of our State. They left a stench in the nostrils of the people of South Carolina that will exist for generations to come." No one in the chamber disagreed with him.

Johnston predicted a new generation of agitators and scalawags would descend upon South Carolina now that the nation's high court no longer upheld white supremacy. "The representatives of these agitators, scalawags and unscrupulous politicians that called themselves white men and used the colored to further their own course are in our midst today," he said.[9] Johnston knew the power of the old familiar stories, of the memory that still lingered of Confederate General Wade Hampton III and the Red Shirts restoring white rule in 1876, of the perhaps embellished story of Hampton on his deathbed reminding white South Carolinians they must remain paternalistic protectors of a formerly enslaved race: "God bless all my people, black and white."

Now, decades later, the 1940s agitators stirring the pot were educated Black editors and lawyers. They had cast aside the old accommodating stories—if they had ever given them credence—for a new and empowering narrative that was a direct threat to long-established customs. Johnston and the other white lawmakers in the House chamber were not ignorant of the rising power of the NAACP and the team of lawyers led by Thurgood Marshall who had won the Texas case. They had read the April headline in Columbia's afternoon paper, the *Columbia Record*, on the day the decision was announced: "Texas Negroes Can Vote, Court Rules; S.C. Action Likely." NAACP president James Hinton, who was also secretary of the Negro Citizens Committee of South Carolina, told the newspaper that $3,400 had already been raised for the fight in the federal court.[10] They had read the no-holds-barred editorials in McCray's *Lighthouse and Informer* newspaper, well-written pieces that aimed to stir the state's Black residents to action. To the white leaders, the editorials bordered on the radical.[11]

Johnston could not resist hearkening back to Tillman, who had succeeded in obliterating the work of the Black Reconstruction lawmakers and cleared the way for the 1895 state constitution that effectively ended voting for the state's Black citizens. "History has taught us that we must keep our white Democratic primaries pure and unadulterated so that we might protect the welfare and homes of all the people of our State," Johnston said. "After these statutes are repealed, in my opinion, we will have done everything within our power to guarantee white supremacy in our primaries of our State insofar as legislation is concerned. Should this prove inadequate, we South Carolinians will use the necessary methods to retain white supremacy in our primaries and to safeguard the homes and happiness of our people." His voice rising, Johnston shouted, "White supremacy will be maintained in our primaries. Let the chips fall where they may!"[12]

Although it is likely most southern politicians had followed the incremental progress of the Texas white primary cases through the federal court system, the South Carolina governor professed to be shocked at the action of the high court in *Smith v. Allwright*. As early as 1927, the Supreme Court contemplated the way Texas Democrats administered their primary and limited who would cast ballots in it. In 1927, in a case known as *Nixon v. Herndon*, Doctor Lawrence Nixon argued that the white primary violated the Fourteenth and Fifteenth Amendments and limited the rights of Black citizens in the state. While the high court unanimously ruled that the Texas law, which allowed the Democrats to limit primary rolls, did violate the Fourteenth Amendment to the

Constitution, party leaders found a workaround. The state legislature removed the offending statutes and enacted provisions that granted authority to the executive committee of the Democratic Party to determine its own rolls. Five years later, Nixon brought a second action. In the 1932 case of *Nixon v. Condon,* the high court, by a vote of 5–4, determined that the Democratic executive committee was again in violation of the Fourteenth Amendment because it did not have the right to determine membership criteria. The Texas legislature then scrubbed the state constitution of all language related to primaries, leaving it up to the Democratic operatives to conduct their own primaries.

Those actions seemed to satisfy justices in the 1934 case of *Grovey v. Townsend.* R. R. Grovey, a Black man, had attempted to vote in the July 28, 1934, Democratic primary but was denied the ballot because of his race. Justice Owen Roberts, writing for the unanimous court, found then that the Democratic Party was a voluntary association that could determine its membership. Since the party's limitations were not endorsed by the state, the justices concluded that the Fourteenth and Fifteenth Amendments to the Constitution did not apply to Grovey's situation. By the time Houston dentist Lonnie E. Smith sued party officials in 1943, the court had come around to Thurgood Marshall's thinking on political parties that discriminate against voters because of race. This time, there was a new slate of justices, the majority of them appointed by President Roosevelt. The justices finally reached the conclusion that primaries, the election that had counted in the solid white South since the end of federal Reconstruction, were an integral part of the electoral process. Marshall, William Hastie and W. J. Durham argued the case before the high court on November 12, 1943, and again in January 1944, after the state of Texas submitted a new brief. The 8–1 decision in *Smith v. Allwright* was a final repudiation of the court's previous analysis of the Texas electoral process. The high court found that Smith's Fifteenth Amendment right to vote was abridged by the party machinery and, because Texas had delegated the election to the Democratic Party, unconstitutional. Roberts, the author of the *Grovey* decision, was the only dissenter in *Smith v. Allwright.* He argued that overturning *Grovey* and rethinking previous decisions in Texas voting cases would ruin the reputation of the court. It would bring "adjudications of this tribunal into the same class as a restricted railroad ticket, good for this day and train only."[13]

James Hinton was buoyed by the *Smith v. Allwright* decision. He made it clear immediately that South Carolina Black leaders were poised to file a complaint in the federal courts to open the primaries to Black citizens. Hinton told the Associated Press the Texas decision was the "go signal" that South Carolina Black leaders needed to press their case.[14] Ten days later, on April 14, the day the special session opened, McCray and his associate editor Osceola McKaine, a World War I veteran who was the key strategist in successful 1941 litigation for equal pay for the state's Black teachers, announced the formation of a new political party. It would be "pledged to contest validity of the lilly [lily] white party at the national (Democratic) convention," according to a page-one story in the Charleston *News and Courier*. The dispatch was short—just four paragraphs—but its location down page from the extensive coverage of the opening day session suggested its significance. Lawmakers at the capitol who commented were unanimous in their assessment of the announcement. The reporter noted: "Virtually every legislator who would comment said, "'That's the thing. Let them organize their own party, and we'll run ours.'" But no lawmaker allowed his name to be attached to the ubiquitous quote.[15]

The day after the special session was gaveled into session, a deadly tornado swept through Georgia and South Carolina around midnight. The tornado tore through a hundred-mile swath of the two states, killing thirty-eight people, seventeen in South Carolina in the Greenwood, Abbeville, and Newberry areas. The American Red Cross reported that 147 homes were destroyed and another 103 were damaged in the two states. Despite the natural disaster, the work of the special legislature went on. In South Carolina, Greenwood County suffered the greatest human toll, with eight dead. But again, the reporting standards of the day did not equate the loss of white citizens with the Black citizens who were also killed. In the Associated Press account of the storm, published in the Monday edition of the *Columbia Record*, the reporter identified by name the white victims of the deadly tornado. Black victims were not listed by name, only by race: In Greenwood, "five Negroes;" in Newberry, "two Negroes." The most dramatic headline involved a young Black girl—"Girl Blown 150 Yds at Greenwood As Mighty Wind Hits," by Banjo Smith, a newspaper staff correspondent. In his first-person front-page account, he explained the deadly capriciousness of the storm, leaving some structures untouched and leveling others. Near the railroad tracks, where some Black residents resided, the houses were destroyed and the storm "tossed a young Negro girl 150 yards and left her lying and stiff with cold until daylight." State Highway Patrolman Tom Blanton found the child in the early morning light and provided this account: "That was the most unusual incident of the storm to me," Blanton told the newspaper. "I found the girl at daybreak, with a gash in the top of her head and as cold and still as death. She had been lying there in the rain all night. And you know, I passed with a few feet of her at 3 o'clock this morning while walking that field, but did not discover her. How she could have been hurled out of the house, and so far, while all the others were left there in the debris is something only a tornado could explain, I reckon." The devastating scene in Greenwood prompted more than a thousand people to utilize their rationed gas and travel to see the devastation for themselves, backing up traffic on the road in and out of Greenwood for hours.[16]

Meanwhile, in the state capitol, the rhetorical storm of protest over the high court's white primary decision continued unabated. On Monday, April 17, 1944, Representative John Long of Union rose on a point of privilege to attack a Black newspaper editorialist at the *Gary* (Indiana) *American*, who had described him as a "hillbilly" ginning up talk of another civil war when his own "forebearers had bit the dust between 1861–1866." Long was outraged, shouting, "We'll fight the Negroes at the polls if I have to bite the dust as did my ancestors." The House chamber "rang with applause" as he said, "If the people of the northern states want to eat, sleep and marry with the Negroes, let them, but I do object to their trying to ram it down our throats." He cautioned that the legislature must be judicious as it worked to remove references to primaries, saying,

> We should make hay slowly here—repeal of these 200 laws may be dangerous. I'm a white man like you, and I can say that as for the Negro voting in my primary, we'll fight them at the precinct meeting, we'll fight him at the county convention, we'll fight him at the enrollment books, and by God, we'll fight him at the polls if I have to bite the dust as did my ancestors.[17]

It was all too much for Modjeska Simkins, who was so agitated at the hot talk pouring out of the state capitol building that she sat down and typed a letter to Governor Johnston. In it, the civil rights activist challenged him to a public debate on white supremacy. "In your presentation, I am challenging you to prove, unequivocally and conclusively,

Modjeska Monteith Simkins helped lay the groundwork for NAACP lawsuits in the 1940s battling unequal teacher pay, the white primary and school desegregation. An outspoken advocate for equality, she could be abrasive to both white and Black people who challenged her. Courtesy of South Caroliniana Library.

that you are superior to me to say nothing of the hundreds of Negroes and other nationally and internationally renowned persons of color."[18] The governor never replied.

On the same day, April 17, the state senate sent to the house sixty-five bills and a joint resolution calling for a constitutional amendment that would remove from the state constitution a requirement that primaries be regulated by the General Assembly. But the senate was mired in debate over how best to allow soldiers overseas to cast ballots in the general election.

Two days later, on the fifth day of the special session, it was Senator George Warren of Hampton County who was doing the shouting as he urged his colleagues to turn their backs on President Roosevelt and "the dictatorship of the Washington crowd." Warren, like "Cotton Ed" Smith in the US Senate, lambasted the Roosevelt administration for allegedly betraying the South as it courted labor and northern Black voters. "If it is necessary to be crucified politically in South Carolina, I am willing to be crucified provided it is on an anti-Roosevelt cross," Warren told lawmakers. In what *The State* newspaper described as "roaring sessions of both houses" the lawmakers sparred over whether they should be paid ten dollars or twenty-five dollars a day for their efforts or just earn traveling expenses as they moved along omnibus bills that acted as a "dragnet" to remove all references to primaries in state statutes.[19]

Leaders of the state's Black colleges, meeting in Denmark, South Carolina, deplored the special session and the hotheaded language emerging from the capitol as a setback to race relations. "There can be no gainsaying the fact that this very act will go a long way in accentuating the tensions between the races as a time when sane and rational thinking is more necessary than ever before," the college presidents, deans, and registrars said in a statement reported in the *News and Courier* on Sunday, April 16. "We cannot expect to live the kind of cooperative, progressive life which is the birthright of every person in a free country, as long as one group uses its powers and prerogatives to prevent the other group from realizing its manhood rights and assume its manhood obligations."

The Black college administrators emphasized the great war effort underway: "We are convinced that the principles and ideals of democracy and Christianity for which the members of all races and nations of the civilized world are fighting and dying are the ends for which we strive in this state."[20] At least one soldier fighting overseas was, like the Black college leaders and the writer Josephine Pinckney, troubled by the machinations of the white supremacists. In an April 13, 1944, letter to the *News and Courier*, T. B. Grubb said he and other soldiers had been ruminating about just what they were fighting for. "It seems to a lot of us in camp who think at all that the idea that we are forced to die for and against—many of us—is the idea that the Huns have of being a super-race who should rule and hold more inferior races in their place. And it seems to us that anyone who cares to think at all would agree with us on that." He went on: "And yet that self-same and identical idea that our country asks us to die in combat is spread all over the Charleston newspapers as one to be upheld against the colored race." He concluded: "So many of us think it would be just as well to stay here and fight and die for our country until this idea of racial superiority is forever eradicated root and branch." He added in parentheses that he was "a soldier writing for group of white soldiers."[21]

Pinckney likely read that letter and took heart from an opinion so contrary to the majority of those who wrote to the Charleston newspaper. In her most famous novel, "Three O'Clock Dinner," published in 1945, she channeled a bit of the despair she had articulated a year earlier. The character of Fenwick Redcliff, patriarch of an old but fading Charleston family, tells his daughter-in-law, Judith: "For years I've been clamoring for an Opposition in the state, be it Republican, Socialist or whatever . . . I've inveighed against the Solid South, against the folly of a one-party system-" When his daughter-in-law suggests he start a new political party, he answers that he wants to "be a Democrat."

"God made me a Southerner, an Episcopalian and a Democrat . . . and in a world of shifting truths these are the principles I like to stand on."[22] The folly of that rigid thinking—shared by the flesh-and-blood white leaders of South Carolina—would be made clear in coming years as the old customs and caste system were swept away in a tidal wave of delayed justice.

CHAPTER 7

Power and Peril of Collaboration

> This is the ONE organization our people have waited
> for and predictions are that NOW WE CANNOT LOSE.
> What is being asked of you is small but it can mean
> for your county the gateway of political freedom.
>
> —John McCray, open letter calling for delegates
> to the inaugural state convention of the
> Progressive Democratic Party, May 17, 1944

As decades passed, the extraordinary session was largely forgotten, an embarrassing relic to a past best left unmentioned.[1] But editor McCray saw that two-week period in April 1944, when white supremacy was laid bare in all its unreconstructed fervor, as the moment the boil was lanced. Ordinary Black South Carolinians, many waiting anxiously for their soldier sons to return home safely, saw that white leaders would never stop looking backwards as the twentieth century moved forward.

If the special session had stirred the blood of unreconstructed white lawmakers determined to keep Negroes in their place, it had elevated to epic proportions the already percolating anger of Black activists. McCray and his well-traveled associate editor Osceola McKaine were seated in the colored gallery of the state capitol (in one 1980s recollection he also placed George Elmore there)[2] as they took in the fiery words of Governor Johnston. "I was looking down his throat," McCray said of the governor, "and the man said, and I quote him almost verbatim: 'When we will have repealed all these laws etc. we will have done everything possible to keep our primaries white. However, should this fail we have other recourse.'" McKaine, a Sumter native and World War I veteran who had spent two decades in Europe as a successful nightclub owner, was barely able to contain his disgust at the veiled threats and legislative mischief, McCray recalled. In those moments, McCray and McKaine began to formulate plans for a separate political party.[3]

McKaine had returned to his native South Carolina when the German Nazis invaded Belgium and quickly immersed himself in civil rights work. It was McKaine who prepared the ground for the NAACP's successful salary-equity lawsuit won by Viola Duvall of Charleston on behalf of Black teachers in February 1944, just two months before the special session. South Carolina had historically paid white teachers far more than their Black counterparts, galling Black teachers and NAACP activists like Septima Clark of Charleston, who had railed against the disparity since the beginning of her teaching career on Johns Island, South Carolina, in 1916. The NAACP's Marshall argued the case before Judge Waring and found, to his surprise, that Waring was not only sympathetic to his argument but also eager to school the state's lawyers on the legal precedent set by a similar case in Virginia.[4] After the Duvall decision case, Clark, who was teaching in Columbia at Booker T. Washington High School, lobbied for a similar outcome for Columbia teachers. Against that backdrop of growing agitation, Union County Representative Long persuaded the South Carolina House of Representatives in February to pass a resolution that affirmed "our belief in and our allegiance to established white supremacy as now prevailing in the South, and we solemnly pledge our lives and our sacred honor to maintaining it, whatever the cost, in war and in peace." The resolution then went on to "firmly and unequivocally demand that henceforth the damned agitators of the North leave the South alone."[5] Hinton and the Reverend E. A. Adams of Columbia replied to Long's affront with a two-page letter that reminded the white lawmaker that the mixing of the races he so abhorred was instigated by white men who "took advantage of Negro women for immoral purposes. Had these women been left alone all Negroes (for the most part) would have been black."

They also assailed Long's concept of white supremacy as the way forward in a postwar South Carolina. "Negroes do not know what is meant by white supremacy, since no one questions the right of any person, White or Black, from developing and advancing, unless, the question of rights enter the picture." The pair said Black South Carolinians were simply asking for the right to cast ballots in primaries, "and the denial of such constitutional rights is UNAMERICAN and UNDEMOCRATIC."[6]

Samuel J. McDonald Jr., a prominent Sumter NAACP activist and state vice president of the Negro Citizens' Committee, was also appalled by Long's rhetoric. In a March 2, 1944, letter to Adams and Hinton, who were also leaders of the Negro Citizens' Committee, McDonald said he believed the resolution was "calculated to block the road toward the end of which the best men and women of both races have been working studiously, prayerfully and hopefully for the past few years," he wrote. "It holds up in shame the gaze of Christian America and to other parts of an astonished civilized world the unbrotherly attitude of a strong, privileged racial group toward a weak, minority underprivileged group of another race, struggling and pleading for a chance to live like other American citizens and to share the democratic way of life."[7]

McCray had already envisioned a separate political party overlaid on the fledgling "Fourth Term for Roosevelt" clubs proposed by McDonald to assist in the reelection of the President. He immediately began arguing for a new political party in the Lighthouse and Informer. That idea gained traction when a Columbia Record newspaper editor publicized the effort. Within a month of the special session, McCray and McKaine had developed the framework that would bear the title, initially, of the Colored Democratic Party. It would be unapologetic in its support of President and Mrs. Roosevelt and defiant toward the white southerners who had become suspicious of the president's liberal leanings on race. McCray would later recount how an "old white woman" had come into the offices of the Lighthouse and Informer with the first donation, her old age pension of $4.50 plus an additional fifty cents. The woman, identified as Margaret Howe, urged him to cast his net wider so that sympathetic white people could also support the party. By the May 24, 1944, convention, the new organization would be known as the Progressive Democratic Party to emphasize its interracial roots. The white press would still refer to it as the Progressive (Negro) Democratic Party.[8]

It may have been Margaret Howe writing under her theatrical name of Margaret Vale, (she had appeared in one New York Broadway play), who penned an opinion piece for the April 2, 1944, special edition of the Lighthouse and Informer. In the draft, Margaret Vale identifies herself as a daughter of a Confederate soldier who had organized the first Ku Klux Klan. She explained the Klan "was organized to restore decent law and order from the horrors of Reconstruction and the depredations of those vultures known as 'carpet-baggers.'" In her piece, titled "Education, Justice, Removal of Fear of Negro Held Solvents of the Race Question,"

Vale hailed the progress of Black South Carolinians and said: "There are things we whites, the race in power, must admit, get together and rectify," including standing up for equal pay, the right to vote and justice in the courts for Black citizens. She said there still existed "a bugaboo of fear and understandable psychic fixation—a sort of 'hang over' of dread" from Reconstruction that Black people would demand what she called "social intermingling." White people must conquer this fear, she wrote. "If the whites in power remain blind to justice, duty, generosity and kindness in giving to the Negroes their equitable rights as tax-paying citizens, then, in my opinion, the Negroes have only one immediate recourse." That option, she noted, was "to take to the courts."[9]

The convention of the newly minted Progressive Democratic Party opened on May 24, 1944, at the Masonic Temple on Washington Street at 12:15 PM with 172 delegates from thirty-nine of the state's forty-six counties. George Elmore was a representative of Richland County and appointed assistant sergeant at arms. At the convention, McKaine delivered the keynote address and proved to be the fire-and-brimstone kind of man who was needed to launch the movement, McCray would later recount in a 1983 oral history. McKaine called May 24 "a history making day" when "Negroes of this state, who have been steadily losing all of their rights of citizenship, have met together to re-assert their rights to unqualified and full citizenship."

In his prepared remarks, McKaine offered up a history lesson on the post-Civil War years of Reconstruction, reminding the delegates that Black men held positions in government and aligned with white lawmakers to achieve progress. In the cadence of a dream sequence, and in contradiction to the Reconstruction memories of white South Carolinians such as Margaret Vale, he painted a sequence of events that he said was a reality, not a fairy tale. "Did I tell you that once upon a time there were eight Negroes from South Carolina in the Congress of the United States? And did I tell you that once upon a time there were 76 Negroes in the legislature here in Columbia?" He called on white people, particularly poor, uneducated white citizens, to join the cause, noting that they too have struggled under the yoke of cynical and ruthless political bosses. He assured the delegates, "We are going to retrieve our lost self-respect and once more we will be respected by our white fellow citizens." The audience "roared with applause."

John McCray, founding editor of the *Lighthouse and Informer,* spearheaded the movement to create the Progressive Democratic Party as a means of defying the all-white political system. He challenged Black people to resist accommodating to segregation and inequality. From the John Henry McCray Papers. Courtesy of South Caroliniana Library, University of South Carolina.

McKaine also hailed McCray as the "fighting editor" who was unafraid of challenging the white power structure. He was, said McKaine, "the dream of many a suffering Negro come true." To demonstrate that the PDP was aligned with the aims of the NAACP, the convention was capped by the appearance of Hinton, the NAACP chief. Hinton had previously aligned with Republicans but was now firmly in the PDP camp. The convention delegates determined that they would challenge the seating of the state's white delegates to the 1944 Democratic National Convention, one of the first bold moves to plant a flag for Black political influence in state and national politics. Eighteen delegates and two alternates were selected, with McCray and McKaine serving as co-chairmen.[10]

On the final day of the Columbia PDP convention, McCray received a telephone call from Robert E. Hannegan, the chairman of the Democratic National Committee. Hannegan asked to meet with PDP leaders hoping to persuade them not to come to the national convention in Chicago. He met in Washington with McCray, A.J. Clement Jr. of Charleston, and the Reverend Roscoe Wilson, a Florence, SC, pastor who would later rise to prominence in Columbia. Despite efforts by the national credentials committee to dissuade them, McCray and his delegation arrived in Chicago determined to have their say. Two women were among the delegation, including Lottie P. Gaffney, a Cherokee County woman who had lost her job as teacher and principal at the Petty Town School in May 1942 after attempting to register at least four times at the Cherokee County Courthouse. A news account in the *Lighthouse and Informer* suggested Gaffney was the victim of two overzealous white trustees who attempted to portray her as incompetent to justify the dismissal. A third trustee had advised against her firing based upon "being a Christian and a believer in justice," and was not asked to sign the letter. McCray had written of Gaffney's plight in a June 28, 1942, column, saying "For Negroes, the cost of democracy is often extreme."[11]

The group arrived on the same train as the white South Carolina delegation led by Senator Maybank, but lost its bid to be seated at the Convention. A few wanted to stage a noisy walkout to publicize their effort, but McCray insisted they remain loyal to the overarching goal of electing Roosevelt to a fourth term. Delegates, buoyed by national publicity in the Black press, returned home determined to boost membership in the PDP and work with the NAACP on lawsuits. In fall of 1944, the PDP nominated McKaine to run for US Senate against Johnston, the governor who had led the April special session and declared his allegiance to white supremacy. Members of the Progressive Democrats reporting from wards around Columbia found election irregularities: officials only handing out the straight Democratic ticket and professing ignorance of where the Republican or Progressive Democrat ballots were located. George Elmore accompanied Aaron Jenkins and his wife, Francena, to Ward 5 where a police officer, "who for some unknown reason had possession of the registration book," inspected their registration certificates. As Elmore and the couple proceeded to a table where various ballots were displayed, "ahead of them in line was a white man who while in the act of collecting ballots for the purpose of making a choice, was told by a man in charge of the ballots in effect, 'You don't want that ballot. It's the ballot of the Negro Democrats.'"[12] At Ward 2, McCray accompanied William Jordan, who was handed the regular Democratic ballot. When he protested, Jordan was told to go to an officer present who told Jordan to "scratch out the name of everybody you don't want to vote for," effectively invalidating his ballot. Jordan noted "only Negro voters, in the polling place at the time, and Negro voters casting the ballot for the Progressive Democratic Party, were directed to said officer."[13] Simkins reported multiple problems at polling places, including instances of obscuring ballots for the Progressive Democratic Party. "In none of these places was there any pretense on the part of managers to work for honest balloting," she reported in her affidavit. "There were many deliberate attempts to make sure that voters, particularly white ones cast the regular democratic ticket. No person in South Carolina who wants to vote anything except the straight OLD LINE South Carolina Democratic ticket can do so with privacy and without probable resulting intimidation and ostracism."[14]

McKaine's campaign served as the needed statewide rallying point for both the party and the NAACP. But on election day, less than three thousand votes were officially recorded for McKaine against Johnston. PDP officials were outraged and claimed voter fraud. But the election underscored to McCray and to Hinton the absolute necessity of mobilizing and organizing a movement to obtain the vote if any progress were to be achieved in South Carolina. As the Progressive Democratic Party tallied up the ingenious devices to prevent Black South Carolinians from registering—keeping registrants waiting in line in Chesterfield County, requiring them to read, write, and interpret the US Constitution in Williamsburg County, announcing open hours and then shuttering the office in Berkeley County—the NAACP began its quest to find a suitable plaintiff to end the white primary in South Carolina. But finding such a person proved to be difficult. Even before the resolution of the Texas white primary case, the Democratic Party had made it routine to purge the names of Black men enrolled in 1942 and 1944. The NAACP and the Progressive Democrats needed to find someone who could obtain a voting certificate in order to attempt to vote in the white primary of 1946.

Marshall, in a June 1944 letter to Florence activist Camille C. Levy, had emphasized the importance of laying that groundwork and recording every person turned away at the polls. "You should make an effort to have all qualified Negroes present themselves at the place of enrollment. Have each person who is refused the right to enroll to make a sworn affidavit giving the name of the person who refused to permit him to enroll and all other particulars."[15] The NAACP planned to forward those to the Justice Department, he said, making it clear that the battle lines were drawn.

CHAPTER 8

"Recognize the Negro Citizen . . . and Give Him the Right to Vote"

Elmore doesn't say he believes in the principles of the Democratic Party. He simply comes before the court and asked that he be infiltrated into the Democratic primary.

—Christie Benet, attorney representing the Richland County Democratic Party, June 1947

When the call went out in May 1945 for a hundred men willing to take the stage in a charity burlesque show, the gregarious George Elmore signed up.[1] The show, *Puffin' Hot,* was going to be "plenty hot," according to organizers, who aimed to raise $100,000 for Columbia's Good Samaritan-Waverly Hospital. The "fast-moving burlesque" was among dozens of events set for that May, including a "Tom Thumb Wedding Array," a "Leading Lady of Fashion" show, and a Mother's Day program that promised to be a joyous occasion, "not a sob sister" affair. In press releases, likely distributed by hospital campaign director Modjeska Simkins, *Puffin' Hot* would feature well-known men in the Waverly community. They included the Black superintendent of schools C. A. Johnson as "The Old Woman in the Show" and businessman A. W. Simkins, Modjeska Simkins's husband, as Mae West, both members of the hospital's board of trustees. Luther Lilliewood and I. P. Stanback were to be featured in a dancing striptease act. Elmore was to perform as Kate Smith, the popular white contralto who sang "God Bless America" on the radio during World War II. Newspaperman McCray was set to portray an "ace reporter and tattler" in a skit called "The Hag Walks." The director was Annie Belle Weston, a professor at Benedict College, who had previously staged a successful show called *The Extravaganza.* She was also active in the Progressive Democratic Party and was a frequent speaker at PDP mass meetings.[2] Organizers sought women to be sponsors for the men as they competed to be "Mr. Hospital Pin-up for 1945."

The show, which was set for May 17 at Booker T. Washington auditorium, attracted the endorsement of the Metropolitan Club and other civic organizations. *"Puffin' Hot* will be 'plenty hot,'" an undated press release proclaimed, "so as they say 'let's get in the groove' and be ready to witness this outstanding production."[3]

The show was postponed once, perhaps because of the need for such a large cast, and there are no newspaper accounts that explain if and when the show took place. But Elmore's prominent role in the planned burlesque suggested both his sense of wry humor as well as his growing role in Black Columbia civic affairs. This was a heady time with the Allied victory over Nazi Germany declared on May 8, 1945, known as VE Day, or Victory over Europe Day. Battles still raged in the Pacific, and it would be several months before Columbians learned that atomic bombs had been dropped on the Japanese cities of Hiroshima and Nagasaki, signaling the end of the war in the Pacific. But the prospect of families reuniting with their soldier sons likely created an air of anticipation and hope in both the white and Black communities. The hospital drive, which aimed to raise the last $35,000 needed for the Black hospital, was embraced by adults and their children. Youngsters clamored to participate in the Tom Thumb wedding review. The little bride and bridegroom who raised the most money would be "married" in a ceremony at Bethlehem Baptist Church. There would be no tears among the small fry, according to organizers: "It is understood that the personal feelings of the little folk will not matter in the least."[4]

Each of Columbia's Black school districts led a fundraising effort, and Simkins made a personal appeal to the students at Booker T. Washington High School to encourage at least a dollar contribution from every home. Those contributing would receive a sticker that could be displayed on home, car, and store windows. Those contributing five dollars would have their names placed in the permanent files of the hospital and those contributing twenty-five dollars would have their names inscribed on hall tablets for display in the new building. The hospital "is an investment in community cooperation," she told the students "not only for health protection but also in the development of a type of dignity and morale that comes only through the accomplishment of major humanitarian tasks."[5]

Black Columbians, fighting on multiple fronts for the vote, better schools, and improved public services, had long complained about the lack of comprehensive medical care at segregated facilities. The city and state had routinely failed to support Black hospitals, with early hospitals relying on businesses and northern philanthropists to keep the small facilities operating. Good Samaritan Hospital was opened in 1910 at 1508 Gregg Street by Dr. William Rhodes and his wife, Lillian Rhodes. Benedict Hospital opened a small facility on its campus that was later merged with Waverly Hospital, founded by Dr. Norman A. Jenkins and his four brothers, according to historical accounts. It was located in the Lysander D. Childs house on the corner of Hampton and Pine Streets. In the 1930s, the Duke Endowment offered to partially fund a new hospital if Good Samaritan Hospital and Waverly Hospital would merge. That merger was stalled, and the money went to the white Columbia General Hospital to build a new segregated wing, a decision that generated controversy in the Black community. In 1938, the merger of the two Black hospitals finally took place, but by that time the Duke Endowment had rescinded its earlier offer. It became the community's responsibility to raise the first $100,000 for the proposed new hospital construction. (The Duke Foundation later agreed to donate $100,000, and another $130,00 in federal funding was granted under the Hill-Burton Act in 1950.) It would be another two years before the hospital opened in 1952.[6]

Elmore's willingness to perform in the hospital burlesque fundraiser suggested he was eager to support a good cause and provide some comic relief for his neighbors. Perhaps it was a combination of appearance, timing, and his trademark affability that also helped him, in spring 1946, obtain the voting certificate that NAACP officials knew was needed as a step toward filing a federal voting lawsuit. McCray expanded on Elmore's quest for registration in a December 6, 1980, column for the *Charleston Chronicle* called "The Way it Was." According to that account, Hinton, the NAACP president, had announced that Black people in Columbia would attempt enrollment in selected wards. "Guinea pigs" had been handpicked. "Enrollment day, round after round was made to the places where registration books were to be available. And, time and again, not a single Black was enrolled," McCray recalled. Whites would enter the establishments and register, but as soon as a Black man entered, the book would be spirited out of sight and under the counter.

"It was near closing time, and the last stop was at the small store on Millwood Avenue, in Ward Nine, manned by a middle-aged white woman. The little store had two display windows, and two rooms. One room was used; the other showed just a counter. The women had told these four persons, all of Ward Nine and handpicked, the registration books weren't there: Rev. Hinton, Dr. R. W. Mance, Rev. E. A. Davis and Rev. F. M. Young." All of the men were active in civil rights. It was Mance who had made an impassioned plea before the Columbia election commission in 1942 to open the primary.

The four men were resigned to try another day, McCray said. "We stood across the street, knowing there was still no guinea pig and prospects were not likely to be for another two years." But then George Elmore drove up. "Almost instinctively, everybody turned his back to George. Elmore was a 'pest' and 'bugged' you – always talking and butting in," McCray recalled. He was secretary of the PDP but had not been among the men the party selected to make the registration attempt. McCray thought Elmore was "just beng nosey." Hinton told him their efforts had been futile that day. Elmore was quiet for a moment and then offered to try, McCray recalled. Soon, the men could see him inside, drinking a Coca-Cola and filling out the registration book. Eventually, he came out and stood on the steps of the store and announced, "She says you other niggers might as well come on in and enroll too." As Elmore later recounted the story, the registrar, believing the light-skinned Elmore was a white man, fussed about the "damn smart alecky niggers" outside. She counseled him that more white people should try to register. He answered politely with a series of "Yes, ma'ams." Only when he revealed his address as the segregated Tree Street did she realize her mistake. On that day, Elmore's loquacious nature, which so irritated McCray and the others, worked in his favor as he disarmed the registrar with his conversation.[7] With certificate in hand, he went to the polls on August 13, 1946, to cast his vote in the primary and was turned away because he was not a white Democrat. The threat of intimidation kept others away as well. Benjamin James Pittman, a sharecropper in Dillon County, said three white female registrars had been kind to Negroes and helped them register. But on primary day, there was a concerted effort, on radio and in the local newspaper, to keep Black people from the polls. "We were busy working tobacco and did not go to the polls," on August 13, he wrote to Robert L. Carter, the NAACP's assistant special counsel. "There was such bitter opposition to colored people voting in South Carolina."[8]

Elmore's action was just what the national NAACP needed to proceed with a legal challenge. Marshall and his New York legal staff had studied the matter continuously since the 1944 action by the South Carolina legislature and had in hand a study undertaken by Columbia University students, he told McCray in a letter dated January 22, 1947. "To make a long story short, we are now ready for legal action in South Carolina and will begin this action in the near future—as a matter of fact just as soon as we can." It would be, Marshall said, "a terrifically tough job," but he said, "I am convinced we are on the right track now." He praised McCray for urging national Democrats not to seat all-white delegations at future conventions.[9]

The next day, Franklin Williams, another of the NAACP's assistant special counsel, wrote to lawyer Boulware seeking names of plaintiffs willing to challenge the primary. "All the affidavits that we have in our office which you sent us are from individuals who were denied the right to register."[10] Williams needed a person who had succeeded in registering but was turned away on the day of the primary. There was growing urgency. On January 30, 1947, Marshall telegrammed Boulware: "Primary suit waiting receipt of affidavits requested from individuals denied right to vote. Please forward immediately."[11] On January 31, 1947, Boulware replied by letter to Williams and enclosed copies of the affidavits, apologizing for the delay. "I don't know if you will use more than one as plaintiff in this case ... The one who is most willing to be used is George Elmore. I would suggest that he be used."[12] Boulware added that NAACP president Hinton "does not mind being made a party." Elmore was not the first choice of some of the state's NAACP leaders, Hinton would later say, but "Elmore" would be the name on the legal documents.

Marshall called on Boulware to search out information on voting in the primary and general elections as well as newspaper and official accounts of the 1944 special session, including the address Governor Olin Johnston made to the all-white legislature. On February 15, Marshall traveled to Washington to meet with a small group of brilliant lawyers and thinkers, including his former Howard University dean and mentor Charles Hamilton Houston, Franklin D. Reeves, William R. Ming, Ruth Weyand, and George Johnson. They spent the afternoon in the Howard University law school going over the details of their legal strategy to destroy the "South Carolina plan" for fear it would spread to other southern states.[13]

Coincidently, on that same evening in Greenville, South Carolina, a white taxi driver, Thomas Watson Brown, was robbed and stabbed to death in Pickens County. A day later, a twenty-four-year-old Black man, Willie Earle, who had been a passenger in Brown's cab, was arrested. He was placed in the Pickens County jail. Two days after the Brown slaying, on February 16, a convoy of taxi drivers drove to the jail and forced the jailer to release Earle. Earle was then driven away, brutally beaten, stabbed, and shot to death. The lynching shocked South Carolina. Governor Thurmond condemned the extra-judicial killing and deployed law enforcement to work alongside the FBI to round up the members of the mob. McCray, accompanied by Elmore, went to Greensville to report on the slaying. Elmore's gruesome photograph of Earle's battered body, patched up by morticians, was on the front page of the *Lighthouse and Informer*.[14] Within days, thirty-one men were arrested and charged in the case, many signing confessions. Against that grim backdrop, Marshall and his team carried on building the case for the white primary challenge. On February 21, 1947, a week after the Washington meeting at Howard University, the NAACP filed a lawsuit in US District Court in Columbia with Elmore as the chief plaintiff. The same edition of the *Lighthouse and Informer* carried news of the primary challenge and a photograph of Elmore.

Marshall and his co-counsel Robert Carter arrived in Columbia early on the morning of May 28, 1947, prepared to take depositions from the defendants in the Elmore trial that day and the following. The Greenville lynching trial had ended a week earlier with a familiar southern outcome: acquittal for all. But there had been plenty of uncomfortable international attention directed at South Carolina, including magazine stories in *Life* and *Time*. The *New Yorker* had sent Rebecca West, fresh from the Nuremberg trials of German Nazi leaders, to dissect southern customs and manners in a searing story called "Opera in Greenville."[15]

As Marshall prepared to take depositions from the defendants in the Elmore trial that day and the following, he had another important case to argue before Judge Waring as well: John H. Wrighten's lawsuit to enter the University of South Carolina law school. Wrighten, a twenty-six-year-old Edisto Island man, was a graduate of the Colored Normal, Industrial, Agricultural and Mechanical College of South Carolina at Orangeburg, commonly known as South Carolina State College (later South Carolina State University). Marshall planned to take depositions from the South Carolina State president on Saturday, May 31, and the USC president and law school dean on Monday, June 2.[16]

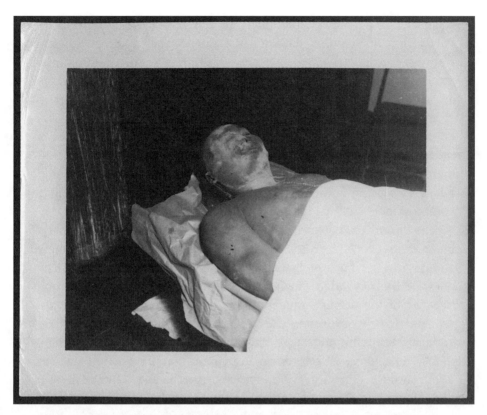

As a freelance photographer for the *Lighthouse and Informer,* George Elmore accompanied John McCray to Greenville, where he photographed the brutalized body of Willie Earle. Earle's February 16, 1947, slaying at the hands of a mob is considered the last lynching in South Carolina. From the John Henry McCray Papers. Courtesy of South Caroliniana Library, University of South Carolina.

There was no question the April 1944 US Supreme Court victory in *Smith v. Allwright* provided Marshall with the legal upper hand in the Columbia courtroom. But the rigid adherence to history and custom in the Palmetto State suggested it would still be a hard slough. Marshall had Boulware, a tall, handsome man with upright bearing, by his side, as well as Carter, his fiery deputy at the NAACP Legal Defense and Education Fund. Christie Benet, a well-regarded Columbia attorney who had served briefly in the US Senate three decades earlier upon the death of Senator Tillman, led attorneys for the Richland County defendants. He was assisted by a respected team that included, among others, state Senator William P. Baskin, a leader in the Democratic Party from Bishopville; state Senator Yancey MacLeod of Columbia; state Senator Edgar Brown of Barnwell; Charles B. Elliott, a Columbia attorney and USC law professor; and Irvine F. Belser, a Yale graduate and Rhodes Scholar who had earned his law degree from the University of South Carolina. Marshall learned to know Benet well, even considered him a friend, according to a recollection of McCray. Marshall commented later that Benet sincerely believed in the separation of the races and the rightness of the Democratic Party's position, although Marshall felt sorry for him for holding that view. "The man is not a racist," Marshall commented. "He is completely sincere and honest."[17]

The Elmore trial opened on June 3 in the US District Court in Columbia with an overflow crowd of predominantly Black spectators, many standing in the back of the courtroom because all seats were occupied. US District Judge Waring was a familiar jurist in the courtroom because of the teacher equalization case. In the opening session, a reporter for the afternoon *Columbia Record* noted that NAACP chief counsel Marshall had "flayed the General Assembly" for its decision in 1944 to remove all references to primaries in its election statutes. The front-page story was prominent but overshadowed by the news of a manhunt for an "armed Negro man" that drew a posse of at least five hundred white men scouring the Edgewood neighborhood of Columbia. Down page was news from Georgia of the beating of a Black man who had testified before a federal grand jury about the July 1946 lynching of four farm workers in Monroe. If Marshall took note of the headlines on his lunch break, the news did not alter his focus.[18]

Marshall insisted that the special session in April 1944, called by Governor Olin D. Johnston, was designed to evade a US Supreme Court decision in Texas that determined primaries were part of each state's election apparatus. "There is no difference between the Legislature which repealed those laws and the Democratic Party. All the members of that body—and the governor—were Democrats," he argued. "They repealed the laws, went somewhere else and promulgated party rules. Even if it's the most private party in the world, if it's exercising the authority of holding an election, it is violating article one, section two and four, of the constitution."

He suggested the legislature's action was akin to repealing a state's policing laws "and letting the Elks enforce the laws."[19] Marshall told the courtroom that the case was not limited to one state or one party. "It applies anywhere in the United States," Marshall was quoted in Columbia newspapers. "This is another step in a long line of cases dating back to the 1880s of Negroes fighting for the right to vote." He contended that the South Carolina Democratic Party was no different than the parties in Louisiana, Texas, Oklahoma, and Maryland, where Black people were now voting. "Recognize the Negro citizen as any other citizen and give him the right to vote."

The following day, June 4, Waring called Senator Baskin, the chairman of the state Democratic executive committee, to the stand to elaborate on the changes in party structure, telling him he wanted facts, not arguments. Baskin testified that the Democratic Party of 1946 was far different than the party of 1942, although he could only name a few alterations. The party organized itself into a new party with a few different rules, he said, including one that made violation of party rules "punishable by expulsion rather than by fine or imprisonment under old party statutes." A new rule also lowered the voting age in the primary to eighteen. Benet also argued that Black voters could create their own party that would run parallel with the white Democrats. "Nobody is forced to join the Democratic Party," Benet said. "The members are those who believe in the same tenets—one of those being that they want to meet with other white Democrats." Benet argued that Black voters, operating within the context of an independent party, could even succeed by "out-voting the Democrats." He said he believed that most Black citizens sought "parallel organizations—not infiltration." Attorney Irvine Belser reminded the court, too, that the general election was open to all. He argued that Black voters "had slept on their hands" by not voting in the general election.

Marshall conceded that a separate party could be established but that would take organization and cash, which Black citizens shut out of the electoral process for decades did not have. But he returned the court to the central issue. "The state made the primary an integral part of the election machinery," he said. "The state built it up through the years, then in 1944 when they repealed the laws, they claim they have a brand-new animal. Well, they haven't. It's the same thing. When the Democratic party furnishes ballots for the general election, that's state action." Marshall drove home the circular logic of his courtroom adversaries. "The rules say that Elmore must be a white Democrat before he can vote in the primary. Elmore is not a white Democrat. He is a Negro. How can he ever become a Democrat? That's the crux of the whole case. I don't see a bit of difference in him standing up at the polls in the general election and in the primary. Grant Elmore the right to cast his ballot in the only place it will count!"[20]

Judge Waring issued his order on July 12, dismissing as "pure sophistry" the argument that the "new" Democratic party, by virtue of removing all references to primaries and elections, could operate privately and independently from federal election law:

> When the General Assembly, answering the call of Governor Johnston, met in extraordinary session, it was wholly and solely for the purpose of preventing the Negro from gaining a right to vote in the primaries as granted under the doctrine of the *Smith v. Allwright* case. There was no concealment as to the reason for this call. And although the General Assembly had repealed all of the laws on the subject, the State Democratic Party, composed of the same persons who voted in the primaries two years before, had its meetings in its same clubs in the same precincts, had the same kind of County Conventions and delegates, had the same kind of State Conventions and delegates, and adopted rules that were almost verbatim to the statutes that had been repealed.[21]

Judge Waring noted that since the 1944 Smith case, Black citizens were now voting in Louisiana, Texas, and Georgia. "I cannot see where the skies will fall if South Carolina is put in the same class with these and other states." Then the federal judge capped his order with these words: "It is time for South Carolina to rejoin the Union. It is time to fall in step with the other states and to adopt the American way of conducting elections."[22]

Four days later, on July 16, 1947, 150 "singing, jubilant delegates" of the Progressive Democratic Party met in special session to formally join the state Democratic Party, the Associated Press reported. McCray presided over the celebratory meeting and encouraged the adoption of a six-point plan to push for expansion of voter registration and fundraising to carry out the work to enroll thousands who had never cast ballots in their lives. McCray declared Waring's decision as "final, ending white primaries everywhere, the most eventful act in our history since Lincoln signed the Emancipation proclamation."

McCray singled out Elmore for "particular gratitude" as well as the "brilliant, daring, thorough and splendid lawyers," Marshall and Boulware. Elmore, described by the Associated Press writer as "corpulent" and "light-skinned," carried in the South Carolina and US flags that framed the speakers' table. The man who had been willing to participate with other community leaders in a hospital charity burlesque was now hailed as a hero who had succeeded on a more significant stage. He was cheered as he offered this modest assessment: "In the words of our other champion, Joe Louis, all I can say is, 'I'm glad I win.'"[23] The year 1947 was likely the high point of Elmore's civic and business life. In coming years, and amid looming troubles, it would be a time he could look back upon and savor.

CHAPTER 9

Suffering Hardships for the Freedom of His Race

Are we to rear a generation of white tricksters and
set an example of dishonesty to eight hundred thousand colored people and expect our state to prosper
in the way of right thinking and right living?
—R. Beverley Herbert, June 1948

Amid the excitement of that July 1947 day, NAACP president James
Hinton warned Progressive Democrats to prepare for seismic political upheaval, even as a handful of white moderates also acknowledged it was time for changing the status quo.[1] White politicians,
after exhausting every legal avenue of dodging the inevitable, would
eventually have to solicit the votes of Black voters. "We must make
a choice between those who have fought us and those who are our
friends," he said, noting that he "had no love in my heart" for US
Senator Burnet Maybank, a staunch white supremacist who had
condemned Waring's decision. McCray also cautioned that Judge
Waring's decision was not the end of the matter. "Yet to be seen and
hurdled are a number of assorted schemes and devices we expect
to be employed by the vanquished upholders of White Supremacy,"
McCray said. He listed difficult literacy tests, a poll tax, the possible
dissolution of the primary, and outright hostility from white county
and city registrars.[2] Hinton sent a telegram to the Democratic executive committee urging "conformity with the decision." In the telegram, Hinton said that the newly enfranchised citizens "pledge full
cooperation, full responsibility and full participation for better government in our state." He also addressed an open letter to Baskin asking that the party "dispense with all racial and color lines" and that
"all feelings and bitterness be forgotten." On July 17, as the state Democratic executive committee met to assess the Waring decision, chairman Baskin responded to a reporter's question about the telegram

with three terse words: "It was read." Shortly after, the committee voted unanimously to appeal.[3]

The state's newspaper editors responded in expected ways. In Charleston, William Watts Ball was apoplectic. "There is nothing left for South Carolinians but to abandon completely the name of the Democratic Party, divorcing themselves from the national party affiliation and reestablishing an exclusive white man's political club under a new title." He also suggested the state abolish the Carolina law school rather than set up a separate school for Black law students. For white South Carolinians, he said, the decisions "mean changes in their ways but not in their determination to maintain separation of white and colored peoples."[4] An editorial in the more moderate *Columbia Record* suggested there was a disconnect between the alarmed white Democrat politicians and the citizens of the state. "Most intelligent South Carolinians have realized for a long time that the day would come when South Carolina would be forced by logic and fair play, if not by the courts, to permit Negroes to participate on a parity with whites in all elections, primaries included," the lead editorial noted. The editorial writer went on to opine that politicians have "a vested interest in preserving the status quo" for fear of dealing with an unknown number of new voters. The editorialist also noted, correctly, that some would also have to rewrite their campaign speeches "to eliminate the appeals to racial prejudice."[5]

Hinton was less sanguine about the alleged new progressiveness of his fellow white citizens, having received his share of threatening mail. Two months earlier, on May 26, 1947, he had received a letter addressed to "My Dear Nigger Leader" from "Local Whites." The letter referenced the February 1946 lynching of Willie Earle in Greenville and suggested extra-judicial justice could be meted out to Hinton if he continued to stir race issues. "I suggest that you give your tounge [tongue] a vacation for if you keep Bellyaching about the way your race is treated you might be using the pick and shovel too."[6] Hinton took such threats seriously. In an incident five years earlier, members of the Ku Klux Klan had gathered at his Heidt Street home to intimidate him. His neighbors armed themselves and guarded the Hinton home from their rooftops. Columbia police declined to intervene. The threats did not abate, and in 1949 Hinton narrowly escaped death when he was kidnapped and beaten by white assailants in Augusta, Georgia.[7]

McCray at the *Lighthouse and Informer* had also fielded anonymous missives as one of the most outspoken and fearless Black figures in the state. Prominent among them was a postcard received in March 1946 and signed by "A Southern Lady." The anonymous writer wondered if McCray and his ilk were trying to start a race war. "The Ku Klux Klan saved our south from just such as you and the Yankees of your mental ability and they will do it again," she wrote from Savannah. "White men settled this country, not negroes, so remember your place."[8]

McCray had seen that southern vitriol play out in cruel, inhumane ways time and time again. He had reported on the blinding of newly returned World War II soldier Isaac Woodard in 1946. McCray had seen with his own eyes the brutalized body of Willie Earle, who was taken from the Pickens County jail in February 1947 and lynched for allegedly stabbing to death a Greenville taxi driver. There were hundreds of other criminal acts perpetuated against Black Americans simply because of their race.

The appeal to the Elmore decision was heard on November 14, 1947, in Baltimore federal court. Hinton, McCray, and Elmore were in the delegation who traveled there to listen to the arguments. Just more than a month later, on December 30, 1947, US District Judge John Parker ruled against the white Democrats. In one of his most eloquent phrasings, Parker wrote, "The disfranchised can never speak with the same force as those who are able to vote."[9]

> The question presented for our decision is whether, by permitting a party to take over a part of its election machinery, a state can avoid the provisions of the Constitution forbidding racial discrimination in elections and can deny to a part of the electorate, because of race and color, any effective voice in the government of the state. It seems perfectly clear that this question must be answered in the negative.[10]

White Democrats were wrong, he said, in arguing that Elmore had no more right to vote in the Democratic primary than "to vote in the election of officers of the Forest Lake Country Club or for the officers of the Colonial Dames of America." He reiterated what the high court justices had ruled in the 1944 *Smith v. Allwright* decision: that primaries were now embedded in the election machinery of the United States. He also provided a history lesson to the defendants, reminding them that

A 1946 anonymous postcard signed by "A Southern Lady" suggested editor John McCray should watch his words and "remember your place." From the John Henry McCray Papers. Courtesy of South Caroliniana Library, University of South Carolina.

the Fourteenth and Fifteenth Amendments were written into the Constitution "to insure to the Negro, who had recently been liberated from slavery, the equal protection of the laws and the right to full participation in the process of government."[11]

Immediately after the appeals court decision, Governor Thurmond issued a "no comment." Baskin also demurred, citing the prospect of an appeal to the US Supreme Court.[12]

Even though the high court had made its position clear on primaries in the 1944 *Smith v. Allwright* decision in Texas, the state's Democratic power structure was not willing to throw in the towel. Members of the executive committee and the rank and file were already restive over President Truman's civil rights stance. Judge Waring had reminded them, in his decision, of the president's view that "we can no longer afford the luxury of a leisurely attack upon prejudice and discrimination" or "await the growth of a will to action in the slowest state or the most backward community." That reference likely galled South Carolinians sensitive to the portrayal in Hollywood and popular culture of an ignorant, hillbilly South. Still despite the sheer futility of the effort, white leaders once again appealed. This time it was not necessary for the attorneys to travel to Washington to argue before the nation's high court. On April 19, 1948, the US Supreme Court declined to review the lower court's decision, stirring that long-awaited celebration in the Elmore household and within the NAACP.

There would be one more attempt to keep Elmore away from the primary. Under the leadership of Baskin, the Bishopville senator and now chairman of the state Democratic party, Democrats devised a loyalty oath that they knew would be unpalatable to Black citizens and some moderate white people. The oath, adopted in May 1948, required voters to swear support for states' rights and opposition to fair housing and equal opportunity in employment. David Brown, of Beaufort, challenged the oath, in *Brown v. Baskin*, with Marshall and Boulware, who had represented Elmore, now serving as counsel to Brown. Brown testified to the court that, after paying his poll tax and registering, his name had been expunged from the election rolls. He was informed that to re-enroll he would have to abide by the new party oath.[13]

The protagonists met again in Waring's courtroom on July 16, 1948. The state's lawyers argued that Brown, who was a member of the Progressive Democratic Party, had no right to vote in the Democratic primary, since he belonged to a rival party. They apparently saw no irony in the argument that Brown and other Black people were excluded by white people from joining the main Democratic party. If that distorted logic struck Waring as odd, he did not belabor it. In the July 20, 1948, opinion issuing a temporary injunction against the oath, Waring reserved his ire for white officials who had deliberately chosen to abide by the order of the Elmore case, which applied only to Richland County, and ignore the opinion that applied to the whole state. Waring wrote:

> The convention frankly set up two standards of qualifications for voting: one applicable to the members of the white race, and the other to Negroes. This of course was in direct contradiction of all law and custom, which must or should have been well known to any students or even casual inquirers in regard to such matters. Such a flagrant disregard of basic rights must have sprung from either gross ignorance or a conscious determination to evade the issue and to refuse to obey the law of the land. It is hardly credible that a convention composed of a large number of persons, many of whom have had long years of experience and were experts in political matters and a number of whom had actually taken part in the presentation and hearings of the Elmore case as attorneys or witnesses, should have been so crassly ignorant.[14]

One of the state's lawyers, Sidney S. Tison, suggested that the judge word his newest order so that "he who runs can read." Judge Waring complied with a vengeance. "The Order will provide that the books be opened to all parties, irrespective of race, color, creed or condition. I'd better put all of those things in there, because, although we are only discussing race here, the next time they may exclude Jews or Roman Catholics or somebody else."[15] Baskin told county registrars to open the voting rolls to all. Three counties, Waring noted with satisfaction, had already defied Baskin and taken steps to open the registration books.

The courts had spoken, but white Democratic leaders once again appealed in hopes of somehow halting the inevitable. They met in US District Court in Charleston in April 1949 to argue that the segregation oath was a private political party matter. On May 17, 1949, Judge Parker, writing for the Fourth US Circuit Court of Appeals, closed the door on further efforts: "We see no reason to modify our holding in Rice v. Elmore.

US Senator Olin D. Johnston, who as governor called a special legislative session in 1944 to maintain white supremacy in elections, dines with his family February 20, 1948, as he boycotts President Truman's Jefferson-Jackson Day dinner. Johnston opposed Truman's civil rights platform. Credit: Harris & Ewing. Courtesy of Harry S. Truman Library & Museum.

On the contrary, we are convinced, after further consideration, that the decision in that case was entirely correct; and little need be added to our opinion there to dispose of every question that is here presented."[16] The clash over the segregation oath signaled the last gasp for South Carolina's white primary. But it was just an exhalation in the civil rights uproar that was percolating within the Democratic Party and throughout the South. Democratic party leaders had met in Columbia in early 1948 and endorsed a resolution "to deplore and condemn the so-called Civil Rights program" promoted by the Truman administration. The leaders also went on record in opposition to the election of President Truman. Olin Johnston, now a US senator, had refused to attend the annual Jefferson-Jackson Day dinner in Washington in February 1948 where Truman was the keynote speaker. The primary decision and the dismissal of the segregation oath confirmed for many white southerners that they must gird now for more assaults on segregation.

Judge Waring had warned his wife that a decision in the white primary case would upend their lives in Charleston. And quickly they saw the insular white Charleston community turn against them. Members of the South Carolina congressional delegation filed articles of impeachment. The rowdiest, law-breaking elements went further, burning a cross on their Meeting Street lawn and chucking a piece of concrete through the front window.[17] As Waring gained accolades outside of the South for the decision, an insulated and angry South Carolina turned inward as they glimpsed the prospect of racial equality—and the possibility of segregation's demise—on the horizon.

Congressman William Jennings Bryan Dorn, who represented South Carolina's Third Congressional District, was among the most vocal Waring critics, absolutely opposed to federal intervention in the South's segregated relations among Black and white residents. On February 9, 1948, Dr. Marion Young of Bishopville chided the first-term lawmaker, suggesting "you have forgotten some of the Christian principles that we used to study and discuss in the S.S. [Sunday School] and the B.T.U. [Baptist Training Union] at the old First Baptist Church in Greenwood." Describing himself as a "country doctor" who strived to treat all men equally, Young asked in his letter, "How can you men speak of 'southern democracy,' and at the same time work so vigorously and vehemently to deprive a large proportion of our population of their inalienable human rights as well as any political rights?"[18]

Dorn replied on March 5, 1948, saying that "strange as it may seem," he opposed civil rights "because I believe in Christianity, because I believe in democracy, and I believe in justice." If the bills pass, he said, "the poor, innocent colored people of the south" will become "tools in the hands of politicians being inflamed with passion and hatred, herded and hauled like sheep to the polls, not knowing for whom they vote or for what."[19] Dorn wrote a letter to Hinton at the NAACP explaining his position this way: "The least said about race consciousness and race prejudice, the better off our Nation will be."[20] While the attacks on Waring were alarming, attorney Boulware could not help indulging in a bit of wry humor over the rising tide of vitriol. In a July 30, 1948, letter to Thurgood Marshall, Boulware forwarded a copy of the *Baskin* decision, adding: "I know you have read what the boys here are trying to do to Judge Waring. Let the heathen rage!"[21]

Herbert, the white Columbia attorney who had continued to engage in some interracial outreach, delivered an impassioned commencement address to the University of South Carolina on June 2, 1948. To the young graduates, he said it was time to lift the yoke of seventy years of second-class citizenship off the backs of Black South Carolinians, who had attained education and served in two world wars and were now "as well informed as their white neighbors." Now, he said, "they have learned in such schools as we have provided for them the great principles and precepts which the founders of our country have laid down for our guidance and we cannot now say to them, 'These things are not for you because of the color of your skin.'" Herbert told the graduates he considered it folly to defy the courts and press for the white primary: "Are we to rear a generation of white tricksters and set an example of dishonesty to eight hundred thousand colored people and expect our state to prosper in the way of right thinking and right living?" The *Southern Christian Advocate*, the newspaper for South Carolina Methodists, published Herbert's address in its June 17, 1948, issue calling it "notable."[22]

Clement, the Charlestonian who was executive secretary of the Progressive Democratic Party, wrote a letter to William Watts Ball on June 1, 1948, chastising the *News and Courier* editor for suggesting that Black voters only want to "get into the Party of the white folks." No, Clement said, "We want to fully participate like any other citizen in 'the only material and realistic election machinery' in this state.'" The current segregated government "is NOT good enough for the Progressive Democrats. We desire no parts of it. It is putrid. Its odor stenches the clear clean air of South Carolina." He warned Ball that "you will soon come to know that the mass of our people are not emotional, not as purchasable as they might have been sixty years ago. We have learned lots in the passing years and we have learned the hard way."[23]

Amid this backdrop, Elmore voted on August 10, 1948, along with an estimated thirty thousand Black South Carolinians who had never cast a ballot in a statewide Democratic primary. The candidates on the ballot were garden variety white segregationist Democrats, led by US Senator Burnet Maybank, who had earlier denounced the Waring decision along with his four opponents. This was Elmore's second time casting a primary ballot—he and his wife, Laura, had voted in the smaller Columbia city primary on April 20, a day after the final review of the US Supreme Court. The high court's decision allowed for about seven hundred Black voters with registration certificates to vote in the Columbia city primary. On that April day, Elmore photographed John McCray, James Hinton, Pete Ingram, state supervisor for the Pilgrim Health and Life Insurance, and J. C. Artemus, state treasurer for the Progressive Democrats, after they had cast ballots. The photograph appeared on the front page of the April 25, 1948, edition of the *Lighthouse and Informer*. The story noted that McCray was among the first to vote after presenting his certificate at 8:03 AM.[24]

John McCray, editor of *The Lighthouse and Informer;* Pete Ingram, state supervisor for the Pilgrim Health and Life Insurance Company; J. C. Artemus, state treasurer for the Progressive Democrats; and James Hinton, state NAACP president, are pictured after casting ballots in the April 20, 1948, Columbia city primary. Photograph taken by George Elmore for *The Lighthouse and Informer.* From the John Henry McCray Papers. Courtesy of South Caroliniana Library, University of South Carolina.

At the statewide August primary, Elmore was a recognizable figure as he stood in the hot sun surveying the lines of eager voters in Ward 9, armed with his own camera to record the day. His photograph had been circulated among Black newspapers as writers detailed each step of his legal case. The *Pittsburgh Courier,* in its May 1, 1948, edition, had saluted Elmore as a "courageous American." McCray, in a July 1947 column for the *Lighthouse and Informer,* had poked fun at those who had sat on the sidelines but rushed to claim credit for the primary victory. "Poor Geo A. Elmore, the only layman in Columbia that had the 'guts' to stick out his neck, the poor NAACP lawyers, Messrs. Harold A. Boulware and Thurgood Marshall, had nothing to do with it, that is if you believe these 'Who Dunnits.'"[25] If he had to give credit, McCray said, it should go to James Hinton "for the master-stroke plan he projected last year," and to the NAACP, the Progressive Democrats, and the Citizens Committee that had raised $6,000 for the fight. "Why can't Negroes, when they have helped do a good job, just let the credit go to the entire race," he lamented. "Most of the men now saying 'I dunnit' were more scared than wild rabbits any time you mentioned 'let's settle this thing' to them." Across the state, leaders reported a "steady Negro vote" but no incidents or altercations. "Both whites and Negroes conducted themselves as everybody except the fear-and-trembling politicians expected," the *Columbia Record* noted the next day.[26] The *State's* editorial writers concurred. While results were not yet in, "the day passed without disorder at the polls just as this newspaper anticipated.[27]

The *Columbia Record* noted that Elmore "was busily snapping pictures of the people waiting in line in Ward 9."[28] But there had been alarming incidents before, during, and after the primary. On August 7, a group of Klansmen, likely from Georgia, "drove half across the State for the dual purpose of obtaining recruits in South Carolina among the less sober white people, and at the same time exhibiting threats against Negroes," the *Lighthouse and Informer* reported in its August 22, 1948 edition. Since July 12, there had been reports of crosses burned in Columbia and Aiken, including one on election day, although the sheriff there disputed that account in newspaper reports. Motorcades of robed figures were seen in Blackville, Ecko, and Williston. A voter in Saluda County received a letter from the Klan, signed in blood, warning him not to vote in the primary election. And in Calhoun Falls, the Reverend Archie Ware, a sixty-six-year-old pastor, was attacked by a band of white men, stabbed and beaten and left unconscious after he left his voting place on August 10. Ware, pastor of four churches in Abbeville and Anderson counties, gave his account to McCray, who ran a front-page story on the attack. According to Ware, he had attempted to register on July 19 and again on July 20. He and a hundred others were able to register until John Black, a candidate for coroner, threatened them. On August 10, after Ware had voted at Calhoun County High School, he was confronted by candidate Black, who was carrying a club. Ware said he moved backward toward two police officers who were guarding the polling place. "Knowing the two officers were right there, I kept backing to them. I had got almost to them when I realized they weren't going to help. So I made a quick turn to the right so I could run." According to the newspaper account, Black struck Ware several times, stunning him. One of the younger men stabbed him in the left thigh. He ran about 150 yards and then collapsed. "They caught up with me. I saw their knives and heard one of them say, 'I got a good mind to cut your throat.'" As it turned out, the overt and covert warnings to stay away from the polls accomplished their purpose—Ware was the only Black person who had dared to vote in the primary. Ware met with McCray and Elmore at the offices of the newspaper, telling them he planned to stay away from his native county for an unknown time. He lamented leaving "his poor people" behind. "They just don't know what to do, nor how it is done. We need help and information," he told the newspaper.[29]

McCray understood that lament. He wrote of the fears among white leaders of "bloc" voting by Negroes, a charge McCray dismissed as ludicrous. Yes, he said, a public meeting was held to distribute to newly minted voters the platforms of the various candidates, exactly what white Democratic leaders had done for years. "What these critics are saying in substance, is that these voters should have been able to figure out which of the candidates were better though no candidate had addressed them, or appeared before them," he wrote in the August 22, 1948, edition. "In other words, the Negroes, in a single day, should be able to forget they are Negroes and close both their eyes and ears to the social system under which they live and the utterances of intolerant candidates who lambast the race." That day may come in 1950 or the next ten years, he said, "but to demand it now is paying too much of a compliment to the race."[30] McCray blamed the mayhem on Governor Thurmond and his embrace of the segregationist States Rights party. In a split screen view of South Carolina politics, the Columbia newspapers reported the primary vote on the same day they featured stories and photos of Thurmond bound for Texas, where he was to accept the presidential nomination of the States Rights party.[31]

By the August statewide primary, Elmore had already begun to experience serious economic repercussions. Some white vendors began to refuse to provide goods on credit or supply him with the bread,

Voters crowd inside one of Columbia's polling places on August 10, 1948. From the John Henry McCray Papers. Courtesy of South Caroliniana Library, University of South Carolina.

crackers, and soft drinks that were part and parcel of his dime-store inventory, a practice known as the "squeeze." The shelves gradually emptied. The Coca-Cola machine, with its signature ice-cold water bath, was no longer serviced and eventually turned off. Donella Wilson lived on Columbia's Heidt Street around the corner from the five-and-dime and shopped there often. "After he got the vote, they (vendors) wouldn't sell him anything," she recalled in a 2003 interview. "He did all he could to make it. He just deteriorated. His wife deteriorated."[32] The only time Cresswell Elmore saw his father cry was the Christmas George Elmore confided to him that he could not afford to buy presents.[33]

Simon Bouie was a boy growing up near the corner of Gervais and Oak Streets. He and his twin brother Sammy delivered the morning and afternoon papers and were known as pranksters in the Waverly community. He recalled memories of pilfering pomegranates from a lady's yard, scaring customers as they exited little neighborhood storefront groceries, running through segregated Valley Park, and "playing dead" outside a parked car to alarm passersby. When he grew up and decided to enter the ministry, his trial sermon at Chappelle AME Church was packed with his Waverly neighbors, who could not fathom that this mischievous boy could now embark upon a serious vocation. But his mind returns to one sad childhood memory: seeing Elmore standing alone outside the Gervais Street store. He asked his grandmother what was wrong with him. "She said, he has had a hard time, son, he has had a very hard time," Bouie recalled. His grandmother didn't explain the full story of Elmore's circumstances, but simply acknowledged he was having troubles. "And then she began to say that he was involved in civil rights, and he used to have a lot of friends, and friends kind of walked away from him and he is kind of left by himself," Bouie said. He went on:

> I didn't understand the significant gains that he had made for us at all until later on in life. But every time my mind reaches back to that picture of him, I remember seeing a very sad man. He would come out every day and he would just stand in front of the store. He was waiting on people to come, apparently. But really a lot of people just stopped going to the store when it got kind of rough. People pulled back from him.[34]

Elmore was not alone in facing backlash. The "economic squeeze" used against Elmore was a tactic deployed across the state as a warning to Black men and women who dared to step out of line. The schemes were more subtle than Ku Klux Klan beatings, cross burnings, and parades, but accomplished the goal of keeping Black people fearful and unwilling to challenge the white status quo. In rural Clarendon County, Black parents were beginning to experience the slow devastation of the "squeeze." In 1947, they tried to obtain a school bus from white school officials to haul their children to a sprawling network of isolated one-room schools. Levi Pearson, who had initiated an NAACP-backed lawsuit on behalf of his son James, was shortly denied, with state lawyers arguing that the Pearsons did not live in School District 22, where the case was filed. Soon, Levi Pearson suffered swift retribution for his daring, as if a blanket had been thrown over a small flame. Journalist Claudia Smith Brinson wrote this of Pearson:

George Elmore was a familiar figure to school children walking up Gervais Street from Waverly School. They often stopped for candy and ice cream at his Waverly Five-and-10-Cents store. Courtesy of the Elmore Family.

No white farmer or distributor allowed the Pearsons to borrow machinery at harvest time or sold them the supplies required for farming. No one would gin Pearson cotton. Fertilizer dealers refused to sell Levi Pearson fertilizer; oil dealers refused to sell him oil. Black people were afraid to talk to the Pearsons; white people wouldn't.[35]

The "squeeze" became a kind of bloodless lynching, more palatable to good white people who had long disdained the rough extra-judicial actions of lawbreakers who had kidnapped, tortured, and killed Black people for offenses, real and imagined.

Elmore's neighbors and acquaintances in the Waverly community found it difficult to witness his transformation from a rotund, jovial community figure to a downtrodden person experiencing emotional and financial turmoil. But there was also fear in assisting him too openly, lest white people take offense. There was also a whispered question about money that Elmore may or may not have received as a result of the trial outcome. Some in the community thought Elmore may have profited by receiving $5,000 in damages in the case, and was hiding the money, his son recounted in interviews.[36] But Elmore never received any sort of financial settlement. Judge Waring had determined that any kind of monetary damages would be decided by a jury, if necessary. That never happened. In a letter to James Hinton, Columbia resident C. Arthur Pompey thought there should be more focus on Elmore than on the leaders of the NAACP and Progressive Democrats who had guided the successful lawsuit. "If any testimonials were to be given and any purses distributed, surely George Elmore deserved to be on the receiving end," Pompey wrote in the August 18, 1948, letter. "He has suffered many indignities and his family had had to undergo many hardships because of his willingness [to] prosecute for the freedom of his race."

Pompey, a trustee with Palmetto Lodge 342 of the Benevolent and Protective Order of Elks, had commenced his letter with a complaint that Hinton had unfairly criticized the Elks in a speech at Allen University. He suggested Hinton, in urging voters to refrain from drinking on Election Day, had slandered his group by portraying the Elks as "liquorheads and roustabouts." Pompey disputed that characterization, noting his lodge had "some of the most highly respected citizens of the Columbia community." He reserved the second part of his letter for concerns about Elmore, saying the Elks and "other thinking people of Columbia," were irked that Elmore was left out of testimonials to the NAACP and PDP organizations.[37]

Elmore distanced himself from the letter, as did the Elks organization. George Woodard, Exalted Ruler of the lodge, said the letter was unauthorized, written and instigated by two or three Republicans under Pompey's signature. He indicated the Elks took no offense at Hinton's suggestions the lodge close on primary day, a story in the August 29, 1948 issue of the *Lighthouse and Informer* noted. Elmore said he regretted the letter. "I don't want charity from anybody," Elmore was quoted in the story. "I have never asked anybody for one cent and I stand today, where I have always stood, with Messrs. Hinton, McCray and Marshall."[38]

The Pompey letter struck a nerve with Hinton, who had devoted hundreds of hours to the NAACP in his very visible role as president and was routinely the target of threats. He faced enormous pressure as the organization prepared to launch a full-throated assault on segregation, and he still had to attend to a myriad of daily racial outrages from police brutality to the lack of school crossing guards. He made it clear he had not personally benefitted from any financial gifts in the wake of the Elmore lawsuit and noted that the recent testimonial was freely given. As to Pompey's assertions about Elmore, Hinton said Elmore "had requested the PRIVILEGE of being the person to file the voting suit." Hinton had not wanted him to be the plaintiff, he said, a fact he said Elmore would affirm. "We felt he had counted the cost, as others in similar cases." Then he added: "I am not GOING TO BE PLACED IN THE POSITION OF DISCUSSING MR. ELMORE, and his condition." Hinton did reveal he had offered Elmore a job with his company, the Pilgrim Health and Life Insurance, at thirty dollars a week, once after the case was filed and again in 1948. The letter offers a window into the tensions that existed as NAACP leaders and lawyers navigated through a labyrinth of legal issues while shoring up the courage of those who were challenging white supremacy. Plaintiffs across South Carolina, including Elmore, had discovered the high cost of upending segregation.[39]

Fragments of the family's struggles would float upward in the years after Black voters claimed the ballot. Elmore's children remembered donations of food and kindnesses shown amid a growing unease and fear about the family's precarious position. The youngest child,

Yolande, recalled returning from a Sunday drive to find a cross burning in front of their house. Packages featuring photographs of lynchings were mailed to the home.[40] By 1949, Elmore had shuttered the five-and-dime store. He still operated a liquor establishment near Millwood Avenue, drove his taxi, and engaged in his freelance photography business. In December 1951, he announced in the pages of the *Lighthouse and Informer* that he was opening a photography studio in space likely provided by McCray.[41] But money was running out and wife Laura's health was in decline. In October 1952, she was hospitalized, her nerves shattered by the pressures from the case. In the spring of 1953, Victory Savings Bank, the city's only Black-owned bank, called the loan on the Tree Street house that Elmore had purchased on March 1, 1943, for the sum of $1,000.[42]

His financial difficulties had played out in a long wave of borrowing that must have seemed quite manageable to Elmore in 1943 when he placed the first down payment on the Tree Street house. On March 4, 1943, Elmore had taken out an initial home mortgage of $800 from Standard Building and Loan Association, to be paid in monthly installments of eight dollars, according to Richland County records.[43] That loan was paid and satisfied on February 1, 1947. But he had not paid his house off in full. In March, a month later, he took out another mortgage from the Home Federal Savings and Loan Association of Columbia, this time for $1,200. His monthly mortgage payment was twelve dollars. That loan was paid and fully satisfied on October 18, 1950. To the casual observer it might have seemed that Elmore was meeting his financial obligations.[44]

But Elmore was spiraling into an untenable financial morass as his debts mounted and his job prospects dwindled in the wake of the lawsuit. In reality, he had not paid off the Home Federal loan with his own money in order to own his home outright. Instead, he turned to Modjeska Simkins and borrowed $2,500 from her on October 17, 1950. That loan was used to pay off the Home Federal loan and provide more cash to the strapped family.[45] The terms of the mortgage included a 7 percent annual interest rate and a requirement that the loan be paid off in four years. Two years later, on May 16, 1952, Elmore paid Simkins by borrowing $2,800 from Victory Savings Bank. Victory Savings was led by Simkins brother, Dr. Henry Monteith, who was a civil rights activist in his own right. The bank was a refuge for Black customers who may have been turned away by white institutions unwilling to loan money. The terms of the mortgage executed on May 16, 1952, included a 7 percent interest annual rate and monthly mortgage payments of thirty-five dollars.[46] But Elmore, out of work and in debt, could not meet his obligations. A year later, on May 27, 1953, Victory Savings called in the loan and on September 8, 1953, Judge E. H. Henderson, ordered the Tree Street house sold at auction. That took place on November 2, 1953. In a bitter irony it was Boulware, the NAACP lawyer who had helped argue the Elmore white primary case, who acted as purchasing agent on behalf of R. E. (Rachel E.) Monteith, the mother of Henry Monteith and Modjeska Simkins. His was the highest bid at $3,054.60.[47]

There had been an effort to save the home for the Elmore children, McCray had written Elmore in December 1954, or perhaps purchase another home in Columbia's Haskell Heights neighborhood for the family to live. But that effort had fallen apart "after Dr. Monteith gave us, rather me, the 'double-cross' in selling the house without first advising us it was going to be sold and allowing the small group working the chance to equal the bid," McCray said in the letter.[48] Elmore had noted to his young son the bitterness of having the loan called, not by a white banker, but by a Black institution.

In the two-page letter, McCray reminded Elmore that he had "been in his corner" for ten years and fought for him in the pages of the *Lighthouse and Informer*. "I have stood behind and beside you, even when everybody else with whom we worked civicly was of another mind." McCray did not elaborate on who had turned against Elmore—"who way back then, became your enemy"—although McCray said he had "written off" two key people he had worked with since 1941 out of loyalty to Elmore. Likely, one of those was Simkins, who had engaged in a bitter, public feud with McCray. The pair had quarreled over voting strategies and the operation of the *Lighthouse and Informer*, which she had helped finance and run. By the time McCray wrote the December 1954 letter, the *Lighthouse and Informer* was shuttered, its equipment and archived newspapers sold off to pay mounting debts. McCray and Simkins were not speaking to each other. The Tree Street home would remain within the Monteith family as part of the properties of the Monteith Holding Company until 1999, when it was sold.

Whether McCray had accurately portrayed the abandonment of Elmore by top NAACP leadership and Progressive Democrats is difficult to assess. In the letter addressed to "My Dear Mr. Elmore," McCray told Elmore he was trying to set the record straight because he had heard that Elmore was upset with him, likely over the sale of the Tree Street home. There was, at least from McCray's writing, a suggestion that others wanted to take credit for the success of the lawsuit and perhaps, in hindsight, wished they had placed their names on the original petition. But there still remained a grassroots effort throughout the state to assist the Elmore family. In May 1954, Sarah B. Reese of Ridgeland, South Carolina, wrote to Modjeska Simkins asking for Elmore's address: "i was appointed as chairman to raise money for him in his distress at Ridgeland SC an i dident have his address," she wrote in the handwritten letter peppered with misspellings. She had sent twenty-five dollars to McCray but needed to verify that he had received the money, "where I can go back to the churches and show them that I did sent it to him."[49]

Following the loss of the Tree Street home, Elmore went to Washington, D.C., to look for work, taking his children and lodging with his sister for about nine months. He had little luck and returned to Columbia in 1955. The family stayed with Laura Elmore's niece, Lillian Delaney Edney, and her family. The Edneys lived in the newly built public housing project of Saxon Homes, near Laura Elmore's elderly parents. But there was only room for the youngest Elmore girls, Vernadine and Yolande, to sleep there at night. George and his son Cresswell slept in their Chevrolet truck outside. Laura Elmore by that time had been institutionalized. Years later, Lillian's daughter, Cynthia Edney, recalled only good memories of having her relatives come stay with them. "I was just happy because they were like big sisters in my house," she said. "You never would have known anything was wrong as far as my Uncle George was concerned because he was always smiling." He found work at a nearby liquor store and indulged her affection for ice pops. "He was always looking down at me and would smile and reach into his pocket and hand me a nickel," Cynthia Edney recalled. "I learned later he had to go the extra mile to get that Popsicle."[50]

CHAPTER 10

A Private Life
Shattered by Violence

I just remember the talk about the cross burning
and the fear.

—Columbia resident Doris Glymph Greene

In happier times—before the cross burnings, before the arrival of
anonymous envelopes filled with gruesome lynching photographs,
before the hospitalizations—Laura Elmore took a moment to sit for a
formal black-and-white portrait in the living room of her Columbia,
South Carolina, home.[1] Her husband, George, was immersed in learning photography, viewing the skill as one more avenue to earn money
for his growing family. He had set up a makeshift darkroom in the
bathroom of the family home at 907 Tree Street, where he would extin-
guish the lights and develop his film into black-and-white portraits of
family groups and babies. The living room became his studio, where
he would set up backdrops and floodlights with the assistance of his
young son, Cresswell. Sometime after the couple purchased the house
in 1943, he persuaded his wife to sit for a "glamour" portrait, the kind
of formal photograph that was popular in the period. It was a simple
portrait of the woman he had wooed and married when she was still
a teenager and he was barely into his twenties. She was dressed in
a cream-colored suit and fashionable black hat with a jaunty plume.
There is, in the tilt of her head and the smile that plays on her face, a
hint that she might be humoring her husband, indulging in his peripatetic efforts to improve the family's fortunes. He seated her against
a white backdrop, a gentle contrast to the beige of her suit. Her face
is smooth and flawless. The bench where she sat is out of the range of
the camera lens, turned sideways from the camera. George Elmore had
already figured out how to employ the photographer's art of having his
subject turn her head, then tilt her chin slightly upwards to capture an
elusive smile.

Laura Elmore photographed by her husband at his home studio sometime after the family moved into 907 Tree Street. Courtesy of the Elmore Family.

Laura Belle Delaney Elmore was in her thirties, a mother of three, when her husband clicked the camera shutter and captured her image in black and white. She was born in 1910 in rural lower Richland County, the sixth child of Maggie and Samuel Delaney. Samuel Delaney was listed in the 1910 US Census as a farmer who tilled on rented land (His name was misspelled as De Laney). Laura's brother, Castor, age twelve in 1910, was also listed as a farm laborer. Her sisters, Manda, Essie, and Willie, were ages ten, six and four. Her brother, Samuel Delaney Jr., was two at the time of her birth.[2] By the 1920 US Census, all of the children were listed as farm laborers except for the youngest children, Laura and Samuel.[3] Sometime between the 1920 and 1930 census, the Delaneys moved into the city of Columbia, where Samuel Delaney found work in a rock quarry. They rented a house at 1110 Blossom Street.[4] Sometime in that decade, too, a teenaged Laura met George Elmore, a young man five years older who had come to Columbia from his home in Holly Hill. Years later, an elderly Columbia resident, Donella Wilson, would recall the image of the young couple walking up Blossom Street, carefree and holding hands. It was a wistful remembrance, recalling a time long before the Elmore family's troubles began.[5]

Laura's parents, the Delaneys, were members of Union Baptist Church, founded in 1907 and located then at 1016 Devine Street, near where the Delaneys lived in Columbia's Ward 1. Their house was an unpainted shotgun house with a dirt yard and unpaved street in front, the kind that populated the poor neighborhoods that fanned out from the state capitol blocks away. Few of the houses had indoor plumbing and most had absentee landlords, but the predominantly Black residents would recall years later a lively, if impoverished, community where residents helped each other and relished their simple lives. Cresswell Elmore remembered as a boy in the 1940s sitting with his maternal grandfather on the wooden porch of the dwelling and enjoying meals cooked by his maternal grandmother, who worked as a domestic.

By the mid-1950s, Blossom Street and the surrounding neighborhoods of Ward 1 were in the sights of city planners determined to eliminate the ramshackle houses and blight that hindered the progress of the capital city. Sometime in 1953, the Delaneys moved into Saxon Homes, a newly constructed low-income Columbia Housing Authority project on Oak Street named for Celia Dial Saxon, a tireless Black educator and founder of homes for orphans and delinquent girls. Saxon, who died in 1935, was a well known figure in Columbia who was determined to improve the lives of Black South Carolinians. The Delaneys, now in their late sixties and early seventies, were likely the first occupants of apartment 10 in building 1 in the garden-style complex of sixty-four buildings.[6] Their residency was not long. Maggie Delaney, Laura's mother, died on July 25, 1954, at the age of seventy-eight; her father, Samuel Thomas Delaney, died four years later on January 29, 1958. He was seventy-four. The unpainted houses along Blossom Street where Laura and her brothers and sisters grew up were eventually razed as Columbia's leaders, Black and white, envisioned a modern downtown of bustling high-rise buildings and an expanded University of South Carolina. By the late 1960s, a basketball arena would occupy the site of the stone Union Baptist Church, which had occupied a visible place on Devine Street for more than a half-century. The church was demolished in 1966 and a new expanded sanctuary was built several miles away on Germany Street in North Columbia. The Ward 1 landmarks that represented the lives of the Delaneys—the church, the storefront groceries, the unpainted wooden houses—would be conjured up only in old black-and-white photographs or in memory.

But all that was far in a future that the young couple could only imagine. Sometime in 1927, when Laura Elmore was seventeen and Elmore was twenty-two, they married. By 1930, the US Census recorded the couple living at 1212 Lyon Street, the first of several unpainted rentals they would occupy before putting enough money down for their first home, a clapboard shotgun-style house on Tree Street in the 1940s. Rent on the Lyon Street house, according to US Census data, was eight dollars a month. Early in their marriage, Laura Elmore was employed as a cafeteria worker, according to census records, while George Elmore drove his cab and worked at a variety of jobs. His sister, Esther Elmore, resided with the couple in the house, a common experience for families, Black and white, seeking to head off the worst of the Depression.[7] Like many people, their lives revolved around family, church, and work. They endured the travails of the Depression as did other South Carolina families. Even before the stock market crash of 1929, families in South Carolina and other southern states were plunged into the darkest economic period they had experienced since the Civil War. Cotton prices fell and what prices didn't devastate, the boll weevil did. Thirty percent of the state's citizens were out of work. Rural share-croppers, white and Black, were hit hardest as families struggled to have enough food to eat and were beset by diseases like pellagra and scurvy. The Internal Revenue Service reported that only 0.70 percent (South Carolina's richest families) of the state's population of 1.7 million

Laura Elmore attended Union Baptist Church as a child and took her children there as they grew up. The church, located on Devine Street, was razed in 1966 to make way for the University of South Carolina's Carolina Coliseum. Stan Schneidmiller, photographer. The State Newspaper Photograph Archive. Courtesy of Richland Library.

had filed income tax returns in 1930 with average net income per return of $3,507. In contrast, 19 percent of New York's 12.5 million residents had filed tax returns that year, reporting an average net income of $5,887. The majority of South Carolinians could not imagine annual incomes that crossed the thousand-dollar mark.[8]

Urban Black families like the Elmores fared slightly better than their rural counterparts, although most people looking back to that period remembered everyone united in poverty. The Elmores were apparently optimistic enough for better days ahead to welcome their first child, Essie Naomi Elmore, on March 12, 1932. Headlines from that day carried news of the frenzied four-way race for president of the German Republic, with the fascist leader Adolph Hitler campaigning, as the Associated Press dispatch noted, "with a banner emblazoned with the policy of 'Nationalism' and a heavy-handed militaristic creed against all enemies of 'Germany for Germans.'"[9] The nationwide hunt was on for the kidnapper of the Lindbergh baby, twenty-month-old Charles Augustus Lindbergh Jr., taken from the home of his famous aviator father and his mother, acclaimed author Anne Morrow Lindbergh. Six years later, Cresswell Delaney Elmore was born on November 8, 1938, an off-year election date that headlines suggested would become a referendum on President Roosevelt's New Deal policies. Four more years passed, and a third child, Vernadine Veranus Elmore, was born on August 2, 1942, during World War II. George Elmore wanted to incorporate the World War II "Double V" campaign in Vernadine's initials to symbolize victory over fascism aboard and victory at home in winning first-class citizenship for Black people. All were home births with a doctor and a midwife assisting in the delivery. After living in a succession of rentals, the family settled at 907 Tree Street, a white frame shotgun house on a dirt street in what was part of the lower Waverly community, a few blocks east of the historic twelve-block Waverly community bordered by Harden, Gervais, Taylor, and Heidt Streets. (That neighborhood would earn historic designation in the latter part of the twentieth century.) Waverly was anchored by two Black colleges founded after the Civil War, Benedict and Allen, and home to thriving Black businesses. The neighborhood, formally annexed into the city in 1913, was Columbia's first documented suburb, according to Historic Columbia, and was initially home to both white and Black residents. It was hailed as a model of upward mobility and a haven for a growing professional class of Black doctors, lawyers, and business leaders. But by the mid-1930s, the Home Owners Loan Corporation (HOLC), a New Deal effort to rescue and restructure the nation's mortgage lending market, had marked the Waverly community and environs with a "D," or "hazardous," rating, for mortgage security. The HOLC designations were written by federal staff with the aid of local real estate lenders, developers, and appraisers in communities across the United States. The more favorable "A" singular designation were reserved for prosperous white neighborhoods, including the rambling Forest Hills suburb that bordered Waverly. There were some favorable elements to the Waverly area, the surveyors noted, including convenience to work, school, and churches and five-cent bus transportation. There was also a new Catholic hospital nearby. "Area between Lady, Heidt, Hampton, and Harden Streets contains highest type negro property in city, majority 2 sty singles; 25 years ago this small potion [portion] of the area was high grade white property," agents wrote in their shorthand description. In the neighborhood description, the agents noted that only eight percent of streets in the area were paved and there was little access to public sewer.

"Vandalism is bad in portion of area north of Richland Street, between Gervais and Taylor Streets, east of lyon and between Heidt, Santee, King and Trenholm Rd. (Gervais st)," the agents noted in their sometimes ungrammatical style. "Difficulty of rent collection exists in the above described portion of the area. Instability of occupants incomes. Dilapidated repair considtions [sic] of may [sic] properties in which living conditions are also unsanitary." The agents noted that "several high class white families" still live in the area.[10]

Did Laura Elmore look around and see what the HOLC agents and the real estate developers saw when they rode down Gervais Street and turned onto her street anchored by a small neighborhood grocery store? Did she contemplate the mix of poverty and dilapidated conditions of some houses around her? Did she wonder why the city sewer system did not connect to the rented houses of her parents on Blossom Street or the poorest segregated neighborhoods of her community? Perhaps, but the reality is she had resided in the countryside or on unpaved streets all her life. And her new home on Tree Street was supplied with indoor plumbing and other amenities that she had not had in the rentals the family had occupied. With three children to attend to and a husband who was emerging as a significant player in the 1940s effort to gain the ballot, Laura Elmore may have begun to realize that her quiet life was gradually altering. Her husband was a founding member of the Progressive Democratic Party, an upstart insurgency aimed at jabbing the white power structure in the eye, and he was relishing the prospect of political change. The Elmore children remember their mother as sensitive and emotional, anchored to their home, indifferent to politics. She was the primary caregiver once her husband claimed some modest success as a taxi driver and budding entrepreneur. George and Laura Elmore had attended school only to the eighth grade; they wanted more for their children. She ferried the children to school and to church. She encouraged her children to attend school faithfully. Cresswell obliged with perfect attendance at Waverly School from the first thru sixth grades.

Elmore did not want his wife working in other people's homes, particularly as a domestic. When he established the Waverly Five-and-10-Cents store, his wife would often help out there. At home, she would assign one household task to young Naomi and Cresswell before she left for the day: Mop the living room and kitchen floors before the elder Elmores returned in the afternoon. But amid outdoor games and friends calling them to play, they often forgot and put off the job until it was nearly closing time, Cresswell Elmore recalled. Their mother rarely scolded them when she returned to still-damp floors. But Cresswell remembered getting "the worst whipping of his life" from his father when he stole a Hershey's candy bar from the A&P grocery store on his way home from school. Even though Hershey's chocolate with almonds was his mother's favorite chocolate bar, she made him return it to the store.

Other memories of the time: The family had a Philco radio in the living room, which was warmed by a coal and wood stove where the children would gather to listen to radio programs. Elmore tuned into Walter Winchell's nightly newscast, the broadcaster's signature staccato opening—"Good evening, Mr. and Mrs. America, from border to border and coast to coast and all the ships at sea"—echoing through the house. Laura Elmore and her relatives and friends often played card games in the afternoons and evenings, including Po-Ke-No, a favorite. There were happy Christmases in those early years on Tree Street, with presents piled high on the Duncan Phyfe sofa in the living room when the children awakened on Christmas morning. Sometime during the war years, the family sat for a formal family portrait at a studio in downtown Columbia, which was run by a white photographer and friend of George Elmore. Cresswell, around age five or six, is dressed in a suit and tie and leans against his mother's leg. Naomi, around age eleven or twelve, stands behind her parents. The parents are serious. The baby, Vernadine, is pensive in a yellow pinafore and white blouse.

The family's domestic life could have remained insulated within the boundaries of the Black community they inhabited except for George Elmore's keen interest in politics. Through his connections in the Waverly community and his work with the NAACP, he decided he wanted to put his name forward when the NAACP sought a plaintiff

Sometime in 1944 or 1945, the Elmore family sat for a portrait at the Lindler Studio in Columbia. Courtesy of the Elmore Family.

to challenge the white primary. From 1946 onward, Elmore's name was championed in the Black community and puzzled over by white political leaders. At the 1947 federal court hearing for *Elmore v. Rice,* the Democratic Party's lawyers complained they knew little of Elmore or his politics, nor did lawyers or reporters include details of his personal and civic life. Sometimes, attorney Belser told the court, when a man considers his rights, "he overlooks the right of the defendants that is in the Constitution—the freedom of assembly and the right that they cannot be compelled to bring into assemblies anyone they don't want."[11] White politicians knew that Elmore identified as a Democrat and had been a member of the Progressive Democratic Party since its founding in 1944. They knew that the PDP had sent out Black voters to attempt to vote in the 1946 Democratic primary and that Elmore had been turned away because of his race.

A week after Elmore appeared in court in June 1947, a cross was burned on Gervais Street, a block from the Waverly dime store and two blocks from the home of the NAACP state president James Hinton. The cross burning and other violence were spawned by a confluence of events, including the white primary trial and a separate, highly publicized, attack on a woman in the Edgewood section of suburban Columbia. In newspaper accounts, the woman reported that a Black man had come into her home for a third time and slashed her arms and choked her, threatening her grandson. A posse of white men, at one point growing to a thousand strong, surrounded her home and roamed the area. Newspaper accounts reported that innocent Black men were stopped and grilled about their whereabouts, prompting the NAACP to demand that the Richland County sheriff intervene. Sheriff Alex Heise ordered the vigilantes to stand down and threatened prosecution if they did not.[12]

Doris Glymph Greene was a child of seven, living with her parents on Barnwell Street, when she overheard her parents speak of the incident and remembered "the absolute fear" that gripped the community. "I just remember the talk about the cross burning and the fear," she said. No one was ever apprehended for the Edgewood incident, and rumors circulated that the attacker was actually the women's former husband, a white man, according to a June 15, 1947, article in the *Lighthouse and Informer.* Shortly after, she remembered her father coming home very upset. "He was concerned because he had witnessed a cross burning, somewhere on Harden Street near Allen-Benedict, around the time of the burning of the cross at the Elmores, and it was the Ku Klux Klan."[13]

That burst of violence, coming rapidly after the trial, was the first of a series of threats that disrupted the tranquility of the private life Laura Elmore had created for her family. Years later, Gloria Schumpert James remembered the anxiety in the community as the court cases unfolded. She lived in a pretty two-story white frame house at 2309 Lady Street with her parents, Frederick Benjamin and Bessie Barber Schumpert. F. B. Schumpert owned his own lumber business, which he had established in Irmo. He was among the most prosperous Waverly residents and able to support community causes. She said her father, like other businessmen who dealt with white clients, would support Elmore and the other NAACP causes in secret by handing over cash rather than taking a prominent community role. "He couldn't afford to be outwardly supportive, or else they would do to you what they had done to George Elmore," she said. As a child, Gloria Schumpert frequented the shops along the nearby block between Oak and Heidt Streets along with other children in the neighborhood. They included Elmore's Waverly five and dime at 2317 Gervais Street, Dantzler's radio and shoe repair shop at 2313 Gervais Street and the "colored" library across the street, with only Hop's Bar and Grill off-limits to youngsters. "I just interacted with Mr. Elmore in the store. He knew that I was Mr. Schumpert's little girl. It was always pleasant."[14]

"It was very contained, very segregated," James recalled of her childhood in Waverly. "The only time you came in contact with white people, the only time we did as children, was when we went downtown. And then you couldn't go to the bathroom. If you had to go to the bathroom, you had to go all the way around to the Greyhound bus station." Waverly parents reminded children of the rules in their interactions with white people—defer to white people passing on the street, sit in the back of the city bus, walk up to the balcony of the movie house—but protected them from the harsher realities of segregation, she said. "I don't think we realized how it was affecting us. Our parents did what they could to protect us from the outside world and the things that were going on. But we could still feel it. When things were going on, you could feel the tension. You could hear your parents whispering," she said. "When George Elmore's case came up, that created a lot of tension in the community. When the teacher equalization was going on, that created a lot of tension because teachers were losing their jobs if they belonged to the NAACP."

On the Sunday after Judge Waring issued his decision, her Sunday School teacher at Second Calvary Baptist Church, Rebecca Stewart, suggested to the class of seven-year-olds a Biblical connection to Elmore's bold action and Judge Waring's ruling. "She was the elevator lady in Haltiwanger's store, which was on the corner of Hampton and Main. Evidently, she was reading the paper the morning after Judge Waring's decision," James recalled. When white ladies stepped inside the elevator, they saw the headlines and began to make critical comments about Judge Waring and the case. "And her retort was 'Well, you know they crucified Jesus.'" That memory of her teacher making a prophetic connection to the struggle for voting rights still sticks with her seventy years later. "She probably couldn't say much, but she said all that she could say and she came to Sunday School and said the rest."

James recalled also the "hand-wringing" among the adults as Elmore faced growing retaliation and economic repercussions. "There was a lot of self-criticism, of why don't we do more. And some realization that we can't provide for him, that we are doing all we can even thought it wasn't enough." The women expressed worry about how Laura Elmore was coping. "He was like a 'hot potato,'" said Columbia attorney Hemphill P. Pride II, who as a youngster visited the dime store often to buy candy. Pride, the son of a dentist, described Elmore as "independent and independent-minded," a man who may have been too optimistic in believing that once the case was decided, he could return to private life without retribution.

A year after the end of the court case, Laura Elmore gave birth to the Elmore's fourth child, Yolande Anita, on September 11, 1949. Over the next few years, the outside world intruded with the arrival of the daily mail and packages, mailed anonymously. Some would show photographs of lynched Black men and threats that this could happen to her husband. She stopped opening the mail and would simply turn over the envelopes to her husband. Yolande Elmore remembered, as a small child, coming back from a Sunday drive to find a cross ablaze on Tree Street. The cheerful Waverly Five-and-10-Cents store, once bustling with goods on the shelves, became a symbol of the white "squeeze" as more and more vendors refused to grant Elmore credit or supply him goods. Elmore shuttered the five and dime in 1949. But he kept up management of two liquor stores nearby, purchasing cases of state-regulated liquor until, as Cresswell remembers it, men came to the store and broke the seals on the bottles, destroying the alcohol. That was 1953, the last year Elmore operated a liquor business. According to state records, he had purchased two hundred cases of liquor with an estimated markup of $2,868 and paid $200 in case taxes. There was no entry for gross profits tax paid. The annual report of the South Carolina Tax Commission on alcoholic liquors sold by retailers July 1, 1952, through June 30, 1953, noted that Elmore was "(OB 3–31–53)," out of business and no longer a retail dealer.[15]

By that point, Laura Elmore had suffered a breakdown that required hospitalization at Columbia Hospital and then commitment to the segregated mental hospital about seven miles from the house on Tree Street. Laura Elmore kept no diary of those times, although there were growing signs that her fragile nerves and her delicate constitution were fraying, according to family recollections. Cynthia Edney, a great-niece, remembered her aunt weeping for no reason. As the family's fortunes declined—the five and dime store shuttered and bill collectors closing in—she likely knew the family home was in jeopardy. Elmore was still working as a photographer, but the income was not enough to prevent the bank from calling the loan on the Tree Street house. Before the family had to move, there was one last celebration—Naomi's spring 1952 graduation from Benedict College. A photograph marking the occasion depicts a pensive Laura Elmore standing by her daughter in cap and gown, along with two of Naomi's paternal aunts, Ines Elmore Harvin and Esther Elmore Swygert. Elmore likely took the picture, capturing the moment the women returned from the ceremony, Naomi holding her rolled-up diploma and the three women still clasping their white gloves and purses.

On October 15, 1952, Laura Elmore was admitted to what was then known as the colored mental hospital or State Park on Farrow Road in Columbia after experiencing convulsions. The family was told she suffered a "nervous breakdown," the common parlance of the day. State mental health officials acknowledged in official reports that conditions at both the white and segregated facilities were marked by inadequate staff, terrible overcrowding, and ramshackle physical structures. There was no question the resources at State Park were

Naomi Elmore, pictured with her aunts, Ines Elmore Harvin and Esther Elmore Swygert (left), and her mother Laura Elmore, on her graduation day from Benedict College, June 1952. Courtesy of the Elmore Family.

even more limited, with fewer physicians and aides and no Black psychiatrists on staff.

That year, the General Assembly appropriated $5 million for improvements at the white State Hospital on Bull Street and the State Training School in Clinton. "Out of these funds there is being constructed four magnificent buildings at the Columbia Division of the hospital for the care and treatment of acutely disturbed patients, a new central kitchen and bakery, together with additional refrigeration facility to replace the inadequate central kitchen justly condemned along with the infamous Taylor Building in which male disturbed patients are still housed," the South Carolina Mental Health Commission reported in its July 1, 1953, annual report to Governor James F. Byrnes.[16] At the segregated State Park facility, building 1 had been renovated into an "attractive dormitory," the commission noted. But there was no effort to achieve any sort of architectural magnificence at the segregated hospital on

Farrow Road. The hospital's maintenance staff did the work "at half the amount that would have been required had it been done on contract" and was also tasked with renovations on buildings 2, 3, and 8. Still, the commission noted, "No institution which has been neglected as the State Hospital has been and which has deteriorated to the extent that it has been allowed to deteriorate can be converted into a modern institution simply by providing 608 beds for acutely disturbed patients. The hospital now houses 5,545 patients. Even when the new buildings are occupied it will remain a woefully overcrowded and dilapidated institution generally."[17]

A month after Laura Elmore's admission to State Park, South Carolina exerted one last punishment on the Elmore family. At a staff meeting of white physicians and one chaplain, her diagnosis was recorded in a log dated November 21, 1952: "Chronic brain disorder—Chronic brain syndrome associated with central nervous system syphilis-meningoencephalitis—with psychotic reaction."[18] Seventy years after that typewritten entry was entered into the mental health records of the state, Laura Elmore's son, Cresswell, read that diagnosis in disbelief and dismissed it as decades-old political deceit. No physician at Columbia Hospital who treated his mother ever spoke of a syphilis diagnosis. No one during her stay at the Columbia hospital or during the time she was committed to State Park facility ever suggested that Laura Elmore suffered from syphilis or suggested that her husband or young children be tested for the sexually transmitted disease. At the time syphilis was commonly viewed as a malady mainly affecting Black and low-income white people.

The records of the South Carolina State Department of Mental Health from that segregated 1950s era have since been destroyed, so there is no file on Laura Elmore beyond cards that explained her entry and exit from the facility. But an examination of the admission records from 1952–1953 shows the prevalence of the syphilis-related diagnosis, particularly among Black patients. A total of 1,671 patients were treated for syphilis and neurosyphilis between July 1, 1952, and June 30, 1953, including 288 white males, 359 white females, 669 Black males and 355 Black females. Most were treated with penicillin.[19]

Among those, thirty-two Black men and seven Black women were admitted with the more serious condition of "chronic brain syndromes with psychotic reaction, associated with central nervous system syphilis," according to the annual report of the South Carolina State Hospital for the year ending June 30, 1953. During that year, nine white men and one white women were admitted with the more serious syphilis-related brain diagnoses.[20]

Until his death in 1959, George Elmore would visit his wife, taking the children with him. They would bring her the Hershey's Kisses candy she called "silver bells." Cresswell Elmore remembered the facility at State Park as dirty and overcrowded, with a pervasive odor of sickness. It was particularly painful for his father to turn into the driveway there. "He had a difficult time going to see her," said Cresswell. His father understood that his political activism had likely contributed to her mental breakdown. "Whenever people came to visit, she would say, 'When is George coming to take me home?'"[21]

Laura Elmore would remain at the segregated South Carolina mental hospital for fifteen years until her children, grown and living in New York, removed her from her home state. In 1967, Laura Elmore was discharged from State Park into the care of her youngest daughter, Yolande, who had turned eighteen that year. She was transferred from South Carolina to Creedmoor Psychiatric Center in Queens and then placed in St. John's nursing home. There, her four children could visit her regularly. Laura Elmore passed away on June 19, 1993, at the age of eighty-three. Her death certificate attributed her demise to natural causes. There was no reference to a brain disorder. Laura Elmore was buried in Randolph Cemetery in Columbia, sharing a tombstone with her husband.

CHAPTER 11

A Patriotic Act
Finally Acknowledged

That was probably the most joyous moment of his
life. Joy and jubilation—he was just so excited that
the challenge he took on was successful.
　　　　　　　　—Cresswell Elmore, November 17, 2022

In the fall of 2022, eighth-grade students in South Carolina public schools learned, for the first time, the story about Elmore and his historic battle to open the state's Democratic primary to Black voters. A newly adopted social studies textbook, the second edition of *The South Carolina Journey*, published by Gibbs Smith Education, detailed lessons on the civil rights movement in South Carolina that had not been previously explained. Among the learning goals for students: "I can describe how South Carolinians began to break through Jim Crow barriers after World War II and influence change at the national level." In an easy-to-understand narrative, students learned that in post-Reconstruction South Carolina, Republicans had little power. The Democratic Party primary determined who would serve in the state's elective offices. Only white voters could cast ballots in that primary. Elmore successfully challenged the all-white primary and won the case. Students learned that Elmore's legal victory "came at a great personal cost" and the text explained that the Ku Klux Klan burned crosses near his home and suppliers refused to provide goods to his business.[1]

Students were asked to ponder this question: "Why do you think his suppliers refused to do business with him after he won the case?" The students learned about what came to be known in the Black community as the "squeeze" with white leaders cutting lines of credit, calling in loans, and engaging in intimidation tactics to prevent Black people from engaging in meaningful civil rights work. The flesh-and-blood Elmore came alive in portraits of him as a young taxi driver in Columbia and then as a middle-aged man standing outside the entrance of the Waverly Five-and-10 cents store he operated on Gervais Street.

It was a moment that the Elmore family had been waiting for all their lives. The eighth-grade lesson—and a similar introduction at the fifth-grade social studies level—was a public acknowledgement of Elmore's bravery in challenging the exclusion of Black voters from South Carolina political life. No longer would the family carry, privately, the memory of a man who was known more by an obscure legal case than by his gregarious boldness. And perhaps, the pain of a generation directly affected by George Elmore's actions would be eased by knowing others now recognize his extraordinary valor.

How Elmore came to be featured in a social studies textbook seventy-five years after he entered a segregated South Carolina courtroom is a labyrinthine story that has its roots in the way that many stories begin, with an act that was bold and life-altering. We now know the outlines of his boldness: the great legal victory in *Elmore v. Rice,* the stirring words of US District Judge J. Waties Waring in admonishing South Carolina to "rejoin the union," the lines that stretched out at precincts across the state with jubilant first-time Black voters. We now know, too, the price he paid for such boldness: the loss of his home and businesses, the institutionalization of his wife, the scattering of his children to live with relatives. Elmore became a nomad as he searched for work, his health failing. With his death in 1959, before the full flowering of the civil rights movement, his story became a footnote to that history.

The telling of the story had stops and starts as fragments emerged in the decades following his death. For many immersed in the civil rights struggles of the twentieth century, the 1940s federal court decisions, first in Texas and then in South Carolina, tempered the hyper-focus on voting rights that had dominated the decade and occupied the full attention of the NAACP and other organizations. They were not so naïve as to think white leaders would give up on efforts to limit Black voter participation; that would be evident in the egregious administration of literacy tests and poll taxes that sprouted throughout the South as ways to thwart voting by underrepresented groups. But as the decade of the 1950s opened, the spotlight angled away from voting rights to public school education, as lawyers took aim at the state of segregated schools in the South. White South Carolinians scrambled to head off calls for political and social integration by belatedly transforming its hundreds of ramshackle Black schools into "separate but equal" facilities. The unheated, crowded wooden schools dotting the rural South Carolina landscape were finally deemed unacceptable by white leaders, who now feared the nation's high court would overturn the 1896 *Plessy v. Ferguson* decision that underpinned segregation. As long as facilities were "separate but equal," the high court had reasoned at the end of the nineteenth century, segregated facilities did not violate the Fourteenth Amendment. But the infusion of millions in state funding in 1953 to upgrade those schools proved a makeshift remedy. On May 17, 1954, a unanimous US Supreme Court said this:

> In these days, it is doubtful that any child may reasonably be expected to succeed in life if he is denied the opportunity of an education. Such an opportunity, where the state has undertaken to provide it, is a right, which must be made available to all on equal terms. We come then to the question presented: Does segregation of children in public schools solely on the basis of race, even though the physical facilities and other "tangible" factors may be equal, deprive the children of the minority group of equal educational opportunities? We believe that it does.[2]

Stunned by the ruling, the loudest and most strident white voices in South Carolina turned away from voting issues to the even more daunting fear of "race mixing" in the public schools and eventually in society at large. This was not to say that registration officials welcomed and encouraged Black people to register—in fact, after 1948, the methods to prevent Black voter registration seemed to get more innovative and bizarre. But the integration of schools ignited an even greater firestorm of protest than that of the 1940s, when white lawmakers insisted that the Democratic primary would remain all white, come hell or high water. There were calls for outright resistance, the establishment of White Citizens Councils to keep potential Black plaintiffs and white sympathizers in line, and a series of frantic, if doomed, strategies to undo the unanimous high court decision. The case, officially known as *Brown v. Board of Education of Topeka, Kansas,* was a series of five cases, including the *Briggs v. Elliott* lawsuit in South Carolina that had emerged out of the deeply segregated and isolated Clarendon County. Those dozens of Black plaintiffs, like Elmore a few years earlier, faced punishing retribution during and after the 1954 decision. Most of the plaintiffs, including small farmers and domestics workers, had lost their livelihoods and, in some cases, the land they sharecropped. The white man's "squeeze" felt by Elmore was applied to the Clarendon parents who had dared to aim for a better education for their children. Fired from his job at a service station, lead plaintiff Harry Briggs farmed for a while but after several years had to leave Clarendon County to find work in Florida, eventually raising his family in New York. His wife, Eliza, was also fired from her job as a maid at the Summerton motel. Other plaintiffs had similar harrowing stories. South Carolina, like other southern states, adopted the concept of "freedom of choice," which allowed each student unrestricted access to attend any school in the district. The hope among segregationists was that both Black and white students would choose their own schools rather than enter a new, unfamiliar environment. As Black South Carolinians rejoiced over the prospect of a better education for their children, white parents fearful of integration attempted to limit the number of Black students in the schools their children attended.[3]

Under the newly defined "freedom of choice" plans, education authorities across the South parsed the high court decision through a lens that suggested the justices did not specifically require integration, but instead simply prohibited discrimination. Elmore, the white primary, and the shouts of defiance from the floor of the South Carolina legislature in 1944 faded in memory. Legal arguments swelled in the wake of the *Brown* decision and a second decision known as *Brown II*, which set forth guidance for local authorities to implement the decision "with all deliberate speed."[4] Thurgood Marshall, the NAACP's chief lawyer on the case, surmised that "all deliberate speed" meant "S-L-O-W." Dodging full integration through whatever means possible became the raison d'etre for most South Carolina politicians. Even as he battled ill health and financial calamity, Elmore was mindful of the public debate surrounding education and still plotting to change the status quo. In 1954, George Sanders Jr., an editorial writer at the *Columbia Record*, spoke with Elmore on issues as wide-ranging as bloc voting and school integration. Elmore, whom the writer described as the "chubby Negro" who launched the assault on the white primary, "is completely serious-minded about the advance of the cause of his race in this state and elsewhere. . . . Certain now that further legal action on voting will be unnecessary, this active member of the National Association for the Advancement of Colored People is avidly watching the pending lawsuit contesting racial segregation in South Carolina public schools," Sanders noted in the piece titled "The Negro's Progress." "He believes that the decision will favor non-segregation, and that the people of the state will accept the verdict of the courts without trouble." The editorial writer was skeptical of Elmore's optimism, noting, "There are several courses of action available to the state in the event that racial separation is banned in public schools." In 1956, when Cresswell graduated from the still segregated Booker T. Washington High School, his father suggested that the time might be right to challenge segregation at the University of South Carolina and other white institutions of higher learning. Not surprisingly Cresswell, having seen the impact of the white primary lawsuit on the family, declined. "That's when I knew I was not the man my father was," he recalled in a 2022 interview. It would be 1963 before the first Black students matriculated at the Columbia university.

As the 1960s began, the fight turned to passage of the federal 1964 Civil Rights Act and the 1965 Voting Rights Act, pieces of legislation championed by President Lyndon B. Johnson and almost universally opposed by southern politicians, with Thurmond, now a US senator, among the most vocal champions of segregation. Finally the discriminatory practices that had long prevented Black Americans from becoming full participants in American life were ending. Discrimination in housing, on public buses and trains, at bowling alleys and restaurants was now illegal. Barriers to voting imposed since the Civil War—poll taxes, literacy tests, harassment, and death threats—ended under the watchful eye of federal examiners. Elmore had only a glimpse of what was to come in the decade of the 1960s. He died on February 25, 1959, in Columbia Hospital of complications from diabetes and pneumonia.

Three months after Elmore's death, John McCray wrote to the Reverend I. DeQuincey Newman, the newly installed state NAACP president, seeking to dispel rumors about conflicts between the NAACP and the Progressive Democrats. In that letter, McCray attempted again to set the record straight on Elmore's enormous contribution to the battle for voting rights. Without mentioning names, McCray told Newman, "On two occasions I have differed strongly with two of your former officers, a state secretary and a president." In an apparent reference to

Hinton, McCray noted "my criticism of the president developed out of his reportedly having offered the late Mr. Elmore work as a yard man around his home at a ridiculously low salary when the man was in dire need; and also out of the persistent attack upon Mr. Elmore for divers and many reasons."

McCray went on: "My reasoning was, and I do not and never will abandon it, that at one time, Mr. Elmore was the organization's big gun, one of whom it (The NAACP) was quite proud and without whom it would not have been able to develop the Richland White Primary suit as soon. . . ."[5] McCray also took aim at Simkins, without naming her, over a testimonial dinner for Judge Waring that did not include invitations to Elmore and other plaintiffs of the 1940s civil rights cases. Elmore was recognized posthumously in late 1959 at the NAACP Freedom Dinner, his Certificate of Merit sent to McCray to tender to the Elmore family.[6]

On June 21, 1981, a little more than two decades after his death and nearly thirty-five years after the end of the white primary, a memorial to Elmore was erected in Randolph Cemetery, the Black cemetery in Columbia that contained the graves of so many Reconstruction lawmakers. The W.E.B. (Waring-Elmore-Brown) organization erected the memorial and inscribed it with these words: "Sacred to the memory of George Elmore, who through unmatched courage, perseverance and personal sacrifice brought the legal action by which black people may participate in South Carolina Democratic Party primary elections—"Elmore vs. Rice, 1947." That day in 1981 was a day of recollection. US District Judge Matthew Perry, South Carolina's first Black federal judge, spoke to a gathering at Sydney Park C.M.E. Church in Columbia about Elmore's legacy. Perry, recalling his visit to the courtroom as a young man to witness the 1947 trial, said what appeared "to be an inconspicuous act" resonated across history. "What I did not appreciate was that it took no small amount of courage for a black man at the time to permit his name on a lawsuit of that time," Perry was quoted in a June 22, 1981, article in *The State*. The speakers that day also reflected how far South Carolina had come in overcoming segregation in public life. In addition to Perry, there was Boulware, Elmore's attorney, who had been appointed a Richland County judge; Columbia Municipal Court Judge Lincoln Jenkins, Perry's former law partner; and state Circuit Court Judge Ernest Finney, who would go on to become chief justice of the South Carolina Supreme Court. Even the headline that day suggested the elusiveness of historical memory: "Gathering Brings Back Past to Honor 'Forgotten' Man."[7]

More fragments emerged in the following decades. In the early 2000s, Waverly resident Donella Wilson, the woman who had remembered Laura and George as a young courting couple, recalled the gradual emptying of the shelves at the Waverly Five-and-10-Cents store and the deterioration of the Elmore family. A half-century after the lawsuit, she still recalled the empty aisles and the harassment, as well as the memory of voting on that momentous day in 1948.

Fannie Phelps Adams, a well-respected retired educator at Booker T. Washington High School, said she believed Elmore represented the doorway to full integration and lamented that he died a pauper. A Black state lawmaker, Representative Joe Neal, remembered his parents telling him of providing food to the Elmores as their situation grew more alarming. The eldest daughter of George Elmore, Naomi, confirmed the direness of the family situation, remembering that she too had to seek help from the corner grocer to supply food for the family.

Elizabeth Wallace, editorial director of Gibbs Smith Education, said the new social studies textbooks by necessity covered a lot of historical terrain. Through compelling, individual stories, she believes it will help modern school children understand a time when signs reading "Whites Only" and "Colored Entrance" were part of the southern landscape. The aim, she said, is to illuminate sometimes hidden history in order to provide students with a comprehensive historical view. "Real estate in our books is precious so we are really cognizant of the stories we are telling and how we are telling them," Wallace said in an August 2022 interview. "And we work really hard to balance. Are we getting the stories of women and other underrepresented people, are we giving a more accurate portrayal of our founding fathers and other people down through history? We don't necessarily want to paint a negative light on people but we want to tell the truth."[8]

For much of the twentieth century South Carolina schoolchildren learned their history from a small volume written and edited by a revered literary and social figure, Mary C. Simms Oliphant. Born in Barnwell County in 1891, she was the granddaughter of an even more towering South Carolina writer, William Gilmore Simms, the South's most prominent antebellum writer. The author of dozens of well-respected frontier novels and works on the American Revolution,

Simms defended slavery, advocated for secession from the North, and portrayed the South as a romantic region. Stunned at the Confederate loss, Simms retreated with his literary companions into a past that no longer existed: "Let us hold ourselves aloof," he wrote to historian and fellow conservative Edward McCrady Jr. of Charleston, "touch not, handle not, taste not anything in common with our invaders; keep up communion among ourselves, as well as we can, in all the ancient circles."[9]

Simms died in 1870, two decades before the birth of his granddaughter, Mary. But when she was asked in 1916 by the South Carolina superintendent of education to edit her grandfather's 1840 school textbook, "The History of South Carolina," she readily agreed. Her updates to the Simms history volume were adopted in 1917 and revised every five years until 1932, according to the South Carolina Encyclopedia. Then Mary Simms Oliphant was tasked with writing an entirely new South Carolina school textbook, *The New Simms History of South Carolina*, on the centennial of her grandfather's volume. It went through nine editions and remained in South Carolina classrooms until 1985. In that textbook, the memory of her grandfather's South loomed large and the vision of a Southland laid waste by Yankee invaders prevailed. White supremacy was understood to be the correct and dominant narrative. Slavery was deemed a necessary, if benign, element of the story of the state. Oliphant adjusted the narrative as the decades past. As conflict loomed in the late 1850s, Oliphant wrote in the 1940s centennial edition:

> South Carolinians were wholly mistaken in two of their most cherished beliefs: First, they felt that slave labor was necessary to the South because farming was the chief interest of this section; second, South Carolina honestly believed that there were so many slaves that their freedom would mean that the South belonged to the black race.[10]

In that same passage, she noted that freeing the enslaved "has not Africanized the South" and issued a belated lament for her fellow Carolinians: "The pity is that South Carolinians had not taken the lead themselves in freeing the slaves and thus saving the country from a brother's war." As she recalled the battles where the Confederacy prevailed—First and Second Manassas, Fredericksburg, Spotsylvania—

she reminded South Carolina children of the great Southern heroes of the day: Wade Hampton, Maxey Gregg, William H. Anderson, Benjamin Huger, among many who led the Confederate army. She painted a grim portrait of the burning of Columbia by Union General William Tecumseh Sherman and the ravaging of the state by marauding bands of Union soldiers. By this point in the war, President Abraham Lincoln had freed the enslaved of the South, and many Black men had fled to fight for the Union side. But Oliphant still pictured South Carolina's slaves as childlike and loyal, writing: "The Negroes had heard so much about the 'Yankees' that they were in deadly terror of them. As Sherman's army marched by him one little darkey cried out in amazement: 'Why, dey's folks! I tought dey was animals!'"[11] There was no mention of free Black people and those who had escaped bondage who had fought for the Union army.

Under Oliphant's pen, the federal Reconstruction period following the war was deemed "the state's darkest day" as white South Carolinians surveyed a state in economic ruins and the reality that forty thousand of their native sons lay dead on the battlefield. Even more alarming was the question of what to do about the newly emancipated freedmen in their midst. While slavery was abolished, she wrote, "Very strict regulations, however, were provided for the freed slaves. Most of the Negroes were ignorant and some of them were almost savages. All were unaccustomed to taking care of themselves. The sudden freeing of the slaves meant a tremendous problem for the whites." Modern day historians would note that the regulations, or Black Codes, imposed a new enslavement among the recently emancipated, with strict rules for working and interacting with white people. And while Oliphant gave a brief nod of admiration to the freedoms of the new 1868 constitution, she framed Reconstruction as a terrible period overall. "The horrors of war were nothing compared to those of this period when Congress was 'reconstructing' the State. It was the darkest and bitterest time we have ever known. The Carpet Baggers, Scalawags, and the Negroes were called Radicals. Backed by United States troops, they took complete charge of affairs. They called themselves the Republican Party in South Carolina and to this day South Carolina Republicans are thought ill of because of the Scalawags and Carpet Baggers."[12] That, of course, changed in the twentieth century as Republicans became the dominant political party.

Elmore's children and their contemporaries read those lessons of war and Reconstruction as they grew up in the 1940s and 1950s. They never learned in official textbooks about the anti-slavery Grimke sisters of Charleston, the underground railroad, or Black Codes. Some Black teachers adapted the lessons to focus on the progress of Black citizens rather than the dismal portrait of ignorance and poverty, although it was imperative they not draw attention from white school officials. In the looming fight over integration, foreshadowed in the battle over the white primary, South Carolina politicians in 1956 passed legislation that made it illegal for state or city employees to be members of the NAACP. Many Black teachers lost their jobs and had to leave the state, although others remained in their posts while supporting the organization in secret.

A Great Depression, two world wars, and industrialization introduced an expanded view of the state by citizens who had traveled outside its borders. The story of the state taught in public schools also changed as lawmakers, led by forward-thinking governors such as Richard Riley (1979–1987), began to fund public education to prepare students for life in a world beyond the South's borders. Educators understood that students must grapple with the knotty complexities of history if they hoped to become educated citizens in a global democracy.

As South Carolina emerged into a more progressive era, new textbooks were adopted in the 1980s and 1990s that began to explain more fully the state's racial complexities and to make sense of what had gone before. The romanticism of the Lost Cause, which painted the South as noble and brave in defeat, gave way to a more comprehensive portrait of the South during the antebellum period, the Civil War, and Reconstruction. The lives of the enslaved, who were ignored or dismissed as minor players in a world where white people reigned supreme, were gradually, if grudgingly, acknowledged. In the 1980s, Governor Riley began a serious examination of the failings of the state's public education system, persuading the legislature to pass the Education Improvement Act, which implemented a comprehensive approach to improving teaching and raising student performance.[13] Subsequent education reforms included the passage of the 1998 Education Accountability Act, which required the State Board of Education to establish specific standards in math, English, language arts, science, and social studies. According to the act, "the standards must be reflective of the highest level of academic skills with the rigor necessary to improve the curriculum and instruction in South Carolina's schools so that students are encouraged to learn at unprecedented levels and must be reflective of the highest level of academic skills at each grade level."[14]

South Carolina requires a comprehensive examination of state standards every ten years. A team of educators develops and revises the standards, which are then released for public comment. The committee may suggest historical events and figures to include. It is up to textbook authors to determine what becomes part of the narrative. Editors are assigned by the textbook company to write particular sections of history and then the passage are sent to reviewers in the state, including historians, college and university professors, and experts at state and local museums. The process takes about three years from development of standards and public comment to the finished textbook.

Around the same time as lawmakers were wrestling with state education standards, University of South Carolina historian Walter Edgar began the arduous work of writing his sweeping *South Carolina: A History*.[15] The 776-page history brought into the historical narrative Black people, women, Native Americans, millworkers, and others who had been only bystanders in the grand cavalcade of historical figures such as the Lords Proprietors, Revolutionary War heroes, and Civil War generals. The book, published in 1999, landed at an important juncture in South Carolina, as its citizens hungered for an expanded view of history beyond the old tales of secession and the Confederacy. "I brought people into the story where they should be," Edgar said in a 2012 interview. "I didn't force anybody into the story."[16] Scholars contributed an explosion of new scholarship into enslavement and rebellion in the nineteenth century and segregation and the Black civil rights struggle in the twentieth century. A new generation of South Carolina students became the beneficiaries of this expanded view of history.

On a crisp fall day in 2022, as thousands of South Carolina schoolchildren were beginning to delve into their new social studies textbooks, the son of George Elmore came to the University of South Carolina. He was there by invitation to tell a class of University of South Carolina Honors College students what his life was like before and after his father agreed to be the plaintiff in the *Elmore v. Rice* lawsuit. The eighty-four-year-old Cresswell recounted scenes of a bucolic childhood growing up in the lower Waverly neighborhood on Tree Street with his older sister Naomi and two younger sisters, Vernadine and Yolande. The street was unpaved and narrow, but he recalled delightful afternoons as children drew circles in the dirt outside their front stoops and shot marbles. At Waverly School, he earned perfect attendance under the watchful eye of principal Cresswell W. Madden, an educator who impressed the elder Elmores so much that they named their only son after him. After school he would return with his mother or father to the Waverly dime store where jars of penny candy, cookies, and ice cream cones awaited him. The store was popular in the neighborhood and a small storefront hub of activity for his Black neighbors, who could scour the shelves for school supplies and household goods.

He described a childhood overflowing with strong family memories. "My experiences in Columbia were very good in my early years and, in my later years, were not so good," he told the class. As a child, he could not walk on the grounds of the university or play in nearby Valley Park because it was for white people only. But the structure of segregation mattered little to him and his family until his father became active in politics and joined the newly formed Progressive Democratic Party in 1944. "He became very interested in changing the politics of Columbia," Cresswell told the class. "I know he was very distraught that you had to pay a poll tax and read to be able to vote."

Cresswell remembers nothing of the courtroom drama of the 1947 *Elmore v. Rice* case. He does not know if his mother attended the three-day trial. But he remembers the jubilation of his father on April 18, 1948, when the US Supreme Court refused to review the case and let the victory in *Elmore v. Rice* stand. "That was probably the most joyous moment of his life," he recalled. "Joy and jubilation—he was just so excited that the challenge that he took on was successful."

The Elmores's happy family life soon gave away to fear and heightened tension as Elmore was subjected to economic reprisals and threats of bodily harm, he recalled. They witnessed cross burnings that destroyed the family's tranquility. After losing his businesses, his home, and his wife to mental illness, Elmore became nomadic, searching for work in Washington and then returning to living out his final days in the Dutch Fork area of South Carolina near Columbia. By the time of Elmore's death in 1959, two of his children, Naomi and Cresswell, had already moved to New York to live, first, with their Aunt Esther Elmore Swygert, and then on their own. Naomi, who had graduated from Benedict College with a degree in music and French, went to work in the federal sector as clerical staff at the Brooklyn Navy Yard and for the Federal Aviation Administration. She married and had two children. She died on August 22, 2022, shortly before her ninetieth birthday. After studying at Queens College and New York University, Cresswell earned certification as an aircraft and powerplant mechanic at the Academy of Aeronautics in Queens and embarked on a decades-long aviation career, first with Pan American World Airways (Pan Am), and then with the Department of Defense in the acquisition and logistics support community acquiring aircraft and logistics support for the US Navy/Marine weapon systems. Vernadine and Yolande, the two youngest daughters, left South Carolina shortly after their father's death in 1959 for New York to live in the home of their aunt, who had welcomed their older siblings. Vernadine was seventeen and Yolande was soon to be ten years old. They finished high school in Jamaica, Queens. Vernadine married and went on to a career with the New York Power Authority. Yolande obtained advanced college degrees, was married, and had two children. She died on July 27, 2021. Except for rare visits, the Elmore girls never returned to South Carolina, finding the memories of their life there too painful to dwell upon.

In the Elmore family, the legacy of their patriarch is cherished each Election Day as a way to remember and honor him. Family members register to vote as soon as they turn eighteen and make sure to vote whenever there is a primary or election, recalling the sacrifice of their grandfather and great-grandfather. Vanessa L. Elmore, born in 1960 a year after her grandfather's death, said she and her two brothers were fortified by stories from her mother and maternal grandmother. The women recalled vividly the bitter story of her grandfather's struggle. Older Black residents would also whisper of his courage, recognizing in Vanessa's physical features something of her grandfather's countenance. "Voting to me, if I don't do early voting, I'm the first one in line on Election Day," she told the class. "I will always vote because he fought so hard and sacrificed so many things." She elicited knowing laughter from the students when she added: "It is something we've instilled in our children. Our children know that if you don't vote, you better not let us find out."

Cresswell told the class the life of the Elmore family was "torn and tattered." But he said he is convinced that his father never privately lamented his personal circumstances nor looked back with remorse at his decision to act. "One thing that my father taught me and said to me: In spite of everything that he went through he would do it again. He never had any regret. And he was glad he won." Cresswell echoed the words of his late sister, Yolande, who described a boldness about their father that set him apart. "I never felt or heard him have a regret," she said in a 2003 interview. "I believe he was visionary."

For years the Elmore family longed for public recognition of George Elmore as a patriot, a South Carolinian who cleared the way for a more democratic way of life. Now the children of George and Laura Elmore and succeeding Elmore generations can turn the pages of a South Carolina textbook along with a new generation of South Carolinians, to learn that story. They can listen as historians place his singular act of bravery in context with other notable moments in a turbulent decade that eventually altered the life of the South and his native state. The man once disdained by white leaders as a potential Communist and agitator now takes his place in the public arena as a patriot, perhaps a visionary, ahead of his time in his own time.

Conclusion

The Legacy of Voting Rights

My great-grandfather, along with many, many,
many others, fought for these rights. And we should
go and express these rights when it's time to. That's
how I feel about it.

—Tiarra M. Elmore, great-granddaughter
of George Elmore

Nearly two decades after the end of the white primary and eight years
after the death of George Elmore, a bright young civil rights activist
was urged to return to South Carolina to register Black voters. James L.
Felder had grown up in Sumter, earned an undergraduate degree from
Clark College in Atlanta, and was armed with a law degree from Howard University. He had served honorably in the US military. As an Army
sergeant and member of the Third U.S. Infantry Regiment known as
"The Old Guard," he served as a pallbearer and guarded the body of
slain President John F. Kennedy. As a child Felder had witnessed strict
segregation in his hometown; as a young man he had marched in civil
rights demonstrations and saw that a revolution was taking place in
his native South. Eighty years of white resistance to Black participation
in elections—a winding tortuous path that historian and law professor W. Lewis Burke described as full of "killing, cheating, legislating
and lying"—was gradually eroding.[1] Vernon Jordan, a rising Black
power broker and head of the Atlanta-based Voter Education Project,
recruited Felder as part of an ambitious southern voter registration
effort that would transform the South's electoral landscape. Reverend Newman, the United Methodist pastor and NAACP leader whose
measured authority and prophetic voice carried protesters through
the 1950s and 1960s, weighed in to ensure Felder would return to his
native state. Modjeska Simkins, still a force to be reckoned with,

added her voice.[2] The Voter Education Project (VEP) operated under the nonpartisan Southern Regional Council and coordinated voter registration drives of five civil rights organizations—the NAACP, the Southern Christian Leadership Conference (SCLC), the Urban League, the Student Nonviolent Coordinating Committee (SNCC), and the Congress of Racial Equality (CORE).

Elmore and the NAACP had cracked open the door to voter registration by smashing the white primary. Since 1948, about fifty thousand Black South Carolinians had managed to successfully register to vote. After the primary victory, Eugene A. R. Montgomery, an NAACP field director, recalled a concerted effort to educate Black citizens who knew virtually nothing about the voting process. "It was part of my job to teach people how to register. None of us had ever voted. None of us had ever registered," Montgomery explained in an oral interview in 1980 with University of South Carolina professor Grace Jordan McFadden. "So, we had this whole educational process to go through." There was, he recalled, an insidious "do-nothing" attitude among ordinary citizens, spawned by the entrenched fear of white retribution. "These were privileges that they had never had before, and it was completely new. So many of them were afraid, let's say, to vote, to go down to register to vote," he said. "And it took quite a bit of time to get them to move forward, to drop that fear, and to understanding the meaning of the ballot and what it could mean to us in South Carolina."[3]

John McCray had earlier attempted to combat that trepidation with a hard-charging editorial aimed at rallying the timid. In a front-page editorial in the May 6, 1950, edition of the *Lighthouse and Informer* headlined "Get Up or Shut Up," McCray said it was time "for the Negro to get up off the ground." He predicted at least two hundred thousand Black citizens, maybe even three hundred thousand, could be qualified to vote in the July 1950 primaries. "They know under what pain they have been put, and of what efforts are exerted to keep them ineffective and dawdling people, the doormats of the race bigots, the Dixiecrats and those who believe and say that when God created man, He meant for one man to keep his foot on the neck of another," he wrote. Now, McCray said, it was time to "slap the racial demagogue in the teeth and perhaps knock out a few of them; and he can do all of these things through the simple expedient of the ballot, the right to full use of which he now has—if he qualifies by June 10, that is; get registered to vote."[4]

McCray's optimism was not matched by the numbers in those early years. The number of registered Black voters plateaued at about fifty thousand as white registrars became more creative in employing tactics to reject Black applicants. Many of those applicants had limited reading and writing skills and were baffled at the convoluted, trick questions often posed to them about the US Constitution. In the Lowcountry, Septima Poinsette Clark had lost her teaching position because she was a member of the NAACP. She began teaching at the Highlander Folk School in Tennessee, which was preparing Blacks and white people in the South to prepare for peaceful integration. At Highlander, Clark and other leaders developed a plan to launch adult Citizenship Schools that would eventually come under the auspices of the Southern Christian Leadership Conference. Clark, her cousin Bernice Robinson, and Esau Jenkins, a community activist who operated a bus from Johns Island to Charleston, set up the first citizenship school on Johns Island in 1957. They recognized that Black citizens could not take their rightful place in society without an appreciation of their constitutional rights. "On Johns Island, in the year of 1948, I saw the condition of the people who had been working on the plantations for many years. And I knew that we were not able to do the things that would need to be done unless we could get people registered citizens," Jenkins wrote in *Ain't We Got a Right to the Tree of Life*, a memoir of life on Johns Island. The success was evident in the numbers in Charleston County alone. "In 1954 in the county [of Charleston] there were 'round about five or six thousand Negroes registered," Jenkins recalled. "In 1964, almost fourteen thousand. So everybody is jubilant for the Highlander Folk School, who have helped them see the light."[5]

With the passage of the 1964 Civil Rights Act and the 1965 Voting Rights Act, southern states were put on notice that they could no longer engage in elaborate subterfuges to suppress the Black vote. And that, according to Felder, is when the tangible power of the ballot box was revealed, not only to shocked white politicians who had historically controlled the vote but to ordinary Black citizens who for generations had avoided the polls as a matter of survival. Nowhere was that more apparent than in the actions of the state's most powerful politician, US Senator Strom Thurmond. As more Black voters became registered, Felder watched as Thurmond took heed of the changing landscape and finally learned how to properly address the state's Black population. "Ol'

Strom Thurmond used to say he couldn't say 'Negro' right. He would say 'nigras, the nigras,'" Felder recalled in a November 2022 interview. Shortening "Negro" to "nigra" was a kind of passive slur that educated white persons could level without appearing to engage in more hateful language. As the VEP's voter registration drive began to reap results during Felder's tenure between 1967 and 1969, Felder witnessed a change in Thurmond's language and demeanor.

"We got 100,000 blacks registered to vote and all of a sudden ol' Strom learned how to say 'Negro,'" Felder recalled. "We got 150,000 registered, and Strom Thurmond was sending out letters 'My Dear Black Constituents, can I be of service to you?'" When the Voter Education Project enrolled two hundred thousand Black voters in South Carolina, "Strom Thurmond was the first of all of the southern congress persons to hire a black staffer. . . . Strom knew how to count votes."[6] Other southern politicians, who like Thurmond had vehemently opposed integration and threatened a second civil war over the race question, also softened their stances when it came to providing constituent services. For Felder, the story illustrated what Black leaders had recognized in their decades-long quest for equal rights: The ballot box was the key to unlocking full American citizenship. Before 1965, there were eight Black elected officials in South Carolina, four in Eastover and four in Beaufort, Felder said. After the Voting Rights Act, hundreds of Black South Carolinians stepped up to run for local boards and councils as well as the state legislature. In 1970, Felder became one of those candidates. Felder, I. S. Leevy Johnson of Columbia, and Herbert Fielding of Charleston, were elected to the South Carolina Legislature, the first Black men to serve in the State House since Reconstruction.

Thurmond had already gone on record against the Civil Rights Acts of 1957, 1960, and 1964. He had engaged in the longest filibuster in the US Senate in 1957 in a dramatic, if unsuccessful, bid to defeat the 1957 legislation. He attempted another filibuster to quash the 1964 Civil Rights Act. A year later, he lambasted the Voting Rights Act, saying it would clear the path for illiterates and criminals to vote in South Carolina and, perhaps, serve on juries. "This proves that Martin Luther King and his kind will never be satisfied," Thurmond told a Columbia television station in February 1965.[7] Even before President Lyndon Johnson signed the 1965 Voting Rights Act into law, Thurmond was seeking refuge in the Republican Party, which now looked to capture disgruntled white southerners fearful of school integration and the prospect of racial equality. Thurmond switched political parties and endorsed Republican Barry Goldwater for president. He claimed there was no longer room in the now-transformed, big-tent Democratic Party for his views on states' rights and federal intrusion into the affairs of the states. Other southern Democrats followed.

Within months of the August 1965 passage of the Voting Rights Act, South Carolina went to court to challenge parts of the legislation that required federal oversight, or preclearance, of voting measures. Under the act, states like South Carolina that had a literacy test and voter registration or turnout of less than 50 percent in the 1964 presidential election had to seek approval from the Department of Justice before enacting any voting laws. The act outlawed the literacy tests that had been infamous in South Carolina as a means of culling voters. On the first day of oral arguments in *South Carolina v. Katzenbach*, South Carolina special counsel David W. Robinson II explained to the justices that South Carolina had a "light" voter registration record because 20 percent of the state's adults were illiterate.[8] In 1964, about 56 percent of eligible voters were registered but only 38 percent cast ballots in the 1964 presidential election. "What Congress has really said by picking these factors is that, South Carolina, if you have a literacy test, if you have a lot of illiterates, you're bound to be guilty of racial discrimination," Robinson said in oral arguments. "This is what I'm asking you, because we have a lot of illiterates and because we keep them from voting, we are guilty of racial discrimination. Now gentlemen, this is just arbitrary."[9] The Supreme Court by a vote 8–1 rejected South Carolina's appeal.

Chief Justice Earl Warren, writing for the majority, said Congress had the power to stop blatant discrimination under the enforcement powers of the Fifteenth Amendment. "The Voting Rights Act was designed by Congress to banish the blight of racial discrimination in voting, which has infected the electoral process in parts of our country for nearly a century," Warren wrote. "The Act creates stringent new remedies for voting discrimination where it persists on a pervasive scale, and, in addition, the statute strengthens existing remedies for pockets of voting discrimination elsewhere in the country." Warren noted that Congress had spent many hours in hearings examining racial discrimination in the South. The House spent three days in debates, while the US Senate spent twenty-six days on the bill's merits. The House approved the bill by a vote of 328–74, and the measure passed the Senate by a margin of 79–18. "Two points emerge vividly from the voluminous legislative history of the Act contained in the committee hearings and floor debates," Warren wrote. "First: Congress felt itself confronted by an insidious and pervasive evil which had been perpetuated in certain parts of our country through unremitting and ingenious defiance of the Constitution. Second: Congress concluded that the unsuccessful remedies which it had prescribed in the past would have to be replaced by sterner and more elaborate measures to satisfy the clear commands of the Fifteenth Amendment."[10]

After 1965, Thurmond and other southern senators embraced a political strategy to slow-walk civil rights and lure traditional white southern Democrats to the modern Republican Party, the Grand Old Party (GOP). That southern strategy deployed during the 1968 presidential campaign of Richard Nixon played on the fears of white southerners and cemented the transformation of the South to a modern Republican stronghold. Harry S. Dent Sr.—a South Carolinian who worked for Thurmond, headed the South Carolina Republican Party, and went on to work in the Nixon White House—was among the key architects of the plan. By coupling appeals for "law and order" with concerns about federal overreach in hot-button issues such as school busing, Nixon and his campaign could claim that race was on the margins. In his 1978 memoir, *The Prodigal South Returns to Power,* Dent claimed the southern strategy was not overtly racist but aimed at returning the South to its rightful place in the nation, no longer viewed as a bastion of illiterates and rednecks as it had been portrayed in Hollywood and in books. By the time he departed politics to become a lay Christian minister in 1981, Dent had determined he owed some penance for the dirty tricks of the Nixon White House. "When I look back, my biggest regret now is anything I did that stood in the way of the rights of black people . . . or any people," he told the *Washington Post.*[11] Dent died in 2007. As years passed few remembered that it was Republicans, under the banner carried by President Abraham Lincoln, who had collapsed the Confederacy and won the Civil War. It was Republicans in Congress who had historically championed the rights of freedmen and made way for the passage of the Thirteenth, Fourteenth, and Fifteenth Amendments.

The Voting Rights Act was reauthorized in 1970, again in 1975, in 1982, and in 2006 with an update to the formula in 1975. Under the 1965 act, South Carolina, Alabama, Alaska, Georgia, Louisiana, Mississippi, and Virginia were required to submit proof that any proposed voting change did not deny or abridge the right to vote on account of race. In 1975, an additional coverage formula was added to address potential discrimination against voters who could not speak or read English. This expanded the number of states or jurisdictions coming under the scrutiny of the Justice Department, although a process of "bailout" was also established. In the intervening years, South Carolina submitted dozens of applications related to its voting and registration practices. As a result of the Voting Rights Act, at-large legislative districts, gerrymandered legislative maps, and other potentially discriminatory practices came under federal inspection and were often abandoned. By 1982, Thurmond cast his vote in favor of the extension of the Voting Rights Act.

The legislation remained resilient through several decades of reauthorization debates. But the South Carolina challenge in 1966 was just the beginning of a barrage of ligation by states and jurisdictions to hollow out the law and remove jurisdictions from Justice Department scrutiny. The biggest blow came in June 2013 in an Alabama case when the US Supreme Court ruled in *Shelby County v. Holder* that the formula used to determine which jurisdictions must be subject to preclearance was unconstitutional.[12] Officials in Shelby County, Alabama, had filed a lawsuit in US District Court arguing that Section 4 and Section 5 of the Voting Rights Act was unconstitutional. South Carolina and six other states that were historically required to submit voting changes filed "friend of the court" briefs on behalf of Shelby County. The district court upheld the constitutionality of the sections as did the appeals court. The high court reversed those decisions. Chief Justice John Roberts, writing for the 5–4 majority, declared that the formula in Section 4 of the Voting Rights Act, last updated in the 1975 reauthorization, was no longer relevant and that the America of the 1960s and 1970s no longer existed.

"Our country has changed, and while any racial discrimination in voting is too much, Congress must ensure that the legislation it passes to remedy that problem speaks to current conditions," Roberts wrote. History did not end in 1965, Roberts noted. "By the time the Act was reauthorized in 2006, there had been 40 more years of it. "In assessing the 'current need' for a preclearance system that treats States differently from one another today, that history cannot be ignored. During that time, largely because of the Voting Rights Act, voting tests were abolished, disparities in voter registration and turnout due to race were erased, and African Americans attained political office in record numbers. And yet the coverage formula that Congress reauthorized in 2006 ignores these developments, keeping the focus on decades-old data relevant to decades-old problems, rather than current data reflecting current needs."[13] For the court's conservative majority, singling out the southern states that had for decades thwarted Black voting was no longer needed and was antithetical to federalism.

But in writing for the minority, Justice Ruth Bader Ginsberg noted that the Department of Justice, between 1982 and 2006, had blocked more than seven hundred voting changes based on a determination that the changes were discriminatory. "The sad irony of today's decision lies in its utter failure to grasp why the VRA has proven effective. The Court appears to believe that the VRA's success in eliminating the specific devices extant in 1965 means that preclearance is no longer needed."[14]

Almost immediately after the Shelby County decisions, states that had previously required Justice Department preclearance began imposing stricter voting regulations. The same day, Texas officials announced that it would put into practice a restrictive voter-identification law that had previously been blocked. Mississippi and Alabama also put into place voter ID legislation that had previously been blocked, according to the Brennan Center for Justice at the New York University School of Law.[15]

South Carolina had already enacted a voter ID law in 2011 that required voters to show one of five photo identifications in order to vote. The Justice Department blocked implementation of the law in December 2011 under the Voting Rights Act, arguing that the law discriminated against minorities.[16] The state sued. Testimony at trial noted about 36 percent of the 178,000 registered voters who did not have a driver's license or Department of Motor Vehicles (DMV) photo identification in 2010 were racial minorities. In October 2012, the US District Court for the District of Columbia approved the new law, but delayed implementation until 2013 elections. Lawmakers said they passed the law in order to prevent people from using fake identifies to vote, although there have been no cases of such voter fraud in the state. Groups such as the League of Women Voters in South Carolina and the American Civil Liberties Union have gone on record in opposition to voter-ID measures, citing the heightened potential for voter suppression.

Now two decades into the twenty-first century, the Republican Party, much like the southern Democratic Party in the post-Civil War and Jim Crow eras, has led the effort to erect guardrails to voting. Conservatives say that is the best way to protect the integrity of elections. Civil rights groups and nonpartisan organizations have long regarded those claims with suspicion, citing the limitations as voter suppression cloaked in modern-day language. The nonpartisan Brennan Center has analyzed voter fraud in the US and determined it would be statistically akin to being struck by lightning. The most common concept of voter fraud—impersonating another voter in order to cast double ballots—has occurred in rare instances, but analysts suggest it more likely involved clerical errors. Still, the debate rages on.

Today in South Carolina, there are more than 3.4 million registered voters, a figure that would likely astound Elmore and the men and women of his generation who fought for the ballot. Black registered voters now hover at one million while white registered voters number 2.4 million. The 1960s-era voting drives that Felder and his colleagues in the Voter Education Project instituted are a thing of the past. But widespread election disinformation has led many Americans to distrust the electoral system and engage in conspiracy theories that have no basis in fact. Civil rights organizations remain vigilant about the continued weakening of the Voting Rights Act, including efforts to limit who can bring cases of alleged discrimination to the Justice Department.

Tiarra Elmore, a great-granddaughter of George Elmore, has ruminated on the legacy of her ancestor in light of modern-day debates over voting and the threat of voter suppression. She worries that the divisiveness and partisanship of the current age threatens democratic institutions and alienates younger voters.[17]

"I feel like my generation, they don't feel like it matters," Tiarra Elmore said in a 2023 interview, that whoever is elected to office, politics remains an insider's game with little impact on the lives of everyday citizens. "They just think it's going to be a messed-up United States."

She has engaged in fierce discussions with her friends to dispute that attitude, armed with a history lesson that cuts close to the bone.

"Look, it's not about what is going on now, it's about what went on in the past," she said, "and how our ancestors and everyone else fought for us to get where we are today.

"Yeah, we still have a long way to go. We do. We still have a very, very long way to go. But we are here now; these are our rights. My great-grandfather, along with many, many, many others, fought for these rights. And we should go and express these rights when it's time to. That's how I feel about it."

ACKNOWLEDGMENTS

I first encountered George Elmore's name in what I thought to be an obscure voting rights case from the 1940s. The year was 2003. I was a journalist at *The State*, South Carolina's capital newspaper, charged with writing a story about voting rights in South Carolina in advance of a civil rights conference. The Citadel in Charleston had organized an impressive four-day event bringing together, after many decades, the people who had fought to desegregate schools, lunch counters, and other public places. The program featured distinguished jurists, including US District Judge Matthew J. Perry, former governors John C. West and Ernest F. "Fritz" Hollings, and noted historians, including John Hope Franklin, Dan Carter, and Peter F. Lau. The ghosts of others who had fought for the end of Jim Crow segregation—or, conversely, pushed back against the end of the white "southern way of life"—hovered over the pristine military campus. Those figures included Levi Byrd, a Cheraw plumber who had built a formidable state NAACP organization in the 1940s; the Reverend Joseph A. DeLaine, who had led rural Clarendon County parents in their fight for equal education; and Judge J. Waties Waring, who had issued a series of groundbreaking legal opinions in the 1940s and 1950s that began to clear a path to full citizenship for the state's Black residents. The conference was both a reckoning and a wrestling with a past that had been sealed off for decades.

Elmore, a portly Columbia five-and-dime store owner, was present in spirit there too. It was Waring who issued an opinion in July 1947 in favor of Elmore, who had challenged the exclusion of Black voters from what was then known as the "white primary." Although I was aware of the impact of the 1965 Voting Rights Act on the South's voting history, I knew little of white primaries or their historical significance. As I leafed through the Elmore case file, I learned that Elmore was, in the language of the times, a Negro, a "duly and qualified elector under the laws and Constitution of the United States." He had presented himself on August 13, 1946, to cast a ballot in Columbia's Ward 9 in the Democratic primary. He was turned away by poll managers because he was not a white person.

From a distance of five decades the case file was intriguing to read. But I was most curious about the man who was willing to place his name on a federal lawsuit in a southern city that was strictly segregated and wedded to the notion of a glorious, if ill-fated, past. Who was George Elmore? Calls to historians and voting-rights experts helped filled in the outlines of his life and the repercussions he suffered. An iconic photograph of a young Elmore from the late 1920s or early 1930s, taken by Columbia photographer Richard Samuel Roberts when Elmore was a taxi driver for Blue Ribbon taxi club, provided a glimpse of his physical presence. There were stories of troubles he suffered in the wake of the lawsuit, economic pressures, crosses burned, bankruptcy. A small monument to Elmore, erected in 1981, sat inside Randolph Cemetery, a resting place for Black Columbia residents since the 1800s.

Still, as I worked toward a newsroom deadline, my search for close relatives—someone to humanize Elmore—was proving fruitless. I finally connected with Vanessa Elmore, an adult granddaughter of George Elmore. Born in 1960, one year after her grandfather's passing, she only knew outlines of his story. She and her brothers, Ronald and Barry, had rarely shared their family's story—"No one would have believed me," Ronald Elmore noted dryly—nor did they expect to see their grandfather's name recorded in any South Carolina history books. But they were passionate about voting and keenly aware of his sacrifice.

They, in turn, led me to an aunt, Yolande Elmore Cole, who provided what I thought was an illuminating observation about her father. There was a boldness about him, said Cole, who was born two years after her father first went to court and was nine years old when he died on February 25, 1959. "I never felt or heard him have a regret. I believe he was visionary." Eventually, I met the other children of George Elmore—son Cresswell and daughters Naomi and Vernadine—who had left an unforgiving South Carolina for the North after the breakup of their family. For a period of time they had also left behind their mother, Laura Delaney Elmore, who had suffered a mental breakdown in the years following the case and been institutionalized.

The Waverly Five-and-10-Cents store anchored the east end of a row of establishments that served the Black community of Waverly in Columbia. The Gervais Street storefront was demolished in 2012, to the chagrin of city leaders and preservationists. Columbia Architectural Survey. Local History Digital Collections. Courtesy of Richland Library.

Occasionally I would return to the story of George Elmore as I continued my daily journalism career. In 2008, when Barack Obama was elected the nation's first Black president, a few people called to remind me that Elmore had a hand in his election, even from a distance of a half century. There was an ill-fated effort in July 2012 to save the Waverly Five-and-10-Cents store Elmore had operated at 2313-17 Gervais Street. But that too disappeared into memory, acknowledged only by an historical marker at the site.

I thought he deserved a fuller journalistic narrative, although I knew there was not much in the historical record on which to hang such a story. He had left behind only a scrapbook of clippings.

In 2015, I left the news business to teach in the journalism school at the University of South Carolina under then dean and former CNN senior Washington correspondent Charles Bierbauer. Conversations with editors at USC Press gave me encouragement. By the fall of 2021

I had a book contract in hand. In January 2022, I was awarded a grant from the university's Racial Justice and Equity Research Fund. The journalism school's grants manager Terri Moorer and associate professor Brooke McKeever guided me through that process. Tom Reichert, who succeeded Bierbauer as dean of USC's College of Information and Communications, supported my research with an incentive award. Andrea Tanner, who, along with Dean Bierbauer had hired me to teach in the journalism school, urged me to teach a class related to my research in the South Carolina Honors College, where she is now an associate dean.

The class, "Voting Rights and Civil Wrongs: Journalism in 1940s-era South Carolina," provided an opportunity to explore with my students the decade that served as a springboard for significant political and social change in South Carolina. As it turned out, none of my Honors College students, including native-born South Carolinians, were aware of seminal civil rights events of the 1940s or the people who inhabited the decade. I could see their quizzical expressions as I ticked off the names of historic figures we would be studying—Elmore, newspaper-man John McCray, teacher and civil rights activist Modjeska Simkins, NAACP leader James Hinton, the blinded World War II soldier Isaac Woodard, federal Judge J. Waties Waring. How did these people fit into the narrative of the 1960s civil rights struggle they had come to know in elementary and high school textbooks? Not handily, as it turned out. But they were eager to read original documents and old newspapers as they studied post-Civil War South Carolina, Reconstruction, Black Codes, and the rise of the Ku Klux Klan. They didn't need me to explain the roots of the Black southern struggle; they found that for themselves in public documents and online archives. They asked good questions, including the perhaps unanswerable question of why decent, ordinary white people in the 1940s did not rise up en masse to protest the devastating lynchings and cross burnings, the attacks on returning soldiers, the economic squeeze suffered by Elmore and others who challenged the status quo. They listened to first-person accounts of growing up in 1940s South Carolina. Cresswell Elmore, George Elmore's only son, was among them. He and two of his adult children, Vanessa and Ronald, told a family story that was "tattered and torn" but still yielded great lessons of sacrifice and patriotism.

Elmore's challenge to segregation was tucked amid an avalanche of lawsuits that eventually led to the passage of the federal 1964 Civil

Rights Act and the 1965 Voting Rights Act. His willingness to participate in the dismantling of voting barriers and segregation shaped his life and, likely, his death. His story is both a South Carolina story and an American story. It is a story that runs like a through line from Civil War South Carolina to the twenty-first century, where Elmore's educated and entrepreneurial descendants enjoy the benefits of American life scarcely dreamed of by their grandfather and great-grandfather. Ultimately, it is a story about patriotism and a belief in the American Creed.

While this narrative is rooted in history, I undertook it as a journalist, relying extensively on interviews bolstered by a deep dive into old newspapers, documents, and personal papers of South Carolinians. Ehren Foley, my editor at USC Press, and I decided we wanted it to be a book that would be accessible to those who may know a lot, or only a little, about a time in South Carolina that is no more. I am grateful for his expertise and his never-wavering belief that the book would become a reality. Any errors in the manuscript are mine. I could not have drawn this portrait of Elmore without the resources of the South Caroliniana Library at the University of South Carolina, South Carolina Political Collections housed inside USC's Ernest F. Hollings Special Collections Library, the South Carolina State Library, the South Carolina Department of Archives and History, Historic Columbia, and the Richland Library, with its fine Walker Local and Family History Center. Special thanks go to Alexander Moore, Henry G. Fulmer, Herbert J. Hartsook, Beth Bilderback, Graham Duncan, Todd Hoppock, Elizabeth West, Dorothy Walker, Kate Moore, Nicholas Doyle, Abigail Cole, Margaret Dunlap, Steve Tuttle, Dawn Mullin, Robin Waites, and Katherine "Kat" Allen, among others. USC history professor Bobby Donaldson, now director of the university's Center for Civil Rights History and Research, provided crucial interpretation of mid-twentieth century life in South Carolina for Black residents. North Carolina videographer Elliot Blumberg and USC journalism school colleague Manie Robinson captured compelling video interviews. Credit goes to Blumberg for the book title. I am particularly indebted to those who were born in pre-World War II South Carolina and shared vivid recollections of growing up in segregated times. They include James L. Felder, Doris Glymph Greene, Melvin S. Hodges, Gloria Shumpert James, Hemphill P. Pride II, and the Rev. Simon Bouie, among others.

No journalist works alone and that is true of me. My family, including my husband, Jay Taylor, and adult children, Catherine Ann Taylor and Henry Taylor, encouraged me on this journey, keeping me fortified with coffee and serving as sounding boards as I shaped the narrative. My sister, Patricia Click, a retired University of Virginia humanities professor who has written and lectured extensively about the freedmen's colony on North Carolina's Roanoke Island, helped me with thorny research questions. My mother-in-law, Ann Taylor Campbell, always offered encouragement. Ben and Annette Sparks, friends and mentors, were early and enthusiastic readers of the beginning chapter, having illuminated the southern struggle for racial justice in their own work. Claudia Smith Brinson, a fellow journalist who has chronicled South Carolina civil rights stories in two critically acclaimed USC Press books, offered unabashed encouragement for the project, as did my wonderful circle of friends who listened to me ramble on about the past. The memory of my late parents certainly guided my work.

Finally, and most importantly, this book could not have become a reality without the family of George Elmore, who were modest in their hopes but always believed that his story and sacrifice should be part of the canon of South Carolina history. Cresswell Elmore was particularly instrumental in bringing his father's story to a larger audience. He sat for innumerable interviews and was always willing to answer questions and plumb his memories about the Elmores's life in 1940s Columbia. As I was working on this book, South Carolina educators determined that the Elmore story and an explanation of the white primary case should be taught to South Carolina public school students as part of their education on the twentieth century civil rights movement. Elmore's photographs and story are now part of the second edition of *The South Carolina Journey,* for eighth grade, and *United States and South Carolina Studies, Part 2,* for fifth grade. After many years, George Elmore has finally taken his place alongside other notable South Carolinians.

NOTES

Introduction

1. Epigraph reference: Letter to Mr. James H. Hinton from C. Arthur Pompey, August 16, 1948, John Henry McCray Papers, box 3, folder 17, South Caroliniana Library, University of South Carolina, https://digital.tcl.sc.edu/digital/collection/p17173coll38/id/7537/rec/5.
2. Gunnar Myrdal, *An American Dilemma: The Negro Problem and Modern Democracy* (New York: Harper & Brothers, 1944), 997.
3. Letter to (Columbia Mayor) Fred D. Marshall from James M. Hinton, August 3, 1945, in John Henry McCray Papers, box 3, folder 17, South Caroliniana Library, University of South Carolina; Letter from J. Clarence Colclough to the Editor of *Lighthouse and Informer* (Columbia, SC), 1943, in John Henry McCray Papers, box 1, folder 2; Letter to President Roosevelt, dated December 13, 1938, asking him to keep Governor Johnston's prejudices in mind, in Modjeska Simkins Papers, General Papers, 1909–1938, Modern Political Collections, University of South Carolina, https://digital.tcl.sc.edu/digital/collection/p17173coll38/id/7546/rec/5; https://digital.tcl.sc.edu/digital/collection/p17173coll38/id/9513/rec/2; https://digital.tcl.sc.edu/digital/collection/mmsimkins/id/555.
4. *Elmore v. Rice*, 72 F. Supp. 516 (E.D.S.C. 1947).
5. Elmore v. Rice, 165 F.2d 387 (4th Cir. 1947); "Court Takes Up Case of Barring Negroes at Box," *Gaffney (SC) Ledger*, November 25, 1947.
6. Brown v. Baskin, 78 F. Supp. 933 (E.D.S.C. 1948), 936–37.
7. The American Presidency Project, "Minor/Third Party Platforms, Platform of the States Rights Democratic Party," https://www.presidency.ucsb.edu/node/273454.
8. "Negro Party Delegates Vote to Join Democrats of State: Plan to Test Waring Ruling at Georgetown," *The State* (Columbia, SC), July 17, 1947.
9. Myrdal, *An American Dilemma*, 485.

Chapter 1: The House on Tree Street

1. Associated Press, "Negro Voting in S.C. Upheld by Top Court," *Columbia (SC) Record*, April 19, 1948; Associated Press, "Party Leaders Confer on Court Decision" *News and Courier* (Charleston, SC), April 20, 1948; United Press, "Columbia Primary May Admit Negroes," *News and Courier* (Charleston, SC) April 20, 1948; Associated Press, "Court Refuses Appeal of S.C. Demos," *Greenville (SC) News*, April 20, 1948; "The 'Shouters'" Lose Final Round in Court," *Tampa (FL) Times*, April 23, 1948.
2. James L. Underwood, interview by author, February 2003.
3. Smith v. Allwright, 321 U.S. 649 (1944).

4. Journal of the Senate of the Second Session of the 85th General Assembly of the State of South Carolina being the Extraordinary Session Beginning Friday, April 14, 1944. Printed under the direction of the Joint Committee on Printing, General Assembly of South Carolina.

5. "Reporter's Beat," *Lighthouse and Informer* (Columbia, SC), April 25, 1948. George A. Elmore Scrapbook, South Caroliniana Library, University of South Carolina.

6. Associated Press, "Highest Court Says Negroes May Vote in Primaries," *The State* (Columbia, SC), April 20, 1948.

7. "The White Primary Goes Out," *Lighthouse and Informer* (Columbia, SC), April 25, 1948.

8. "Death Knell of White Primary," editorial, *Afro-American*, May 1, 1948.

9. Elmore v. Rice, 72 F. Supp. 516 (E.D.S.C. 1947), 528.

10. Valley Park was founded in 1893 as Shandon Pavilion and is now known as Martin Luther King Jr. Park. Historic Columbia has documented the history of Valley Park and recorded voices on its website of those who played in the park or tried to desegregate it. https://www.historiccolumbia.org/tour-locations/2300-greene-street.

11. Elmore v. Rice, 72 F. Supp. 516 (E.D.S.C. 1947), 521.

12. Associated Press, "Senator Smith Walks Out of Convention as Negro Minister Offers Prayer," *News and Courier* (Charleston, SC), June 25, 1936; Associated Press, "Senator E. D. Smith Walks Out of Conclave," *The State* (Columbia, SC), June 25, 1936; "Party Adopts Platform; Smith, Four Others Quit," *News and Courier*, (Charleston, SC) June 26, 1936; "Senator Ellison D. Smith Walks Out for Last Time," *The State* (Columbia, SC), June 26, 1936; "Exactly Right," *News and Courier* (Charleston, SC), June 26, 1936.

13. "ELECTIONS: Curtains for Cotton Ed," *Time*, August 7, 1944, https://content.time.com/time/subscriber/article/0,33009,886159,00.html.

14. "Blease Rebuked For 'Obscene' Poem On DePriest and Hoover: Blease Poem Is Expunged from Record," the *Afro-American*, June 22, 1929; Daniel W. Hollis, "Cole Blease: The Years between the Governorship and the Senate, 1915–1924," *South Carolina Historical Magazine*, January 1979, 1–17.

15. "Senator Smith Walks," 2.

16. Olin D. Johnston, address to the joint assembly, Journal of the Senate, 4.

17. Letter from James A. Hoyt to Fitz Hugh McMaster, December 17, 1938, in Papers of Fitz Hugh McMaster, box 2, 10 MSS, December 2, 1938–December 24, 1938, South Caroliniana Library, University of South Carolina.

18. Letter from Fitz Hugh McMaster to William Watts Ball, December 22, 1938, in Papers of Fitz Hugh McMaster, box 2, 10 MSS, 2 December 2, 1938–December 24, 1938.

19. Monthly labor review, *US Department of Labor, Bureau of Labor Statistics* 44, no. 4 (April 1937).

20. On April 19, 1948, William Powell and Ella Raines starred in *"The Senator Was Indiscreet"* at the Carolina Theatre; Frank Sinatra and Fred MacMurray starred in *"Miracle of the Bells"* at the Palmetto Theatre, while The Ritz featured *"Dangerous Year."* Cary Grant and Constance Bennett starred in *"Topper,"* *The State* (Columbia, SC), April 19, 1948.

21. Hill's Columbia (Richland County, SC) *City Directory* 1943, vol. XIV (Richmond, VA: Hill Directory Company), 533.

22. Cresswell D. Elmore, interview by author, June 28, 2004; John Henry McCray, "The Way It Was," *Charleston Chronicle*, December 6, 1980, in papers of John Henry McCray, box 7, folder 5, https://digital.tcl.sc.edu/digital/collection/p17173coll38/id/17407/rec/1.

23. Cresswell Elmore, interview.

24. McCray speech, document about the Elmore case, May 14, 1962, in papers of John Henry McCray, box 3, folder 4, https://digital.tcl.sc.edu/digital/collection/p17173coll38/id/6944/rec/1.

25. Elmore affidavit, August 13, 1946. NAACP papers, Part 4, Voting Rights Campaign, 1916–1950. Manuscripts Division, Library of Congress, https://congressional.proquest.com/histvault?q=001517-010-0001&accountid=13965.

26. Alderman Duncan, Associated Press, "Decision Promised Soon on Primary," *The State* (Columbia, SC), June 5, 1947.

27. Associated Press, "Highest Court."

28. Associated Press, "Governor Thurmond 'Shocked' At Ruling of High Court," *The State* (Columbia, SC), April 22, 1948.

29. Hugh Munn, "Negroes Line Up in Ward 9 to Vote in Democratic Primary," photograph, *The State* (Columbia, SC), August 11, 1948.

Chapter 2: Amid a Rural Landscape, Spasms of Violence

1. Epigraph reference: "Negro Boy Murdered by Dorchester Mob." *The State* (Columbia, SC), August 24, 1906.

2. US Census Bureau, 13th Census of the United States, Federal Census Population Schedules, 1910.

3. US Census Bureau, 13th Census of the United States, 1910, "Statistics for South Carolina," 607, https://www2.census.gov/library/publications/decennial/1910/abstract/supplement-sc.pdf.

4. "Statistics for South Carolina," 608.

5. Henry Orlando Marcy, Harriott Cheves Leland, ed., "Diary of a Surgeon in US Army South Carolina 1865," South Caroliniana Library, University of South Carolina, 15, 27–28.

6. Marcy, "Diary of a Surgeon," 37–39.

7. Brevet Major George Ward Nichols. *The Story of the Great March: From the Diary of a Staff Officer* (New York: Harper & Brothers, 1865), 150. https://archive.org/details/storyofgreatmarc00innich/page/n11/mode/2up?ref=ol&view=theater.

8. Nichols, *Story of the Great March*, 159.

9. Nichols, *Story of the Great March*, 155.

10. The Statutes at Large of South Carolina, Volume XIII, Containing the Acts from December 1861 to December 1866 (Columbia, SC: Reprinted by Republican Printing Company, State Printers, 1875), 268. https://archive.org/details/statutesatlargeo13repu/page/n7/mode/2up.

11. The Statutes at Large of South Carolina, 276, https://archive.org/details/statutesatlargeo13repu/page/276/mode/2up.

12. Larry McIntyre, "The South Carolina Black Code and It's Legacy," (master's thesis, University of North Carolina at Charlotte, 2016), University of North Carolina at Charlotte ProQuest Dissertations Publishing, 10117988, 57–65, https://www.proquest.com/openview/ee86a7d4b5b84a0b0fed765be017e840/1?pq-origsite=gscholar&cbl=18750.

13. William A. Gladstone, collector, *William A. Gladstone Afro-American Military Collection: Special Field Orders, No. 15, Headquarters, Military Division of the Mississippi, by Major General W. T. Sherman, re "young and able bodied negroes must be encouraged to enlist," mentions bounties paid and locations for settlement of freed Negr,* William A. Gladstone Afro-American Military Collection, Manuscript Division, mss83434, box 3, item 256, https://www.loc.gov/item/mss83434256/.

14. *Constitution of the commonwealth of South Carolina, ratified April 16, 1868, together with the Constitution of the United States of America* (Columbia, SC: C. A. Calvo, jr., state printer, 1885), https://www.loc.gov/item/14008433/.

15. "The Great Ring-Streaked and Striped Negro Convention, Desecration of the Charleston House," *Charleston Mercury,* January 14, 1868. Each day the newspaper offered up "Incidences of the Ringed-Streaked and Striped Convention" along with "Sketches of the Delegates to the Great Ringed-Streaked and Striped Convention."

16. "Our Late Legislature and the Ensuing Convention," *Charleston Daily Courier,* November 25, 1867.

17. Underwood, interview.

18. Remarks of Francis Cardozo on *Proceedings of the Constitutional Convention of South Carolina, held at Charleston, S. C. beginning January 14th and ending March 17th* (Charleston, SC: Denny & Perry, 1868), 826.

19. Remarks of Richard Harvey on *"Proceedings of the Constitutional Convention, 1868,"* 830.

20. *Address. In the Convention of the Colored People of Southern States, begun to be holden in the City of Columbia, South Carolina, on Wednesday, the eighteenth day of October 1871,* Broadsides, leaflets, and pamphlets from America and Europe, Library of Congress, https://www.loc.gov/item/2020779318/.

21. James. S. Pike, *The Prostrate State: South Carolina Under Negro Government* (New York: Loring & Mussey, 1935), 12.

22. Pike, *"Prostrate State,"* 67–68.

23. Rod Andrew Jr., *Wade Hampton: Confederate Warrior to Southern Redeemer* (Chapel Hill: University of North Carolina Press, 2008), 386–391.

24. William Jennings Bryan Dorn and Scott Derks, *Dorn: Of the People, A Political Way of Life* (Orangeburg, SC: Sandlapper, 1988), 23.

25. *Federal Writers' Project: Slave Narrative Project, Vol. 14, South Carolina, Part 1, Abrams-Durant.* 1936, 15, Federal Writer's Project, United States Work Projects Administration (USWPA), Manuscript Division, Library of Congress, https://www.loc.gov/item/mesn141/.

26. "Gen. Hampton's Great Speech," *News and Courier,* July 6, 1878, in Andrew, "Wade Hampton," 434.

27. Andrew, *"Wade Hampton,"* 435.

28. George B. Tindall, *South Carolina Negroes 1877–1900.* (Columbia: University of South Carolina Press, 1952), 37.

29. Tindall, *South Carolina Negroes,* 40.

30. Edward E. Baptist, *The Half Has Never Been Told: Slavery and the Making of American Capitalism* (New York: Basic Books, 2014), 59–65.

31. Mary J. Miller, ed., booklet, "The Suffrage: Speeches by Negroes in the Constitutional Convention. The Part Taken by Colored Orators in Their Fight for

a Fair and Impartial Ballot," (1895, Place of publication not identified; Publisher not identified), 7.

32. Miller, "The Suffrage," 16, 18.

33. "Speech of Senator Benjamin R. Tillman, March 23, 1900," *Congressional Record*, 56th Congress, 1st Session, 3223–24.

34. "Mob's Victim Found at Reevesville," *The State* (Columbia, SC), January 16, 1904.

35. "Negro Boy Murdered by Dorchester Mob, *The State* (Columbia, SC), August 24, 1906.

36. "Another Lynching," *Orangeburg (SC) Times and Democrat*, August 23, 1906. (*Times and Democrat* identified the youth incorrectly as Ben Ethridge.)

37. A. H. Seats, "Dan Etheredge Killed by Mob," *The State* (Columbia, SC), August 21, 1906.

38. "Gov. Heyward Appeals in Vain For the Law," *The State* (Columbia, SC), August 17, 1906; "Black Fiend: Brave Young Woman Fights for Life and Honor Against a Fiend," "Fiend Caught: And Governor Heyward Goes to the Scene and Tries to Save Him," "Fiend Lynched: Within Hearing of the Scene of His Awful Crime," *Manning Times*, August 22, 1906.

39. "White Brutes Murder Black Brutes," *Gaffney (SC) Ledger*, August 21, 1906.

40. "State Can't Punish Mob," *Gaffney Ledger*, August 21, 1906.

Chapter 3: Hard Work, Racial Uplift, and Card Parties

1. Epigraph reference: Helen Kohn Hennig, *Columbia: Capital City of South Carolina, 1786–1936*, (Columbia, SC: R. Bryan, 1936), 306.

2. Cresswell Elmore, interview.

3. US Census Bureau, 16th Census of the United States, Federal Census Population Schedules, 1940.

4. US Census Bureau, 14th Census of the United States, State Compendium, 1920, Summary for the United States, by Divisions and States—Population, Agriculture, Manufacturing, Mining, 56, https://www2.census.gov/library/publications/decennial/1920/state-compendium/06229686v38–43ch2.pdf.

5. Walsh's Columbia South Carolina City Directory, 1925, Vol. XXIX (Asheville: Commercial Service, 1925), 537.

6. Postcard, Columbia, SC, Main Street, showing retail section, Postcards of the Midlands, Walker Local and Family History Center Digital Collections, Richland Library, https://localhistory.richlandlibrary.com/digital/collection/p16817coll6/id/1239/rec/4.

7. Rev. E. A. Adams, "The American Negro," *Palmetto Leader* (Columbia, SC), January 10, 1925, https://historicnewspapers.sc.edu/lccn/sn93067919/1925-01–10/ed-1/seq-1.pdf.

8. "Booker T. Washington Delivers the 1895 Atlanta Compromise Speech," History Matters (website), George Mason University, from the original on January 27, 2006, https://web.archive.org/web/20060127085119/http:/historymatters.gmu.edu/d/39/.

9. M. F. Ansel, *Inaugural Address of M. F. Ansel, Governor, to the General Assembly of South Carolina*, January 15, 1907 (Columbia, SC: Gonzales and Bryan, State Printers, 1907), 7, Inaugural_Address_1907-1–15.pdf.

10. David H. Jackson Jr., "Booker T. Washington in South Carolina, March 1909," *South Carolina Historical Magazine*, July 2012, 198.
11. Jackson, "Booker T. Washington," 207.
12. "The Greatest Event in the History of Allendale County," *Palmetto Leader* (Columbia, SC), January 4, 1930.
13. "N.A.A.C.P Begins Fight on Texas Primary Law." *Palmetto Leader* (Columbia, SC), April 11, 1925.
14. City Directory of Columbia, S.C. 1927 (Columbia, SC: The State Company, 1927), 584.
15. Richard Samuel Roberts, author, Thomas L. Johnson and Phillip C. Dunn, eds, *A True Likeness: The Black South of Richard Samuel Roberts, 1920–1936* (Columbia, SC: Bruccoli Clark, Chapel Hill, NC: Algonquin Books, 1986), 48.
16. *Garnet and Black*, 1927, Garnet and Black Yearbooks, 1899–1994, University of South Carolina, South Caroliniana Library, 383, https://digital.tcl.sc.edu /digital/collection/garnetblack/id/32829/rec/14.
17. Charles S. Johnson, *The Economic Status of Negroes: Summary and Analysis of the Materials Presented at the Conference on the Economic Status of the Negro, Held in Washington, D. C., May 11–13, 1933, under the Sponsorship of the Julius Rosenwald Fund* (Nashville: Fisk University Press: 1933), 18.
18. "Farm Employment, November 1, 1934," Crop Reporting Board, Bureau of Agricultural Economics, US Department of Agriculture, https://downloads .usda.library.cornell.edu/usda-esmis/files/x920fw89s/h989r4790/3b591b322 /FarmLabo-11–13–1934.pdf.
19. "25.—Farms—General Statistic," US Department of Commerce, statistical abstract of the United States, 1934 (Washington, DC: Government Printing Office, 1934), 564.
20. US Census Bureau, 15th Census of the United States, 1930; Columbia, Richland, South Carolina; 8B; Enumeration District: *0028;* FHL microfilm: 2341944.
21. "Thousands See Crowning of Sesqui Queen." *Columbia (SC) Record*, March 23, 1936.
22. "Oldest Citizen Acclaimed," *Columbia (SC) Record*, March 23, 1936.
23. "Capital's Greatest Crowd Sees Sesquicentennial," *The State* (Columbia, SC), March 24, 1936.
24. "Thousands See Pets Marching, *The State* (Columbia, SC), March 25, 1936.
25. "History-Graph of Columbia, South Carolina in Celebration of its Sesquicentennial, 1786–1936," Maps of Columbia and Richland County Digital Collection, Richland Library, Columbia, SC, https://localhistory.richlandlibrary .com/digital/collection/p16817coll16/id/13/rec/1.
26. C. A. Johnson, "Negroes" in Hennig, *Columbia: Columbia: Capital City of South Carolina, 1786–1936,* 303.
27. Johnson in Hennig, 305.
28. Johnson in Hennig, 306.
29. "Welcome Teachers," *Palmetto Leader* (Columbia, SC), March 21, 1936.https:// historicnewspapers.sc.edu/lccn/sn93067919/1936–03–21/ed-1/seq-4.pdf
30. "Belk's Installs Lounging Room for Coloreds," *Palmetto Leader* (Columbia, SC), March 21, 1936. https://historicnewspapers.sc.edu/lccn/sn93067919/1936–03 –21/ed-1/seq-1.pdf.

31. Cresswell Elmore, interview.
32. "Radio News," *Palmetto Leader* (Columbia, SC), January 2, 1937. https://historicnewspapers.sc.edu/lccn/sn93067919/1937–01–02/ed-1/seq-7.pdf.

Chapter 4: "Difficulty with the White People"

1. Epigraph reference: Melvin S. Hodges, interview by author, August 2022.
2. For a comprehensive account of the attack on veteran Isaac Woodard and the aftermath, see Richard Gergel, "Unexampled Courage: The Blinding of Isaac Woodard and the Awakening of President Harry S. Truman and Judge J. Waties Waring, (New York: Farrar, Straus and Giroux 2019).
3. Gergel, *Unexampled Courage*, 12–23.
4. Orson Welles, "Orson Welles Commentaries," *Orson Welles on the Air*, 1938–1946, July 28, 1946, Indiana University Bloomington, Lilly Library, https://orsonwelles.indiana.edu/items/show/2169.
5. Welles, August 11, 1946.
6. Edgar T. Rouzeau, "Black America Wars on Double Front for High Stakes, *Pittsburgh Courier*, February 7, 1942. "Nation Lauds Courier's 'Double V' Campaign," *Pittsburgh Courier*, March 7, 1942.
7. Eugene Talmadge, "Returning to the Governor's Mansion: Fighting for an All-White Primary," excerpt from a 1946 campaign radio speech, Kennesaw State University, Georgia Journeys: Legacies of World War II, website. https://georgiajourneys.kennesaw.edu/items/show/423.
8. Greg Bluestein, "Lynching Probe Reached Dome," Associated Press in *Atlanta Journal-Constitution*, June 16, 2007.
9. "55 years later, a reopened GBI probe and new call for justice may shed light on Moore's Ford lynching," *Atlanta Journal-Constitution*, March 11, 2001; Brad Shrade, "No charges as probes of '46 lynchings end," *Atlanta Journal-Constitution*, December 28, 2017; Moore's Ford lynching GBI investigative file, contributed by *Atlanta Journal-Constitution*, January 30, 2018, https://www.documentcloud.org/documents/4359004-GBI-Moore-s-Ford-File.html.
10. For a nuanced and evocative account of the NAACP in the 1940s, see Patricia Sullivan, *Lift Every Voice: The NAACP and the Making of the Civil Rights Movement* (New York: New Press, 2010), 318–23.
11. Gergel, *Unexampled Courage*, 115–32.
12. "Vindication for Shull," *The State* (Columbia, SC), November 7, 1946.
13. "Federal Usurpation," *Columbia (SC) Record*, November 9, 1946.
14. Charles E. Wilson, *To Secure These Rights: The Report of the President's Committee on Civil Rights* (New York: Simon & Schuster, 1947). See Truman Library and Museum for online version, https://www.trumanlibraryinstitute.org/civil-rights-symposium-history-11/.
15. President Truman's Address Before the NAACP, June 29, 1947, *Tru Blog*, Truman Library Institute, https://www.trumanlibraryinstitute.org/historic-speeches-naacp/.
16. Executive Order 9981, July 26, 1948, General Records of the United States Government, Record Group 11, National Archives.
17. 103 Cong. Rec., S16429 (Part 12, weekly ed. August 22, 1957–August, 30, 1957), statement of Sen. Thurmond; S16401 (statement of Sen. Knowland); S16402 (statement of Sen. Thurmond); S16403 (statement of Sen. Knowland). https://

www.senate.gov/artandhistory/history/resources/pdf/Thurmond_filibuster_1957.pdf

Chapter 5: Battle Lines at Home and Abroad

1. Epigraph reference: "City Election Board to Forward Negroes Request for Suffrage," *The State* (Columbia, SC), April 23, 1942.
2. Letter from James M. Hinton to Thurgood Marshall, May 5, 1942, NAACP Papers, Part IV, Voting Rights Campaign, 1916–50, Reel 10, 709–10.
3. The life and work of Levi Byrd is explored extensively in Peter F. Lau, *Democracy Rising: South Carolina and the Fight for Black Equality since 1865* (Lexington: University Press of Kentucky, 2006), 107–28.
4. "County Refuses to Back Move for Negro Vote," *The State* (Columbia, SC), May 5, 1942.
5. Letter from Louise Bailey to R. Beverley Herbert, May 6, 1942, Papers of R. Beverley Herbert, box 1, folder 16 (civil rights), South Caroliniana Library, University of South Carolina.
6. Letter from E. C. Townsend to R. Beverley Herbert, May 5, 1942, Papers of R. Beverley Herbert, box 1, folder 16 (civil rights).
7. Letter to Colored Citizens Committee from R. B. Herbert, April 23, 1942, Papers of R. Beverley Herbert, box 1, folder 16 (civil rights).
8. "Negroes Enrol for City Vote," *Columbia (SC) Record*, March 17, 1942.
9. "City Election Board to Forward Negroes Request for Suffrage," *The State* (Columbia, SC) April 23, 1942.
10. Henry Cauthen, "Negro Ballot Seen Blocked in Party Move," *Columbia (SC) Record*, May 20, 1942.
11. Cauthen, "Negro Ballot," 7.
12. "Negro Suffrage in Primary Urged by 21 White Citizens," *The State*, May 18, 1942.
13. "Negro Suffrage," 12.
14. For an in-depth examination of the work of interracial organizations, including the Southern Regional Council, during the 1930s and 1940s, see John Edgerton, *Speak Now against the Day: The Generation before the Civil Rights Movement in the South* (New York: Alfred A. Knopf, 1994).
15. Pamphlet, *Southern Conference on Race Relations*, Durham, NC, October 20, 1942, contributed by University of North Carolina at Chapel Hill, 5, https://archive.org/details/southernconferen00sout/mode/2up.
16. *Southern Conference on Race Relations*, 3–4.
17. *Southern Conference on Race Relations*, 12–13.

Chapter 6: "We'll Fight the Negroes at the Polls"

1. Letter from Josephine Pinckney to R. Beverley Herbert, R. Beverley Herbert Papers, April 21, 1944, box 1, folder 17.
2. Smith v. Allwright, 321 U.S. 649 (1944).
3. "Negroes Will Not Be Allowed to Take over Elections in SC, Maybank Asserts in US Senate," *The State* (Columbia, SC), April 14, 1944.
4. Pinckney to Herbert letter, April 21, 1944.
5. Mark Warren, "Smith Alarmed over Negro Vote Decision, Urges S.C. to Wake Up, Flays New Deal," *Columbia (SC) Record*, April 6, 1944.

6. "Johnson Not Alarmed on Negro Vote," *The State* (Columbia, SC), April 6, 1944.

7. "Johnston Says Will Keep White Supremacy," *The State* (Columbia, SC), April 15, 1944.

8. "To Save State from Reconstructed Court," *News and Courier* (Charleston, SC), April 4, 1944.

9. Journal of the Senate, of the Second Session of the 85th General Assembly of the state of South Carolina Being the Extraordinary Session Beginning Friday, April 14, 1944, (Columbia, SC: Joint Committee on Printing, General Assembly of South Carolina, 1944); 4; "Johnston Says Will Keep White Supremacy," *The State* (Columbia, SC), April 15, 1944; 1. "House Sets Salary at $10 A Day," *Columbia (SC) Record*, April 15, 1944; Jimmy Price, "Scene as Governor Arrives for Special Session," photograph, *Columbia (SC) Record*, April 15, 1944.

10. "Texas Negroes Can Vote, Court Rules; S.C. Action Likely," *Columbia (SC) Record*, April 3, 1944.

11. For a rich examination of the role of South Carolina's Black press and the impact of the extraordinary session, see Sid Bedingfield, *Newspaper Wars: Civil Rights and White Resistance in South Carolina, 1935–1965* (Urbana: University of Illinois Press, 2017).

12. *Journal of the Senate*, of the Second Session of the 85th General Assembly of the state of South Carolina Being the Extraordinary Session Beginning Friday, April 14, 1944, (Columbia, SC: Joint Committee on Printing, General Assembly of South Carolina, 1944), 5.

13. For an exploration of the Texas primary case, see Darlene Clark Hine, *Black Victory: The Rise and Fall of the White Primary in Texas*, (Columbia: University of Missouri Press, 1979); with essays by Steven F. Lawson and Merline Pitre new edition, 2003; and Charles L. Zelden, *The Battle for the Black Ballot: Smith v. Allwright and the Defeat of the Texas All-White Primary* (Lawrence: University Press of Kansas, 2004).

14. Associated Press, "Dixie Reaction Varies on High Court Rule of Negro Voting," *The State* (Columbia, SC), April 4, 1944.

15. Associated Press, "State Negroes to Form Party." *News and Courier* (Charleston, SC), April 15, 1944.

16. "Tornado's Death Toll Reaches 38, with 17 in S.C.," *Columbia (SC) Record*, April 17, 1944; Banjo Smith, "Girl Blown 150 Yds at Greenwood as Mighty Wind Hits," *Columbia (SC) Record*, April 17, 1944.

17. "House Lauds Attack on Negro Press," *Columbia (SC) Record*, April 17, 1944; Associated Press, "Scores of Laws on Primaries are Repealed; Long Willing to 'Bite the Dust' to Prevent Negroes from Voting," *News and Courier* (Charleston, SC), April 18, 1944; "SC Legislature Rushes Scores of Bills for White Primary," *News and Courier* (Charleston, SC), April 18, 1944.

18. Letter to Governor Olin Johnson, dated April 17, 1944, challenging him to debate the validity of the concept of white supremacy, Modjeska Simkins Papers, General Papers, 1940–1949, https://digital.tcl.sc.edu/digital/collection/mmsimkins/id/428/rec/1.

19. "House Insists on $10 a Day for Session." *The State* (Columbia, SC), April 20, 1944; "Senators Tangle in Exchange on Roosevelt."*The State* (Columbia, SC), April 20, 1944.

20. Associated Press, "State Negro College Leaders 'Deplore' Special Session," *News and Courier* (Charleston, SC), April 16, 1944.

21. "To the *News and Courier*," letter from T. B. Grubb, *News and Courier* (Charleston, SC), April 13, 1944.

22. Josephine Pinckney, *Three O'Clock Dinner* (New York: Viking Press, 1945), 21.

Chapter 7: Power and Peril of Collaboration

1. Epigraph reference: Letter from John Henry McCray (addressed to fellow citizen), May 17, 1944, in John Henry McCray Papers, box 2, folder 21, Politics, Feb.–June 1944. https://digital.tcl.sc.edu/digital/collection/p17173coll38/id/2084/rec/1.

2. John McCray oral history interview, 1983 June, part 4, William Gravely Oral History Collection on the Lynching of Willie Earle, Department of Oral History, University of South Carolina.

3. Bedingfield, 64–66.

4. *Viola Louise Duvall, et al. v. J. F. Seignous* 1943 Case No. 108. Online Exhibit, "Somebody Had to Do It: First Children of School Integration," includes "School Equalization," Lowcountry Digital History Initiative, College of Charleston, https://ldhi.library.cofc.edu/exhibits/show/somebody_had_to_do_it/struggle_for_equal_ed/school_equalization.

5. "House Hits Northern Agitators." *Columbia (SC) Record*, February 29, 1944; "House Wants No Meddling in Race Affairs by Northerners." *The State* (Columbia, SC), March 1, 1944.

6. Letter from E. A. Adams and James M. Hinton to John D. Long, Representative of Union County, March 1, 1944, John Henry McCray Papers, box 1, folder 3, Journalism, https://digital.tcl.sc.edu/digital/collection/p17173coll38/id/9516/rec/3.

7. Letter to Dr. E. A. Adams and J. M. Hinton from S. J. McDonald, March 2, 1944, John Henry McCray Papers, box 2, folder 21, Politics, Feb.–June 1944, https://digital.tcl.sc.edu/digital/collection/p17173coll38/id/2074/rec/1.

8. Bedingfield, 71, "The Way It Was," *Charleston (SC) Chronicle*, March 13, 1983. 3" Mp.

9. Rough draft of an opinion piece entitled Education, Injustice, Removal of Fear of Negro Held Solvents of the Race Question, April 2, 1944, John Henry McCray Papers, box 1, folder 3, Journalism, https://digital.tcl.sc.edu/digital/collection/p17173coll38/id/9523/rec/1.

10. Osceola McKaine, keynote address of the inaugural meeting of the Progressive Democratic Party, Arthur A.R. Clements Jr. Papers, South Caroliniana Library, University of South Carolina, box 8, "Progressive Democratic Party, May 1944–Apr. 1983 and no date."

11. "School Board Fires Teacher for Trying to Register, Vote," *Lighthouse and Informer* (Columbia,SC), June 28, 1942, in NAACP Papers, Voting Rights Campaign, 1916–1950, Group II, box B-215, reel 10, 675–76.

12. An affidavit by Aaron Jenkins, Francena Jenkins, and George A. Elmore about the wrongful procedures of the polling place for Ward 5, Columbia, SC, in the 1944 election, John Henry McCray Papers, box 2, folder 23, https://digital.tcl.sc.edu/digital/collection/p17173coll38/id/11953/rec/4.

13. An affidavit by William Jordan about the wrongful procedures of the polling place for Ward 2, Columbia, SC, in the 1944 election, John Henry McCray Papers, box 2, folder 23.

14. An affidavit by Modjeska Monteith Simkins about the wrongful procedures of the polling place for Ward 4, Columbia, SC, in the 1944 election, John Henry McCray Papers, box 2, folder 23.

15. Letter from Thurgood Marshall to Camille C. Levy, June 8, 1944, 16. Library of Congress, reproduced from the manuscript, https://hv.proquest.com/pdfs/001517/001517_010_0779/001517_010_0779_From_1_to_69.pdf.

Chapter 8. "Recognize the Negro Citizen . . . and Give Him the Right to Vote"

1. Epigraph reference: Alderman Duncan, Associated Press, "Decision Promised Soon on Primary," *The State* (Columbia, SC), June 5, 1947.

2. Meeting flier of the Progressive Democratic Party, John Henry McCray Papers, box 3, folder 36. https://digital.tcl.sc.edu/digital/collection/p17173coll38/id/8646/rec/3.

3. Press release about a hospital burlesque fundraiser entitled "Puffin' Hot," Modjeska Simkins Papers, Good Samaritan Waverly Hospital, General, N.D. (1 of 2), https://digital.tcl.sc.edu/digital/collection/mmsimkins/id/3687/rec/1.

4. Press release about stage attractions that are part of the hospital fundraising drive, Modjeska Simkins Papers, Topical Papers, Good Samaritan Waverly Hospital, General, N.D., https://digital.tcl.sc.edu/digital/collection/mmsimkins/id/3689/rec/1.

5. Press release about the Waverly-Good Samaritan Hospital, Modjeska Simkins Papers, Topical Papers, Good Samaritan Waverly Hospital, General, N.D., https://digital.tcl.sc.edu/digital/collection/mmsimkins/id/3692/rec/1.

6. Sarah Conlon, *"A hospital built by them, for them": The Good Samaritan-Waverly Hospital Building Fund Campaign and the evolution of black healthcare traditions in Columbia, South Carolina,"* University of South Carolina, University of South Carolina ProQuest Dissertations Publishing, 2012, 1516712, https://www.proquest.com/pqdtlocal1006876/dissertations-theses/hospital-built-them-good-samaritan-waverly/docview/1038140906/sem-2?accountid=13965.

7. John McCray, "The Way It Was," December 6, 1980, John Henry McCray Papers, box 7, folder 5, Legal Size, Journalism, *Charleston (SC) Chronicle* ("The Way It Was"), 1980–1986, https://digital.tcl.sc.edu/digital/collection/p17173coll38/id/17407/rec/6.

8. Letters from Benjamin James Pittman to the NAACP, July 2–3, 1946, August 17, 1946, NAACP Papers, Part IV, Voting Rights Campaign, 1916–1950, reel 10, frames 820–823, 842–843. Library of Congress, reproduced from the manuscript, 46–49, 68–69. https://hv.proquest.com/pdfs/001517/001517_010_0779/001517_010_0779_From_1_to_69.pdf.

9. Letter from Thurgood Marshall to John McCray, January 22, 1947, NAACP Papers, Part IV, Voting Rights Campaign, 1916–1950, reel 10, frame 848.

Library of Congress, reproduced from manuscript, 5. https://hv.proquest.com/pdfs/001517/001517_010_0874/001517_010_0874_0001_From_1_to_50.pdf.

10. Letter from Franklin Williams to Harold Boulware, January 23, 1947, NAACP Papers, Part IV, Voting Rights Campaign, 1916–1950, reel 10, frame 851. Library of Congress, reproduced from manuscript, 8. https://hv.proquest.com/pdfs/001517/001517_010_0874/001517_010_0874_0001_From_1_to_50.pdf.

11. Telegram from Thurgood Marshall to Harold Boulware, January 30, 1947, NAACP Papers, Part IV, Voting Rights Campaign, 1916–1950, reel 10, frame 852. Library of Congress, reproduced from the manuscript, 9. https://hv.proquest.com/pdfs/001517/001517_010_0874/001517_010_0874_0001_From_1_to_50.pdf.

12. Letter from Harold R. Boulware to Franklin Williams, January 31, 1947, NAACP Papers, Part IV, Voting Rights Campaign, 1916–1950, Reel 10, 853. Library of Congress, reproduced from the manuscript, 10. https://hv.proquest.com/pdfs/001517/001517_010_0874/001517_010_0874_0001_From_1_to_50.pdf.

13. Memorandum to Charles Houston, George Johnson, W. Robert Ming Jr., Frank Reeves, and Miss Ruth Weyand, February 8, 1947, NAACP Papers, Part IV, Voting Rights Campaign, 1916–50, reel 10, frame 861. Library of Congress, reproduced from the manuscript, 18. https://hv.proquest.com/pdfs/001517/001517_010_0874/001517_010_0874_0001_From_1_to_50.pdf.

14. Special correspondent, "Officers Nab Earle Lynchers; 28 Taxi Drivers, 3 Others to Face Trial on Charges Pressed by State and County," *Lighthouse and Informer*, March 2, 1947; The body of Willie Earle, view 1 and 2, Papers of John Henry McCray, box 8, folder 62, photographs, Willie Earle Lynching.

15. Rebecca West, "Opera in Greenville," *New Yorker*, June 14, 1947, 31–65.

16. Wrighten v. Board of Trustees, 72 F.Supp.948 (E.D.S.C. 1947).

17. "They Laughed All the Way," John Henry McCray Papers, box 2, folder 20, Journalism, Writings, n.d., https://digital.tcl.sc.edu/digital/collection/p17173coll38/id/1689/rec/2.

18. Tina Cannon, "Court Hears White Primary Arguments, *Columbia (SC) Record*, June 3, 1947; Mark Warren, "Posse Hunts Attacker," *Columbia (SC) Record*, June 3, 1947.

19. "Party Denies Exercising Government Functions," *The State* (Columbia, SC), June 4, 1947.

20. Tina Cannon, "White Primary Decision Pends, *Columbia (SC) Record*, June 4, 1947.

21. Elmore v. Rice, 527.

22. Elmore v. Rice, 527.

23. Associated Press, "Negro Party Delegates Vote to Join Democrats of State," *The State* (Columbia, SC), July 17, 1947.

Chapter 9: Suffering Hardships for the Freedom of His Race

1. Epigraph reference: R. Beverley Herbert, "A Plea for Better Race Relations: An Address Delivered at the Commencement Exercises," June 2, of the University of South Carolina, *Southern Christian Advocate* 112, no. 25 (June 17, 1948): 5.

2. "Negro Democrats See Vote Problems Ahead," *Columbia (SC) Record*, July 16, 1947.

3. "SC Democratic Party Will Appeal Case," *The State* (Columbia, SC), July 14, 1947. "Maybank Attacks Court Ruling on Negro Voting," *The State* (Columbia, SC), July 14, 1947; Associated Press, "Negroes Ruled Eligible in Primaries," *The State* (Columbia, SC), July 13, 1947; "Democratic Committee Orders Appeal," *The State* (Columbia, SC), July 18, 1947.

4. "Federal Court Decisions," *News and Courier* (Charleston, SC), July 13, 1947.

5. "Must Have Surprised," *Columbia (SC) Record*, July 17, 1947.

6. Letter to James M. Hinton from local whites, May 27, 1947, John Henry McCray Papers, box 3, folder 17, https://digital.tcl.sc.edu/digital/collection /p17173coll38/id/7531/rec/5.

7. For an evocative and full portrait of the life of James Hinton and an account of his kidnapping, see Claudia Smith Brinson, *Stories of Struggle: The Clash over Civil Rights in South Carolina* (Columbia: University of South Carolina Press, 2022): 2–3, 20–22.

8. Postcard from a southern lady to J. H. McCray, March 11, 1946, John Henry McCray Papers, box 1, folder 05. https://digital.tcl.sc.edu/digital/collection /p17173coll38/id/9735/rec/5.

9. Rice v. Elmore, 165 F.2d 387 (4th Cir. 1947), 392.

10. Rice v. Elmore, 389.

11. Rice v. Elmore, 392.

12. Associated Press, "Court Voids Ban against Negro Voting," *The State*, (Columbia, SC) December 31, 1947.

13. Brown v. Baskin, 78 F. Supp. 933 (E.D.S.C. 1948), Brown v. Baskin, 80 F. Supp. 1017 (E.D.S.C. 1948).

14. Brown v. Baskin, 78 F. Supp. 933, 940–941.

15. Transcript of July 16, 1948, hearing in *Brown v. Baskin* before Hon. J. Waties Waring Charleston, SC, 45, South Caroliniana Library, University of South Carolina.

16. Baskin v. Brown, 174 F.2d 391 (4th Cir. 1949), 394.

17. Gergel, *Unexampled Courage*, 210–12.

18. Letter from Dr. Marion Young to Rep. William Jennings Bryan Dorn, February 9, 1948, William Jennings Bryan Dorn Papers, Box 31, Topical File 1, 1947–49, Civil Rights Folder 1, Modern Political Collections, University of South Carolina.

19. Letter from Rep. William Jennings Bryan Dorn to Dr. Marion Young, March 5, 1948, in William Jennings Bryan Dorn Papers, Box 31, Topical File 1, 1947–49, Civil Rights Folder 1,

20. Letter from Rep. William Jennings Bryan Dorn to James M. Hinton, secretary of Negro Citizens' Committee of South Carolina, William Jennings Bryan Dorn papers, Box 31, Topical File 1, 1947–49, Civil Rights Folder 1.

21. Letter from Harold R. Boulware to Thurgood Marshall, July 30, 1948, NAACP Papers, Part 4. Voting Rights Campaign, 1916–1950, Group II, box B-213, reel 9, 405, also Library of Congress, https://hv.proquest.com/pdfs/001517/001517 _009_0392/001517_009_0392_From_1_to_94.pdf.

22. Herbert, "A Plea," 3.

23. Letter from J. H. Clement Jr. to Editor of the Charleston News & Courier, June 1, 1948, A.J. Clement Jr. Papers, box 8, "Progressive Democratic Party, May 1944–Apr. 1983 and no date."

24. George A. Elmore, "Cast First Ballots," photograph, *Lighthouse and Informer* (Columbia, SC), April 25, 1948.

25. "Who Done it?" *Lighthouse and Informer*, July 27, 1947. George A. Elmore Scrapbook, South Caroliniana Library, University of South Carolina.

26. "South Carolina Democrats Get In Good Day's Work," *Columbia (SC) Record*, August 11, 1948.

27. "Yesterday's Primary," *The State* (Columbia, SC), August 11, 1948.

28. "Vote Is Heavy, Order Prevails: All Is Quiet As Many Negroes Cast Ballots," *Columbia (SC) Record*, August 10, 1948.

29. "Rev. Archie Ware Flees Home After New Threats Are Made on His Personal Safety," *Lighthouse and Informer* (Columbia, SC), August 22, 1948.

30. "Too Much of a Compliment," *Lighthouse and Informer (Columbia, SC)* August 22, 1948.

31. Robert Jeffrey, "States' Righters Enroute to Rally, *Columbia (SC) Record*, August 10, 1948; Jimmy Price, "Thurmond Off for Houston," photograph, *Columbia (SC) Record*, August 10, 1948; Associated Press, "Dixiecrat Campaign to Open Today at Houston," *The State* (Columbia, SC), August 10, 1948; Robert Jeffrey, "Delegates Gather for Texas Rally," *The State* (Columbia, SC), August 11, 1948.

32. Donella Wilson, interview by author, February 2003.

33. Cresswell Elmore, interview.

34. Rev. Simon Bouie, interview by author, June 2023.

35. Brinson, *Stories of Struggle*, 43.

36. Cresswell Elmore, interview.

37. Letter to Mr. James H. Hinton from Mr. C. Arthur Pompey, August 16, 1948, John Henry McCray Papers, Box 3, Folder 17. https://digital.tcl.sc.edu/digital/collection/p17173coll38/id/7537/rec/5

38. "Letter by Pompey Denounced by Elks," *Lighthouse and Informer* (Columbia, SC), August 29, 1948.

39. Letter to Mr. C. Arthur Pompey from James M. Hinton, August 17, 1948, John Henry McCray Papers, box 3, folder 17, https://digital.tcl.sc.edu/digital/collection/p17173coll38/id/7533/rec/5.

40. Naomi Elmore Green, interview by author, June 2004; Yolande Cole, interview by author, February 2003.

41. Ad for Elmore photo studio opening, *Lighthouse and Informer* (Columbia, SC), December 22, 1951, https://historicnewspapers.sc.edu/lccn/sn92065442/1951-12-22/ed-1/seq-2.pdf.

42. Richland County, South Carolina, Book F-K of Deeds, involving the sale of 907 Tree Street from J. Richard Allison M.D. to George A. Elmore, 183.

43. Richland County, South Carolina, Mortgages, Book JY (microfilm), 72, $800 mortgage taken out by George A. Elmore from Standard Building and Loan Association, satisfied, February 1, 1947.

44. Richland County, South Carolina, Mortgages, Book KG (microfilm), 3. $1,200 mortgage taken out by George A. Elmore from Home Federal Savings and Loan Association, satisfied October 18, 1950.)

45. Richland County, South Carolina, Mortgage of Real Estate, Book 80, 155–57, $2,500 mortgage taken out by George A. Elmore from Modjeska M. Simkins, October 17, 1950, satisfied and cancelled May 16, 1952.

46. Richland County, South Carolina, Mortgage of Real Estate, Book 116, 524–26. $2,800 mortgage taken out by George A. Elmore from Victory Savings Bank, May 16, 1952.

47. Richland County, Court of Common Pleas, Harry M. Lightsey, master, granted R. E. Monteith sale of 907 TreeStreet, vol. 122, 190–91.

48. Letter to Mr. Elmore from John Henry McCray, December 6, 1954, John Henry McCray Papers, box 2, folder 30, 1951–1955, https://digital.tcl.sc.edu/digital/collection/p17173coll38/id/3408/rec/5.

49. Letter from Sarah Reese offering to help with George Elmore's mortgage, Modjeska Simkins Papers, General Papers, 1950–1956, https://digital.tcl.sc.edu/digital/collection/mmsimkins/id/896/rec/7.

50. Cynthia K. Edney, interview by author, January 2009.

Chapter 10: A Private Life Shattered by Violence

1. Epigraph reference: Doris Glymph Greene, interview by author, February 2013, July 2022.

2. Bureau of the Census, 13th Census of the United States Year, 1910; Census Place: Lower, Richland, South Carolina; Roll: T624_1471; Page: 4b; Enumeration District: 0096; FHL microfilm: 1375484.

3. Bureau of the Census, 14th Census of the United States, 1920; Census Place: School District 7, Richland, South Carolina; Roll: T625_1708; Page: 5B; Enumeration District: 101.

4. Bureau of the Census, 15th Census of the United States Year, 1930; Census Place: Columbia, Richland, South Carolina; Page: 5B; Enumeration District: 0017; FHL microfilm: 2341944.

5. Donella Wilson, interview.

6. Hill's Columbia (Richland County, SC) City Directory, 1954. (Richmond: Hill Directory Co. Inc., 1954), 206.

7. Bureau of the Census, 15th Census of the United States, Columbia, Richland, South Carolina; Page: 8B; Enumeration District: 0028; FHL microfilm: 2341944.

8. US Treasury Department, *Statistics of Income for 1930: Compiled from Income Tax Returns and Including Statistics from Estate Tax Returns* (Washington, DC: United States Government Printing Office, 1932), 67–68, https://www.irs.gov/pub/irs-soi/30soirepar.pdf; "$7,000,000,000 Drop in Incomes in 1930, Tax Returns Show," *New York Times*, November 30, 1930.

9. Associated Press, "Politics Boils in Fatherland," *The State* (Columbia, SC), March 12, 1932; *Associated Press*, "Eaglets Kidnapers Baffle All Efforts," *The State* (Columbia, SC), March 12, 1932.

10. Nelson, Robert K., LaDale Winling, et al. "Mapping Inequality: Redlining in New Deal America," edited by Robert K. Nelson and Edward L. Ayers, *American Panorama: An Atlas of United States History*, 2023, https://dsl.richmond.edu/panorama/redlining/map/SC/Columbia/.

11. "Party Denies," *The State* (Columbia SC), June 4, 1947.

12. "Posse Hunts Attacker," *Columbia (SC) Record*, June 3, 1947; "Hunt Continues for Edgewood Home Prowler," *Columbia (SC) Record*, June 4, 1947; "Reward Hiked After Second Assault Try in Edgewood," *The State* (Columbia SC), June 4, 1947; "Negroes 'Terrorized,' Burnings, Rumors Disturb Columbia in Case Officers Find Hard to Solve," *Lighthouse and Informer* (Columbia, SC).

13. Doris Glymph Greene, interview by author, February 2013, July 2023.

14. Gloria Schumpert James, interview by author, January 2023, June 2023.

15. "Annual Report of the South Carolina Tax Commission on Alcoholic Liquors to the Governor and General Assembly, Columbia, SC, 1954" in Reports and Resolutions of South Carolina to the General Assembly of the State of South Carolina, Regular Session Commencing January 13, 1953, Vol. 1 (Printed under the direction of the State Budget and Control Board), 19.

16. "130th Annual Report of the South Carolina State Hospital for the Year ending June 30, 1953," (Printed under the direction of the State Budget and Control Board) 5, http://hdl.handle.net/10827/19182.

17. "130th Annual Report," 6.

18. Staff book, South Carolina State Hospital, July 1, 1952, through June 30, 1953, South Carolina Department of Archives and History.

19. "130th Annual Report," 15.

20. "130th Annual Report," 52–55.

21. Cresswell Elmore, interview.

Chapter 11: A Patriotic Act Finally Acknowledged

1. Timothy Hicks, Donald Stewart, and Fritz Hamer, *The South Carolina Journey, 2nd edition* (Gibbs-Smith Publisher, Education Division, 2021) 302–3.

2. Brown v. Board of Education of Topeka, 347 U.S. 483 (1954).

3. For a comprehensive narrative of the NAACP's fight for school integration, see Kluger, *Simple Justice*, Sullivan *Lift Every Voice* and Brinson, *Stories of Struggle*.

4. Brown v. Board of Education of Topeka, 349 U.S. 294 (1955).

5. Letter from John McCray to the Rev. I DeQuincey Newman and Billie S. Fleming regarding rumors of the Progressive Democrats hampering the work of the local NAACP efforts, p. 3; John Henry McCray Papers, box 5, folder 07, Topical, NAACP, 1954–59, https://digital.tcl.sc.edu/digital/collection/p17173coll38/id/13554/rec/1.

6. Letter from I. DeQuincey Newman to John McCray about the Certificate of Merit that was awarded to the late George A. Elmore, John Henry McCray Papers, box 5, folder 07, Topical, NAACP, 1954–59, https://digital.tcl.sc.edu/digital/collection/p17173coll38/id/13578/rec/1.

7. Patsy V. Pressley, "Gathering Brings Back Past to Honor 'Forgotten' Man," *The State* (Columbia, SC), June 22, 1981.

8. Elizabeth Wallace, interview by author, August 2022.

9. Mary Simms Oliphant, Alfred Taylor Odell, and T. C. Duncan Eaves, eds., *Letters of William Gilmore Simms*, Vol. 5 (Columbia: University of South Carolina Press, 1956), 306–7.

10. Mary C. Simms Oliphant, *The New Simms History of South Carolina, 1840–1940* (Columbia, SC: State Company, 1941), 227.

11. Oliphant, *New Simms History*, 251.

12. Oliphant, *New Simms History*, 254, 256.

13. L. Roger Kirk, "The South Carolina Education Improvement Act of 1984," *Journal of Education Finance* 11, no. 1 (Summer 1985): 132–45.

14. Education Accountability Act, 1998, Act No. 400, Chapter 18, Article 3, Section 59–18–300. https://www.scstatehouse.gov/sess112_1997-1998/bills/850.htm.

15. Walter Edgar, *South Carolina: A History* (Columbia: University of South Carolina Press, 1998).

16. Carolyn Click, "At USC, Edgar Is History." *The State* (Columbia, SC), May 27, 2012.

Conclusion

1. W. Lewis Burke, "Killing, Cheating, Legislating, and Lying: A History of Voting Rights in South Carolina after the Civil War." *South Carolina Law Review* 57 (2006): 859- 888.

2. James L. Felder, interview with author, November 2022, December 2022.

3. Eugene A.R. Montgomery, "Quest for Civil Rights: Eugene A.R. Montgomery." November 7, 1980, interview by Dr. Grace Jordan McFadden. From the series *"Quest for Human / Civil Rights-Oral Recollections of Black South Carolinians."* Moving Image Research Collections, University of South Carolina.

4. John McCray, "Get Up or Shut Up," *Lighthouse and Informer,* May 6, 1950, 1.

5. Lincoln Jenkins in Guy and Candie Carawan, *Ain't You Got a Right to the Tree of Life: The People of John's Island, South Carolina, Their Faces, Their Words and Their Songs* (Athens: University of Georgia Press, 1989), 149– 50.

6. Felder interview, November 2022.

7. Thurmond on Voting Rights. WIS-TV News Collection. February 1965. Civil Rights Films from Moving Images Collection, University of South Carolina. https://digital.tcl.sc.edu/.

8. *South Carolina v. Katzenbach,* 383 U.S. 301 (1966).

9. Oral arguments, "South Carolina v. Katzenbach." Oyez. https://www.oyez.org/.

10. Earl Warren and Supreme Court of The United States. *U.S. Reports: South Carolina v. Katzenbach, 383 U.S. 301.* 1965. Periodical, 308. https://www.loc.gov/.

11. "A Repentant Harry Dent Will Follow the Lord," *Washington Post,* August 22, 1981.

12. *Shelby County v. Holder,* 570 U.S. 529 (2013).

13. John Roberts and Supreme Court of The United States. *U.S. Reports: Shelby County v. Holder, 570 U.S. 529.* 2012. Periodical. 29, 24. https://www.loc.gov/.

14. John Roberts and Supreme Court of the United States, (R. Ginsberg, dissenting). *U.S. Reports: Shelby County v. Holder, 570 U.S. 529.* 2012. Periodical, 64. https://www.loc.gov/

15. Tomas Lopez, "'Shelby County': One Year Later," Brief. Brennan Center for Justice, New York University School of Law, June 24, 2014. https://www.brennancenter.org/.

16. Charles Savage, "Justice Dept. Cites Race in Halting Law Over Voter ID," *New York Times,* December 23, 2011, A1. https://www.nytimes.com/.

17. Tiarra M. Elmore, interview with author, January 2023.

BIBLIOGRAPHY

Interviews

Adams, Fanny Phelps, interview by author, February 2003, October 2009.
Bouie, Rev. Simon, interview by author, June 2023.
Cole, Yolande Elmore, interview by author, February 2003.
Donaldson, Bobby J., interview by author, March 2023.
Edney, Cynthia K., interview by author, January 2009.
Elmore, Cresswell D., interview by author, May 2004, June 2004, July 2004, July 2022, November 2022.
Elmore, Darnell, interview by author, February 2023.
Elmore, Ronald C., interview by author, March 2003, November 2022.
Elmore, Tiarra M., interview by author, January 2023.
Elmore, Vanessa L., interview by author, February 2003, July 2022, November 2022.
Farmer, James O., interview by author, February 2003.
Felder, James L., interview by author, December 2022, November 2023.
Green, Naomi Elmore, interview by author, June 2004.
Greene, Gloria Glymph, interview by author, February 2013, July 2022, June 2023.
Hodges, Melvin S., interview by author, July 2022, October 2023.
James, Gloria Schumpert, interviewed by author, January 2023, June 2023.
Pride, Hemphill P., II, interview by author, November 2022, July 2023.
Quan-Soon, Vernadine Elmore, interview by author, July 2022.
Underwood, James L., interview by author, February 2003.
Wallace, Elizabeth, interview by author, August 2022.
Wilson, Donella B., interview by author, February 2003.

Newspapers

Afro-American (Baltimore)
Atlanta (GA) Journal-Constitution
Charleston Daily Courier (Charleston, SC)
Charleston Mercury (Charleston, SC)
Columbia Record (Columbia, SC)
Gaffney Ledger (Gaffney, SC)
Greenville News (Greenville, SC)
Lighthouse and Informer (Columbia, SC)
Manning Times (Manning, SC)
News and Courier (Charleston, SC)
Palmetto Leader (Columbia, SC)

Pittsburgh Courier
Southern Christian Advocate (Charleston, SC)
The State (Columbia, SC)
Times and Democrat (Orangeburg, SC)
New York Times
Washington Post

Manuscripts

Belser, Irvine Furman. *"A Southern Dilemma: A Possible Way Out."* Undated speech delivered to the Kosmos Club, Columbia, SC, in Caroline Dick McKissick Belser Dial Papers. South Caroliniana Library, University of South Carolina, Columbia, SC.

Clement, A.J. Jr. Papers, 1926–1986. South Caroliniana Library, University of South Carolina, Columbia, SC.

Dorn, William Jennings Bryan. Papers, 1912–1995. South Carolina Political Collections, University of South Carolina, Columbia, SC.

Elmore, George A. Scrapbook, compiled 1947–1956. South Caroliniana Library, University of South Carolina, Columbia, SC.

Herbert, Robert Beverley. Papers, 1879–1974. South Caroliniana Library, University of South Carolina, Columbia, SC.

Herbert, R. Beverley. *What We Can Do About the Race Problem*. 16-page pamphlet. Columbia: Publisher not identified, 1948. South Caroliniana Library, University of South Carolina, Columbia, SC.

Kahler, Sophie. "The Evolution of Columbia's Neighborhoods: 1937 to Present." (2021). Senior Theses, 432, https://scholarcommons.sc.edu/senior_theses/432, https://storymaps.arcgis.com/stories/fe2f41e8b9af4227966bcf53ae7e9783.

McCray, John Henry. Papers, 1929–1989. South Caroliniana Library, University of South Carolina, University of South Carolina, Columbia, SC.

McMaster, Fitz Hugh. Papers, 1782–1960. South Caroliniana Library, University of South Carolina, Columbia, SC.

Moore, Winfred B. "Soul of the South: James F. Byrnes and the Racial Issue in American Politics, 1911–1941." in *The Proceedings of the South Carolina Historical Association 1978*, James O. Farmer, ed. 42–51. South Carolina State Library Digital Collections, http://hdl.handle.net/10827/23297.

NAACP Legal Defense and Educational Fund. Records, 1915–1968. Library of Congress, on microfilm, NAACP Papers, The Voting Rights Campaign, 1916–1950, Group II.

Simkins, Modjeska Monteith. Papers, 1909–1992. South Carolina Political Collections, University of South Carolina Libraries, University of South Carolina.

Periodicals, Speeches, Oral Histories, Online Resources

Address. In the Convention of the colored people of the Southern states, begun to be holden in the City of Columbia, South Carolina, on Wednesday, the eighteenth day of October. 1871. Broadsides, leaflets, and pamphlets from America and Europe, Library of Congress. https://www.loc.gov/item/2020779318/.

Bedingfield, Sid. "John H. McCray, Accommodationism, and the Framing of the Civil Rights Struggle in South Carolina, 1940-48." *Journalism History* 37, no. 2 (Summer 2011).

Boulware, Harold R. Sr. "Quest for Civil Rights: Judge Harold R. Boulware Sr."
    Interview by Grace McFadden (September 23, 1980). From the series Quest
    for Human/Civil Rights–Oral Recollections of Black South Carolinians.
    Moving Image Research Collections, University of South Carolina.

Briggs, Harry and Eliza. Video interview (October 25, 1985) for PBS *American
    Experience* documentary series *"Eyes on the Prize."* Washington University
    Film & Media Archive. http://mavisweb.wulib.wustl.edu:81/mavisSearch.

Burke, W. Lewis. "Killing, Cheating, Legislating, and Lying: A History of Voting
    Rights in South Carolina after the Civil War." *South Carolina Law Review* 57
    (2006): 859–888.

Conlon, Sarah. *"'A Hospital Built by Them, for Them': The Good Samaritan-Waverly
    Hospital Building Fund Campaign and the Evolution of Black Healthcare Tradi-
    tions in Columbia, South Carolina,"* MA thesis, University of South Carolina,
    2012. ProQuest.

Equal Justice Institute. "Lynchings in America." https://eji.org/reports/lynching
    -in-america/.

"Federal Writers' Project: Slave Narrative Project, Vol. 14, South Carolina, Part 3,
    Jackson-Quattlebaum." 1936. United States Work Projects Administration
    (USWPA), Manuscript Division, Library of Congress. https://www.loc.gov
    /item/mesn143/.

Frederickson, Kari. "'The Slowest State' and 'Most Backward Community':
    Racial Violence in South Carolina and Federal Civil-Rights Legislation,
    1946–1948." *South Carolina Historical Magazine* 98, no. 2 (1997): 177–202. http://
    www.jstor.org/stable/27570230.

Gaddis, Elijah, and Seth Kotch, directors. "A Red Record." An online project of
    the University of North Carolina at Chapel Hill to document lynchings in the
    American South. https://lynching.web.unc.edu/.

Haram, Kerstyn M. *"The Palmetto Leader's* Mission to End Lynching in South
    Carolina: Black Agency and the Black Press in Columbia, 1925–1940." *South
    Carolina Historical Magazine* 107, no. 4 (October 2006): 310–333. https://www
    .jstor.org/stable/27570843.

Herbert, R. Beverley. "A Plea for Better Race Relations: An Address Given at the
    Commencement Exercises at the University of South Carolina," June 2, 1948.
    Reprinted in *Southern Christian Advocate* 112, vol. 25 (June 17, 1948): 5.

Jackson, David H. "Booker T. Washington in South Carolina, March 1909." *South
    Carolina Historical Magazine* 113, no. 3 (July 2012): 192–220. URL:https://www
    .jstor.org/stable/41698114.

Kahler, Sophie, and Conor Harrison. "'Wipe Out the Entire Slum Area':
    University-Led Urban Renewal in Columbia, South Carolina, 1950–1985,"
    Journal of Historical Geography 67 (January 2020): 61–70. https://doi.org/10
    .1016/j.jhg.2019.10.008.

Klarman, Michael J. "The White Primary Rulings: A Case Study in the Conse-
    quences of Supreme Court Decisionmaking." *Florida State University Law
    Review* 29, iss. 1, (2001). http://ir.law.fsu.edu/lr/vol29/iss1/2.

Lau, Peter F. "Freedom Road Territory: The Politics of Civil Rights Struggle
    in South Carolina during the Jim Crow Era." PhD diss., Rutgers, The State
    University of New Jersey, 2002.

Lewis, John, and Archie E. Allen. "Black Voter Registration Efforts in the South."
    Notre Dame Law Review 48, iss. 1 (October 1, 1972): 105–32.

Marcy, Henry Orlando. Diary of a Surgeon in US Army, South Carolina, 1865. Transcribed and edited by Harriott Cheves Leland. South Caroliniana Library, University of South Carolina.

McDonald, Laughlin. "An Aristocracy of Voters: The Disfranchisement of Blacks in South Carolina," *South Carolina Law Review* 37, iss. 4 (1986): 557–582.

McIntyre, Larry. "The South Carolina Black Code and its Legacy." MA thesis, University of North Carolina at Charlotte, 2016. ProQuest.

Mickey, Robert K. "The Beginning of the End for Authoritarian Rule in America: *Smith v. Allwright* and the Abolition of the White Primary in the Deep South, 1944–1948." *Studies in American Political Development* 22 (Fall 2008): 143–82.

Montgomery, Eugene A. R. "Quest for Civil Rights: Eugene A. R. Montgomery." Interview by Dr. Grace Jordan McFadden (November 7, 1980). From the series Quest for Human/Civil Rights–Oral Recollections of Black South Carolinians. Moving Image Research Collections, University of South Carolina.

Nelson, Robert K., LaDale Winling, Justin Madron, Riley Champine, Chad Devers, Nathaniel Ayers, Annie Evans, et al. "Mapping Inequality: Redlining in New Deal America." Edited by Robert K. Nelson and Edward L. Ayers. American Panorama: An Atlas of United States History, 2023. https://dsl .richmond.edu/panorama/redlining.

Report of the Secretary to the Anti-Lynching Committee, January 21, 1921. NAACP Collection, Manuscript Division, Library of Congress. www.loc.gov/item /mss34140_02/.

Richey, Staci, and Lydia Mattice Brandt. Columbia: Downtown Historic Resource Survey. South Carolina Historical Books Collection, State Library, Columbia, SC. DAH_Downton_Historic_Resource_Survey_Report_2020-09-28.pdf (13.05 MB)

Roberts, John G., and Supreme Court of The United States. "U.S. Reports: *Shelby County v. Holder*, 570 U.S. 529 (2013)." US Reports, Library of Congress. https://www.loc.gov/item/usrep570529/.

Simkins, Modjeska Monteith. "Oral History Interview with Modjeska Simkins, G-0056-1 and G-0056-2." Interview by Jacquelyn Hall. Southern Oral History Program Collection, University of North Carolina at Chapel Hill, 1976.

South Carolina. *Constitution of the Commonwealth of South Carolina, Ratified April 16, 1868, Together with the Constitution of the United States of America*. Columbia, SC: C. A. Calvo, jr., state printer, 1885. Library of Congress. https://www .loc.gov/item/14008433/.

State Budget and Control Board. *One Hundred and Thirtieth Annual Report of the South Carolina State Hospital: For the Year Ending June 30, 1953*. South Carolina State Library. https://dc.statelibrary.sc.gov/server/api/core/bitstreams /53e69d43-701d-4a4c-985a-4f5c09afaa79/content.

Time. "Elections: Curtains for Cotton Ed." August 7, 1944. https://content.time .com/time/subscriber/article/0,33009,886159,00.html.

Tindall, George B. "The Question of Race in the South Carolina Constitutional Convention of 1895." *Negro History Bulletin* 15, no. 4 (1952): 59–68. http:// www.jstor.org/stable/44212519.

US Census Bureau, Federal Census Population Schedules, 1910–1940. US Department of Commerce.US Census Bureau, 13th Census of the United States,

1910. Statistics for South Carolina. Published in connection with the abstract of the census. US Department of Commerce.

US Department of Labor. *Handbook of Labor Statistics, 1936 edition*. Washington, DC: United States Government Printing Office, 1936.

Wallace, D. D. "The South Carolina Constitutional Convention of 1895." *Sewanee Review* 4, no. 3 (May 1896): 348–60.

Waring, Julius Waties. "The Reminiscences of J. Waties Waring, 1957." Interviewed by Harlan B. Phillips and Louis Morris Starr. Columbia Center for Oral History, Columbia University, 1972. https://dx.doi.org/10.7916/d8-22t5-sm51.

Warren, Earl, and Supreme Court of the United States. "U.S. Reports: *South Carolina v. Katzenbach*, 383 U.S. 301 (1966)." US Reports, Library of Congress. https://www.loc.gov/item/usrep383301/.

West, Rebecca. "Opera in Greenville." *New Yorker*, June 14, 1947.

Books

Andrew, Rod, Jr. *Wade Hampton: Confederate Warrior to Southern Redeemer*. Chapel Hill: University of North Carolina Press, 2008.

Ball, William Watts. *The Editor and the Republic: Papers and Addresses of William Watts Ball*. Edited by Anthony Harrigan. Chapel Hill: University of North Carolina Press, 1954.

Ball, William Watts. *The State That Forgot: South Carolina's Surrender to Democracy*. Indianapolis: Bobbs-Merrill, 1932.

Baptist, Edward E. *The Half Has Never Been Told: Slavery and the Making of American Capitalism*. New York: Basic Books, 2014.

Bedingfield, Sid. *Newspaper Wars: Civil Rights and White Resistance in South Carolina, 1935–1965*. Urbana: University of Illinois Press, 2017.

Brinson, Claudia Smith. *Stories of Struggle: The Clash Over Civil Rights in South Carolina*. Columbia: University of South Carolina Press, 2020.

Burton, Orville Vernon. "'The Black Squint of the Law': Racism in South Carolina." In *The Meaning of South Carolina History: Essays in Honor of George C. Rogers Jr.*, edited by David R. Chesnutt and Clyde N. Wilson, 161–185. Columbia: University of South Carolina Press, 1991.

Carawan, Guy, and Candie Carawan. *Ain't You Got a Right to the Tree of Life?: The People of Johns Island South Carolina–Their Faces, Their Words and Their Songs*. 2nd ed. Athens: University of Georgia Press, 1994. First published 1966 by Simon and Schuster (New York).

Chesnutt, David R., and Clyde N. Wilson, eds. *The Meaning of South Carolina History: Essays in Honor of George C. Rogers Jr.* Columbia: University of South Carolina Press, 1991.

Crawford, Vicki L., Jacqueline Anne Rouse, and Barbara Woods, eds. *Women in the Civil Rights Movement: Trailblazers and Torchbearers, 1941–1965*. Bloomington: Indiana University Press, 1993.

Dorn, William J., and Scott Derks. *Dorn: Of the People, a Political Way of Life*. Orangeburg, SC: Sandlapper, 1988.

Edds, Margaret. *Free at Last: What Really Happened When Civil Rights Came to Southern Politics*. Bethesda, MD: Adler & Adler, 1987.

Edgar, Walter. *South Carolina: A History*. Columbia: University of South Carolina Press, 1998.

Edgar, Walter, ed. *South Carolina Encyclopedia*. Columbia: University of South Carolina Press, 2006.

Edgerton, John. *Speak Now against the Day: The Generation before the Civil Rights Movement in the South*. New York: Alfred A. Knopf, 1994.

Ellison, Ralph. "An American Dilemma: A Review." In *Shadow and Act*, 303–17. New York: Random House, 1964.

Gergel, Richard. *Unexampled Courage: The Blinding of Sgt. Isaac Woodward and the Awakening of President Harry S. Truman and Judge J. Waties Waring*. New York: Farrar, Straus and Giroux, 2019.

Gravely, William B. *They Stole Him Out of Jail: Willie Earle, South Carolina's Last Lynching Victim*. Columbia: University of South Carolina Press, 2019.

Hennig, Helen Kohn, ed. *Columbia: Capital City of South Carolina, 1786–1936*. Columbia, SC: R. Bryan, 1936.

Hicks, Timothy, Donald Stewart, and Fritz Hamer, *The South Carolina Journey*, 2nd ed., Kaysville, UT: Gibbs-Smith Education, 2021.

Hine, Darlene Clark, *Black Victory: The Rise and Fall of the White Primary in Texas*. New essays by Steven F. Lawson and Merline Pitre. Columbia: University of Missouri Press, 2004.

Holden, Charles J. *In the Great Maelstrom: Conservatives in Post-Civil War South Carolina*. Columbia: University of South Carolina Press, 2002.

Hudson, Janet G. *Entangled by White Supremacy: Reform in World War I-era South Carolina*. Lexington: University Press of Kentucky, 2009.

Hurston, Zora Neale. *Dust Tracks on a Road*. Philadelphia: J. B. Lippincott, 1942.

James, John G. *The Southern Students Hand-Book of Selections for Reading and Oratory*. New York: A. S. Barnes, 1879.

Kluger, Richard. *Simple Justice: The History of Brown v. Board of Education and Black America's Struggle for Equality*. New York: Alfred A. Knopf, 1976.

Lau, Peter F. *Democracy Rising: South Carolina and the Fight for Black Equality since 1865*. Lexington: University Press of Kentucky, 2006.

Lowe, Stephen H. *The Slow Undoing: The Federal Courts and the Long Struggle for Civil Rights in South Carolina*. Columbia: University of South Carolina Press, 2021.

Mickey, Robert. *Paths Out of Dixie: The Democratization of Authoritarian Enclaves in America's Deep South, 1944–1972*. Princeton, NJ: Princeton University Press, 2015.

Moore, Winifred B., Jr., and Orville Vernon Burton, eds. *Toward the Meeting of the Waters: Currents in the Civil Rights Movement of South Carolina during the Twentieth Century*. Columbia: University of South Carolina, 2008.

Myrdal, Gunnar. *An American Dilemma: The Negro Problem and American Democracy*. New York: Harper & Brothers, 1944.

Nichols, Brevet Major George Ward. *The Story of the Great March: From the Diary of a Staff Officer*. New York: Harper & Brothers, 1865.

Oliphant, Mary C. Simms, *The Simms History of South Carolina*. Columbia, SC: State Company, 1932.

Oliphant, Mary C. Simms, *The New Simms History of South Carolina–Centennial Edition, 1840–1940*. Columbia, SC: State Company, 1940.

Oliphant, Mary Simms, Alfred Taylor Odell, and T. C. Duncan Eaves, eds. *Letters of William Gilmore Simms, Vol 5*. Columbia: University of South Carolina Press, 1956.

Pike, James S. *The Prostrate State: South Carolina under Negro Government.* New York: Loring & Mussey, 1935.

Pinckney, Josephine. *Three O'Clock Dinner.* New York: Viking, 1945.

Roberts, Gene, and Hank Klibanoff. *The Race Beat: The Press, the Civil Rights Struggle, and the Awakening of a Nation.* New York: Alfred A. Knopf, 2006.

Roper, John Herbert, Sr. *The Magnificent Mays: A Biography of Benjamin Elijah Mays.* Columbia: University of South Carolina Press, 2012.

Sullivan, Patricia. *Lift Every Voice: The NAACP and the Making of the Civil Rights Movement.* New York: New Press, 2010.

Tindall, George B. *South Carolina Negroes 1877–1900.* Columbia: University of South Carolina Press, 1952.

Underwood, James L. *The Constitution of South Carolina. Vol. IV, The Struggle for Political Equality.* Columbia: University of South Carolina Press, 1994.

Underwood, James Lowell, and W. Lewis Burke, Jr. *At Freedom's Door: African American Founding Fathers and Lawyers in Reconstruction South Carolina.* Columbia: University of South Carolina Press, 2005.

Yarbrough, Tinsley E. *A Passion for Justice: J. Waties Waring and Civil Rights.* New York: Oxford University Press, 1987.

Zelden, Charles L. *The Battle for the Black Ballot: Smith v. Allwright and the Defeat of the Texas All-White Primary.* Lawrence, KS: University Press of Kansas, 2004.

INDEX